Chic Ironic Bitterness

10·20·07

To Judy —
Thanks for being such
a great mentor to my
sister. Hope you enjoy
the book — and if not,
please use as doorstop.

Kind Regards,

R. Jay

Chic Ironic Bitterness

R. Jay Magill, Jr.

THE UNIVERSITY OF MICHIGAN PRESS

Ann Arbor

Copyright © by the University of Michigan 2007
All rights reserved
Published in the United States of America by
The University of Michigan Press
Manufactured in the United States of America
⊗ Printed on acid-free paper

2010   2009   2008   2007   4   3   2   1

A CIP catalog record for this book is available from the British Library.

Library of Congress Cataloging-in-Publication Data

Magill, R. Jay (Ronald Jay), 1972–
    Chic ironic bitterness / R. Jay Magill, Jr.
        p.   cm.
    Includes bibliographical references and index.
    ISBN-13: 978-0-472-11621-8 (cloth : alk. paper)
    ISBN-10: 0-472-11621-5 (cloth : alk. paper)
    1. United States—Intellectual life.   2. United States—Politics
and government—1989–   3. United States—Social conditions—1980–
4. Irony—Social aspects—United States.   5. Trust—Social aspects—
United States.   6. Politics and culture—United States.
7. Television and politics—United States.   8. Romanticism—History.
9. Irony—History.   10. Social contract—History.   I. Title.

E169.12.M15   2007
973—dc22   2007019164

FOR MY PARENTS,

Ronald and Bonnie Magill,

AND MY GRANDPARENTS,

Harold and Kathryn Magill &
Edmund and Evelyn Kling, Jr.

Entire strata of the population have been living
for a considerable period in an *inner somewhere-else.*
They do not feel bound to what are called the
fundamental values of society.

—Peter Sloterdijk,
The Critique of Cynical Reason (1983)

Preface

This book began vaguely in 1999. Not that any of it was written but for a small review of Jedediah Purdy's book *For Common Things* on a satire website that two friends and I had started—*The Saucepot Review*—which has since, like all dead websites, become a portal for porn.

Now eight years later, the topic of irony as a social attitude, as a form of social critique, is even more palpable and—as Borat so deftly displayed—has even greater effects on political and national identity. September 11, as it shook everything else in the world, only further widened the cultural fault line between the "serious" pundit and the ironic critic. As political speech and culture over the past half-dozen years have become increasingly grave, bleak, and eerie, seriousness has somehow become the litmus test of true patriotism. Yet as we've had to adjust to the rhetoric and living conditions in the shadow of terrorism, the fanaticism of religious groups, and the publishing of cartoons about religious figures, irony as a method of wry, skeptical detachment has thankfully proven itself to be far from dead, as many predicted and some even hoped for.

When Stephen Colbert spoke at the White House Correspondents' Association Dinner in April 2006, it shoved into high relief the tension between the serious and ironic modes of public engagement. Colbert's tone did not register with many in the audience of decorated military folk, high officials, Hill workers, media bigwigs, and Pentagon types. The blows were hard. Laughs were nervous. The president grew noticeably incensed. Tension, sweatingly palpable, scented the room.

The performance glaringly opened up the faults of the present and of politics, making for awkward, weighty silences. Yet scarcely a network mentioned it. Many claimed the performer had bombed.

Colbert's speech, however, far from being insignificant, was a visible emanation from within a culture swimming with knowing assumptions about its nation's power, politics, and pragmatism. Ironic debasing of the Colbert variety is motivated by a sort of entrenched disgust with the state of our national being. It is, as it's long been, a method of critique that gets to the heart of this disgust with economy and stealth. It seems at times an alternative, in our cosmopolitan minds, to actual revolution.

Raising its perky head most alertly when it sees a dreaded state of affairs passing as normal, the ironic, satiric turn seen so frequently of late is a way to distance oneself from threats to integrity. Indeed more than a figure of speech, the ironic worldview, when performing, does something else rarely examined in debates about it in the recent past: it paradoxically and secretly preserves the ideals of sincerity, honesty, and authenticity by momentarily belying its own appearance. It must vigilantly maintain the split between the social role and the inward self to shield what is valuable. For the satirically inclined, trust is now based on the mutual and silent recognition of purposeful artifice. In a culture dense with spin, it's one of the most honest things we have going.

While irony and satire have been used since the Greeks for lambasting those in power—and used in American literary culture since the beginning of this fair Republic—ironic critique has grown into the dominant operative strategy of social criticism in popular culture over the past decade, particularly as seen on shows such as *The Daily Show, The Colbert Report, South Park, The Simpsons, Family Guy, Curb Your Enthusiasm, Extras, The Office, Chappelle's Show,* and, of course, in *The Onion.* Crucially, this book is not a hellishly dry academic analysis that will ruin everything great about these shows. I like TV too much to betray it with too much thinking. Instead, this book is a foray into both cultural criticism and intellectual history to examine what motivates the larger ironic sensibility being utilized by these shows, a certain cultural bitterness legitimated through trenchant disbelief—an intellectual heritage of irony as a private revolt against the world, particularly one seen as increasingly unstable, ambivalent, open to interpretation, and of dubious moral authority.

In this sense, we're still Romantics. Ever since European romanticism, leaping the chasm from the eighteenth to the nineteenth centuries, this hovering mode, this turn inward, this skeptical remove was recommended—initially by writers, poets, philosophers—as a steady armor against society itself, against the self's impending invasion by technology, scientific understanding, politics, and commercialism. And against the abuse of language, too, that brittle thread of trust.

Romanticism got its jump start by clinging to—however now inconvenient to discuss given religion's divisive role—some rather Protestant values in the face of this onslaught, namely those of inwardness, privacy, sincerity, and a sense of authentic connection to others and to oneself. As a mode of social engagement, irony, based ultimately in Romantic ideology, instead of being fundamentally anti-everything, is, then, at root a Protestant stance: it attempts to critique exteriorities and convey the hidden truth of inwardness. Thus, efforts by some pundits to oppose irony and cynicism with sincerity or earnestness have not understood that sincerity of moral vision can no longer, in a cultural moment that so often seems a frightening yet absolutely predictable joke, be spoken literally to have any effect. Moral vision loses its power—for those deeply aware of its recurrent misuse—when it is cheapened by ready-made, cliché-laden, speech-writer-prepared, pedantic literalism.

I regret that there is much to this topic that could not be included in this book for lack of time and my own effort. Clearly, detachment/cool/irony as forms of social resistance have been around in any number of American cultural productions for ages—African American, gay, punk, Jewish (which would require several volumes to address), ethnic "others"—as well as in the works of countless artists and writers, all in need of a sort of psychic armor against a dominant political and commercial culture trying to smother existing ways of life with ever-increasing expediency and absorption. Our current ironic mode is comprised of all of these.

What is most interesting now, however, is that such an attitude, such distancing, is no longer hemmed off to cultural enclaves. Now, instead, enormous swathes of Americans feel the need to armor themselves against their very own culture, one that seems to comes at, instead of from, them: "Entire strata of the population have been living for a considerable period in an *inner somewhere-else*" wrote the German philosopher Peter Sloterdijk in 1983. "They do not feel bound to what are called the fundamental values of society." They respond with a "chic bitterness," a term coined by Sloterdijk and which I've adapted. These two attitudes—chic ironic bitterness and civic trust—have only intensified in opposition, particularly so in the United States. And civic trust, embodying our fundamental social values and discussed so habitually over the last decade, has slowly suffered and retreated, has become a problematic whose reasons must be discovered and analyzed.

But for millions of us who are to some extent ashamed of our culture and national behavior, proud of its ideals yet conscious of the state of politics and knowledge in the early twenty-first century, the answer is clear: trust has been abused and thus withheld from those undeserving of it. It has been replaced by a justified, antagonistic remove. We now have a resolute understanding of how things get done in the world— we're so often reminded by a thousand reality shows and ominous political statements—and we know it ain't pretty. *Realpolitik* has unabashedly become life. Significantly, however, we wish it were otherwise.

The public ironists and satirical outlets of today are not simply experiencing a random blessing; no, they are giving voice and functionality to a frustration felt by so many that have enacted this psychological stance as a distance from a culture and politics that embarrasses them. They retain a vague but very real social hope in the ideals that politics needs but has forgotten. But as they suspect that's cheesy, too, they'll never speak it.

This concludes my application for/absolute guarantee for never getting a job at *The Daily Show.*

—RJM
Philadelphia, Pennsylvania, and Hamburg, Germany
April 2007

Acknowledgments

None of this would have been possible without the early backing and guidance of the University of Michigan Press, particularly in the figure of my editor, Jim Reische. He showed early and confident support of the manuscript and has been a keen and hilarious editorial partner throughout. Most importantly, Jim shared the feeling that something about the topic of irony in America, though by 2007 intellectually passé, was still alive and, moreover, flourishing—something worth readdressing at length. For his mutual understanding and encouragement I am indebted. Mary Bisbee-Beek, who deftly handled promotion of the book and got off the starter's block early, has been a total joy to work with; we'll always have Paris. To Phil Pochoda, director of the University of Michigan Press, for taking on the risk of this discipline-crossing venture, I am enormously grateful.

Chic Ironic Bitterness began as a dissertation at the University of Hamburg, Germany, under the watchful eyes of Americanists Bettina Friedl and Hans-Peter Rodenberg. They offered sound advice and encouragement consistently and were swift to introduce literature and figures I would have otherwise missed. An additional advisor to this project was the political scientist William Chaloupka of Colorado State University and author of *Everybody Knows: Cynicism in America* (Minnesota, 1999). A solid and reliable source of critique since the beginning, Bill gave generously of his time and advice, and for that I am both thankful and humbled. He embodies something sorely missing from so many academics: an ability for write clearly for a broad audience.

To previous academic influences, I owe thanks to Allen Bäck at Kutztown University, Donald Kuspit at Stony Brook University, and to Dr. Robert Coles of Harvard University, all of whom have lent valued guidance and insight. I am grateful as well for the correspondence of Daniel Horowitz of Smith College, Boston College's Alan Wolfe, Harvie Ferguson at the University of Glasgow, and Werner Sollors at Harvard. I'd also like to recognize the sound advice of Don Herzog of the University of Michigan Law School, an early and advantageous reader of the original manuscript.

First books offer a rare opportunity for the public acknowledgment of long-standing private encouragement. I would like therefore to coronate in print much-owed gratitude to my parents, Bonnie and Ronald Magill, and my siblings, Scott and Liz. Congratulations to the former + Lindsay Bruckner. The latter + husband Rob Hanawalt = Chase. Welcome to the world, nephew. My deep appreciation, as well and of course, to Barb and Rick Parkhurst; Edmund, Else, Ed, Judy, Jed, and Adria Kling; and to the Esher, Brannan, and Maka families.

As I've bored many a friend and colleague with various parts of this manuscript, I'd like to apologize to them here. For years of inspired conversation, my gratitude to Dan R. Gluibizzi, Brett Huggett, Evan Lyon, Jolie Scena, Adrienne Lamb, Kelly Hanlon, Niko Günther, John Luther, and Bill Coleman. Thanks also to James Meacham, R. Norris Clark, Jennifer Romolini, Michelle Lamuniere, Kirk Kicklighter, Mark Solley, Trevor Hall, Jill Petty, Toby Lester, and Todd Pruzan for words both personal and professional. I owe particular thanks to William Ganis of Wells College, who delivered meticulous edits and spent hours talking over arguments. Christine Mehring of Yale University and Georg Weizsäcker of the London School of Economics made life less painful by boosting my written German over the first-grade level. *Vielen Dank.* My genuine thanks also to the guys and gals at Oh! Bryon's for some truly great afternoons during this long process.

This book was inspired by four philosophers—Richard Rorty,

Charles Taylor, Richard Sennett, and Peter Sloterdijk. All four have sparked for me true intellectual exhilaration, left tasty stylistic bread-crumbs, and stirred great aspirations for writing about big things in a clear and fiery way. To them my continued and humble admiration.

Surely not least: for her enduring support, ideas, editorial wisdom, translating stamina, stunning beauty, and always entertaining *Miss-brauch* of the English language, my gratitude and love to Tanja Maka, one of the best advisors—and worst cynics—ever.

Contents

Fun,
pop
culturey,
refs to
known
things

More
serious,
less fun,
but more
substantial

Again
like
beginning

You Are Being Sarcastic, Dude

Indication of alienation. The clearest sign that two people
hold alienated views is that each says ironic things to the
other, but neither of the two feels the other's irony.
　　—Friedrich Nietzsche, aphorism 331, *Human, All Too Human* (1878)

"Here comes that cannonball guy—he's cool."
"Are you being sarcastic, dude?"
"I don't even know anymore."
　　—Two teenagers at Hullabalooza, *The Simpsons* (1996)

I remember verbatim the above three lines from an episode of *The
Simpsons,* that always calibrated cultural barometer.* Originally aired
in 1996, this Simpsonian haiku remains just as telling today. And one
can imaginatively supply a last line: "Whatever." Further reflection is
just not worth the time or effort.

In the scene, the two teenagers are in a crowd watching the Cannonball Guy—Homer Simpson himself—about to be blasted in the
stomach with a cannonball. Homer's grinning, goggled enthusiasm
runs strictly contrary to the sentiment of the rock-and-freak show he

---

***The Simpsons,* episode 724, "Homerpalooza," season 7; airdate June 19, 1996.
Unfortunately, since the arrival of *South Park* three years after this episode, the
Simpson family, trailblazing pioneers all, have sort of lost their calibration.

is in, Hullabalooza, which is all about being cool (nonchalant, rebellious, subtly angry).* After the first adolescent kid tells the other that Homer is cool, he does not, upon reflection, recognize his own relationship to what he said; he is alienated from what he means. Was he being sarcastic? Did he "mean" what he said? If he did, why didn't he know it? If he didn't, why did he say it? His friend clearly doesn't understand him either.

Alas, Homer Simpson is not cool. But it's the last statement, "I don't even know anymore," that suggests the abundance of sarcasm the concert-going dude normally uses has put him in state where he no longer recognizes the meaning of his own words. This is why it is funny. But something else, too: Here, in the midst of a cartoon parody of a real-life outdoor concert created with the express intention of bonding its individualist visitors together in a frenzy of rebelliousness, Nietzsche's aphorism lurches to life: alienation reigns.†

Sarcasm like the kind used by the slacker caricature above is, of course, a member of the big, happy irony family. And what a family it is. A few of its more memorable faces (and by name completely forgettable) are:

---

*Headliner bands at the actual Lollapalooza in 1996 included the both angry and not-so-angry sounds of Rage Against the Machine (not just angry, ragingly so), Metallica (napstangry), Cocteau Twins (high), Soundgarden (goateed angry), Waylon Jennings (uh . . .), Cheap Trick (definitely), Violent Femmes (equals out), The Tea Party (huh?), Wu Tang Clan (urban anger vs.), Steve Earle (country displeasure), Devo (whip it, anger), The Ramones (anger, be sedated), Rancid (tattooed anger), Shaolin Monks (anger cleansing), Screaming Trees (see: Soundgarden), and Psychotica (anger at eyeliner, mostly). Ice-T (then, definitely angry) debuted his band Body Count and the song "Cop Killer" (about killing cops) at the first Lollapalooza in 1991. Lollapalooza is now sponsored by AT&T. Ice-T now plays a cop on *Law & Order: SVU.*

†Perry Farrell said that when he was looking for bands "to play Lollapalooza, honestly, aside from the music . . . I look at the players and decide, oddly enough, if I'd like to sit down and eat with them." http://www.cnn.com/2003/SHOWBIZ/Music/08/29/mroom.farrell/index.html.

Antiphrasis: irony of one word, often derisively performed through patent contradiction. Referring to a tall person, one says, *What's up, shortie?*

Paralipsis: drawing attention to something in the very act of pretending to ignore it. *It would be inappropriate for me at this time to reveal the senator's Oxycontin addiction.*

Epitrope: turning the interpretation of a statement over to one's hearers in a way that suggests evidence of something without having to state it. The Irishy hoodlum band House of Pain blurting, *Come and get some of this* (i.e. you really don't want any of "this").

Sarcasm: use of mockery or bitter verbal taunts. In reference to a bad grade, *Great job, genius!* Or: *Here comes that Cannonball Guy—he's cool.*

Mycterismus: mock given with an accompanying gesture, scornful countenance, or enthusiastic banter. Drawing the lip up at the corner as one says, *No doubt of that, Sir!!*[1]

Of course, you need not go far to find examples of speech like this in everyday life. It's just normal talking. It ain't no thing. We use irony and sarcasm effortlessly to show that we're not idiots, that we are on the same level as our conversational partner, and that they, in turn, are part of our club (of course, speaking *about* irony, like right here, cancels this out, reveals the secret-club password, and so on).

As intellectually taboo as it seems to talk about it, however, something so huge cannot but be addressed. The use of irony adds a certain spice of insiderness to all conversations. It makes us feel as though we are among the now-massive elect who understand way the world works. Talking to someone who does not get it immediately ends discussion or prompts a new kind of distanced interaction.* Normally,

---

*A dialogue in the April 9, 2007 *Newsweek* illustrates this well. Pastor Rick Warren of *The Purpose Driven Life* and Sam Harris of *The End of Faith* and *Letter to A Christian Nation* are talking about God. Warren: "I look at the world and I say, 'God likes variety.' I say, 'God likes beauty.' I say 'God likes order,' and the more we understand ecology, the more we understand how

however: Down with the flu? "Just awesome"; flat tire on I-95 while heading to see your favorite band/comedian/*Twenty-Fifth Annual Putnam County Spelling Bee* in New York? "Super." Context-dependent examples are everywhere. With the proper bodily and tonal cues—the true transmitters of irony—any expression makes a magic transformation for the audience that's in on the joke. Entire performances can take place under such guise, just like *The Colbert Report* or Borat's *Cultural Learnings of America for Make Benefit Glorious Nation of Kazakhstan* (2006). You'll find this performative stance in basically anything by Sacha Baron Cohen. Or Ricky Gervais. Or a thousand more who entertain by skewering. Body language, inflection, context, and tone translate invisible ideas into received meaning to those in wait of it. This is why e-mail can be such a poor communicator of irony, reduced as it is to the options of "scare quotes," *italics*, emoticons (☺), or YELLING. But among the closest of minds, no outward signs at all.

In short, the ways in which we express intentions through language are frequently askew of their literal meaning. And we're not talking in allegories, synecdoches, metonyms, or in constant metaphors. No, irony's power, in its own right, beyond its entertainment value, is a kind of talking and expressing that conveys a broader comprehension of social reality, political preferences, and power, all by manipulating the rules of language itself.

Ironic speech, then, aside from bringing together like minds, allows the speaker to be what G. W. F. Hegel, that German philosopher/stringy-haired obligatory reference, called "negatively free": that is, able to *feel free* by negating the existence of something else, liberating oneself from commitment to meaning. It is not serious about seriousness; it cannot be bound by what is *said*. Instead, it is undetermined,

---

sensitive that order is." Harris: "Then God also likes smallpox and tuberculosis." Warren: "I would attribute a lot of the sins in the world to myself." Harris, hilariously: "Are you responsible for smallpox?" Warren, obviously: "I am responsible to do something about it . . ." One can almost hear the gelatinous rolling of Harris's eyes at Warren's escape into the moral-human-highground and out of logical contradiction (pp. 49–50).

unaccountable to actual verbal utterances. It refuses to be governed, to abide, to commit to meaning. Irony is, as one of its taxonomists, J. Hillis Miller, has said, "the mode of language which cannot be mastered." Or, more deftly, as Stephen Colbert has:

> I can retreat from any statement I've ever made on *The Daily Show* without anyone impugning my credibility because I've never claimed any. But a pundit has to back up what he says with statistics and some study from the Pew Research Center. . . . I don't. And so I can say anything because I'm not asking you to believe that I mean it. I'm just hoping that you'll laugh at what I say. [But that] doesn't mean I don't mean it.[2]

He's not asking you to believe that he means it, but that doesn't mean that he doesn't. Mean it. See? Predictably, the ironic figure of speech "looks down, as it were, on plain and ordinary discourse immediately understood by everyone," Søren Kierkegaard—that other obligatory reference/Danish/debonair writer wrote in 1841. "It travels in an exclusive incognito . . . looks down from its exalted station . . . on ordinary pedestrian speech. . . . [and] regards virtue as a kind of prudishness."[3] He forgot to mention here that it also requires a community of those who understand a constellation of shared references and those who don't. There is no joke like an inside joke. ; -)

I'll be citing the Pew Research Center in a few pages to back this up.

While ironic speech alone does not an ironist make, ironic speech and gestures are good signs that the speaker has a sort of self-regarding distance from the everyday world, from the quotidian *boringness* of large swathes of American commercial culture. There is something antagonistic and slippery about the ironist character as he's been described. And this is why this attitude has been characterized by some—and for some time—as withholding, disengaged, uncommitted, relativistic, and haughty. And because of this association, many social observers and political pundits have regarded shows like *The Simpsons*, *Murphy Brown*, or *The Daily Show* (which Robert Novak does not watch) as symbols of America's fraying or imperfect moral fabric. When American popular culture, everyday speech, and urban punditry communicate in a way where words bear little relation to their literal meanings, where a snide detachment shadows all comments, then the culture is awash in irony, cynicism, skepticism, and easy sarcasm. Misregistration abounds. Meaning slips. We're doomed.

As will become increasingly clear, irony has been described as a general sensibility and not just a rhetorical device. We have known this for more than two hundred years, since the first Romantic arched an eyebrow in skepticism towards society's imposed roles and expectations. Yet the (relatively) recent debate about irony and civic trust went into mini-convulsions every time some social critic employed the term in reference to a social malaise or an attitude. This kind of reaction was particularly apparent in the debate following books such as Jedediah Purdy's *For Common Things: Irony, Trust, and Commitment in America Today* (1999) and after 9/11 with *Vanity Fair's* Graydon Carter and *Time's* Roger Rosenblatt proclaiming the "death of irony."

Some commentators' claimed that the word was being misused, that irony was solely a literary term that had been simplemindedly conflated with cynicism, sarcasm, anomie, and plain old wit. They simply didn't want to see irony entering into the current debate about moral values. Instead, they wished to limit it squarely to the realm of aesthetics, wrongly assumed to be amoral. Elise Harris' *Nation* review of Dave Eggers' *A Heartbreaking Work of Staggering Genius* (2000), supposedly but hardly an ironic novel, asked, "What is this dread 'irony' that everyone loves to hate? Nothing that corresponds to the dictionary definition of the rhetorical trope. They don't mean the deadpan statement of the opposite of your literal meaning, or the way an event turns out the opposite of expectations."[4] Dave Eggers himself addressed this concern in the reverse chapters of his book (*Mistakes We Knew We Were Making*) in increasingly difficult-to-read type in a section called "Irony and its Malcontents." Irony for Eggers was the most overused and wrongly assigned word ever. So, "Well. Well. Ahem. Well. Let's define irony as the dictionary does," he writes, "*the use of words to express something different from and often opposite to their literal meaning."*

> You know how much it pains me to use that word. . . . I have that
> *i*-word here only to make clear what was clear to, by my estima-
> tions, about 99% of original hardcover readers of this book: that
> there is almost no irony, whatsoever, within its covers. But to
> hear a few people tell it, this entire book, or most of it, was/is
> ironic.*

---

*Dave Eggers, *A Heartbreaking Work of Staggering Genius* (New York: Vintage, 2000), 33 (of the reverse paperback, *Mistakes We Knew We Were Making*).
For what it's worth, I agree with the author, Dave Eggers, about
A.H.W.O.S.G., one of the most beautiful, alive, energetic, life-giving, and
internal-dialogue-correlating books I've ever read. It is a funny book, and
there are moments of irony, but it is not an ironic book; it rarely takes aim at
anything snarkily. Rather, it hits directly in the chest (those Hippie Sticks are
not described as "a wonderful invention," but rather, as "fucking stupid hippie
sticks," or something like that).

Why some readers—mostly dusty literary types, one imagines—thought
Eggers's work so ironic: in a culture inured to spin, false sincerity, and more
jargon than an actionable paradigm, the mode of bone-breaking honesty and
deadpan observation is oddly *disbelieved* and *found to be funny* because it is done
in a manner contrary to the normal mode of ideological spin, business-speak,
and strategic euphemisms. All Eggers seemed to be doing, simply and in the
best-of-the-humanities tradition, was to describe what was going on around
him in plain language. Microbrewed beer is "beer that was brewed on the
premises." This is funny because the normal phrase for that beer is confusing
and made to seem more complex than it actually is. But it is not ironic.
Rather, "it's funny because it's true" (accredited to Homer Simpson/George
Meyer). Direct expression, with no tricks, gimmickry, or irony, has come to
be *interpreted ironically* because the default interpretive apparatus says, "He
can't really mean THAT!" When a culture becomes ironic about itself *en masse*,
simple statements of brutal fact, simple judgments of hate or dislike become
humorous because they unveil the absurdity, "friendliness," and caution of
normal public expression. It's funny because it's true. Honestly. We're all
upside down now.

The title of Benjamin Anastas' 1999 *New Republic* article—"How Did A Literary Device Become A Public Enemy?"—about the irony debate following the publication of Jedediah Purdy's book, also highlighted Anastas' confusion about irony's dual existence as both a literary trope and a social attitude. He was confused (more aptly: Socratically feigned confusion) about the idea that irony could be an *attitude* towards public life, positing instead that irony is "nothing more than a literary device."[5] He wondered how something as trite as a trope could become such a deplorable public nuisance and why some people are using a fallacious definition of "irony" that conflates "cynicism, sometimes parody, sometimes sarcasm, and sometimes plain old vice."[6] Likewise, *Harper's* editor, Rodger Hodge, asked, "How is it that an ancient and venerable figure of speech long associated with Socrates, Plato, Boccaccio, Shakespeare, and Cervantes . . . came to be the cause of so much unhappiness?"[7]

These are all fair, understandable accusations. The word, for better or worse, has come to signify cynicism, parody, sometimes sarcasm, and plain old vice. And by the 1990s, irony, in some more academic circles, in fact, had come to delimit an entire type of social character. Though the concerns of these critics are warranted, what is interesting is not that irony has been imbued with moral qualities, but why.

There are good and interesting reasons for the conflation: irony's moral dimension—though it seems the most honest thing we have going—has often been conceived of as unserious, untrustworthy, insincere, and incapable, fundamentally, of human connectedness or true belief. And for those on both sides of the political aisle fretting over the state of American society, irony poses a social *problem*. It reveals the ambivalence inherent in our ethical relationships with fellow citizens—our promises, political responsibilities, civic duties—and, closer to home, our intimate relations with friends, colleagues, and neighbors. The ironist, the oft-repeated argument goes, is fundamentally a bad citizen. He is as well to some, a bad American.

Yet irony as a device used as social critique has a long tradition in America, from the satires of Sarah Kembell Knight, Joseph Green, and

Francis Hopkinson, to William Byrd's jocular *History of the Dividing Line betwixt Virginia and North Carolina* (1728); from the Connecticut Wits (John Trumbull, Timothy Dwight [grandson of Jonathan Edwards], and Joel Barlow) to the riotously imaginative Washington Irving, whose satirical *History of New York* [by Diedrich Knicker-bocker] (1809) made him immediately famous, and about which Sir Walter Scott declared made his "sides hurt from laughter." Thomas Nast, Mark Twain, H. L. Mencken, Dorothy Parker, Ambrose Bierce, George Ade, Ring Lardner, Robert Benchly, S. J. Perelman, Art Buch-wald, Joseph Heller, Mort Sahl, Art Spiegelman, Jules Feiffer, Woody Allen, Garrison Keillor, *et al., et al., et al.!* And slightly earlier there's Philip Freneau, the eighteenth-century Revolutionary poet who wrote feverish satires against Tory sentiment even during his early days as James Madison's roommate at Princeton.

Freneau and another classmate, Hugh Henry Brackenridge—whose *Modern Chivalry* lampooned the problems of democracy in a western Pennsylvania backdrop—deployed irony to a higher cause: American independence, anti-Federalism, and the very birth of the Republic. Theirs was irony in the mode of satire, a utilitarian literary weapon with a well-honed tradition reaching from Xenophon to Jonathan Swift. Of course, there is an entire literary history of examples of irony and satire used in realm of American letters to critique culture and society, particularly when aimed at those in power or those whose interests ran contrary to the benefit of the general populace.[8] As much as some of these writers were criticized in their own time, they just as often found an enormously receptive audience ready to understand and sympathize.

This is exactly the same today.

The Argument

Contemporary American life is, frankly, somewhat of a nightmare. Our everyday existence is in a constant siege state, beset by affronts to our moral character and identity, not to mention actual threats to actual living we're constantly reminded of. This is not to demean the realities of those things. But in the culture wars of the 1990s, and even more so in the aftermath of September 11, 2001, Americans struggled hard to make sense of a national identity fraught with division. Throughout this discussion many pundits and commentators, particularly in the late 1990s, argued that in order to save our nation, to get the country back on track, Americans had to reject the pithy skepticism nurtured by pop culture and the intellectual elite. This attitude was often associated with a decline in the now-famed coinage, civic trust.*

Why has irony been portrayed as the behooded harbinger of civic Armageddon in the United States?

Among the tracts in the 1990s vying for a return to basics were Robert H. Bork's *Slouching towards Gomorrah* (1996), Stephen L. Carter's *Civility* (1998), Robert Bellah and company's *Habits of the Heart* (1985/1996), Amitai Etzioni's *The Spirit of Community* (2004), and Robert Putnam's feverishly discussed *Bowling Alone: The Collapse and Revival of American Community* (2000). Herein, discussions of private morality, pop culture, civility, and trust obsessed those concerned with the social health of the nation. Appropriately, Marc and Marque-Luisa Miringoff's *The Social Health of the Nation* claimed to show "how America is really doing."[9] Articles in *Atlantic Monthly, The Weekly Standard, The Chronicle of Philanthropy, The Wall Street Journal, The New Republic, Reason, The American Prospect, Commentary, Commonweal, The Public Interest, The National Interest*, and other nationally minded publications were engaged in a heated debate about why incivility was reigning in America and what could be done to get civil behavior back in the running. Often these works, from across the political spectrum,

---

*Curiously, there is no good translation of this term in German, French, or Italian.

urged a return to a better time (in the future), when society was (could be again) more civil, kind, and believing. For America to return to the nobility of its unique historical errand it had to shed, in effect, its detachment from the public good, its concern with the self, its frivolity. This concern, we were told, became even more urgent after the terrorist attacks of September 11, 2001, when, incongruously and curiously, the punditocracy counterattacked by calling for a return to seriousness and a permanent end to, of all things, irony.

This was a disastrous move, not least because the complaints that fueled the attack on irony—that society had become too selfish, civically unconcerned, hypocritical, self-absorbed, that we had lost our sense of proportion and self-restraint and humility—are legitimate and important ones. Irony can be a very useful critical tool for pointing out such flaws. The enormous reception of *The Daily Show* and *The Colbert Report* evidences this point.* The declaration of a War on Irony disregarded irony's liberating powers, particularly as contrasted against the utter craziness of fanatical belief—militant Islamicist (Talibanian, Al-Qaedian) or militant Christianist (Pat Robertsonian, Jesus Camp-ian)—evidenced in irony's leavening power against the Mohammed cartoon situation or Katrina being sent by God to attack New Orleans for its gay partying revelry.† Pundits and editors who went after irony, both pre- and post-9/11, neglected to credit its long-

---

*The *Washington Post* announced on October 9, 2006, that Jon Stewart and Stephen Colbert will not, in fact, be running for the office of president of the United States in 2008. Barry Levinson's *Man of the Year* will have to be archived until 2012 to become Nostradamic. Stewart said at the *New Yorker* Festival in October 2006 that T-shirts promoting the possibility "are a real sign of how sad people are" and that "nothing says 'I am ashamed of you, my government' more than 'Stewart/Colbert 08.'" True that.

†Art Spiegelman addresses this point nicely in an article entitled "Drawing Blood," *Harper's* (June 2006). Moreover, Spiegelman's entry to the counter-cartoon competition sponsored by an organization in Holocaust-denying Iran featured a concentration camp prisoner standing in a long line waiting for incineration, laughing hysterically, saying, "The funny thing is, none of this is really happening!"

entrenched ability to patently hold off lies, hypocrisy, fanaticism, and insincerity since its inception as permanently engaged social criticism—a bastard child of the Enlightenment.

While reading about and thinking through this topic, then, I have been concerned with asking these questions: why has irony figured so prominently in the American debate over civil society? What is it about irony and its relationship to morality that strikes such a public nerve? Why, in effect, did irony assume a moral quality? What are irony's philosophical assumptions? Is irony inherently a liberal position? Why? What attributes of the good citizen does the ironist supposedly lack or contradict? And, importantly, why has irony been portrayed as the behooded harbinger of civic Armageddon in the United States? Do ironists make civic culture less healthy, or is an unhealthy civic culture, caused by other events and situations, making people ironically detached? What is it about the ironist's personality or character that is quintessentially anti-civic?

The task of the present work—which moves from light and bantering in the first two chapters to some more weighty (i.e., somewhat somnolent but necessary) material in the chapters following, then back again—is to find out why this happened and to propose a different outcome, one in which irony is recalled as a liberating cultural and personal force; one that, when used wisely, can be a psychological strategy for maintaining personal integrity in the face of a complex and often contradictory world, one filled with plentiful handfuls of "sincerity-marketing" politicos and images of fulfillment attained by sacrificing all inner measures and passions, all defenses against being *made* into something.*

To be sure, there is a protective dimension to this kind of detachment; it is, ultimately, though its own face belies it, no joke. It values, above all, the sacredness of integrity, of locating souls of like tenor, of

---

*Theodor Adorno wrote, "The artist today does not become an artist. He avoids being made into something else."

sincerity, authenticity, and maintaining a private vision of a better society and culture. It enables individuals to distance themselves from a culture and politics they regard as worthy of disavowal. It is in this sense that irony comes close to, as Kierkegaard wrote, "a species of religious devotion."

CHAPTER ONE

Good Morning, America

Insofar as irony becomes conscious of the fact that existence has no reality, thereby expressing the same thesis as
the pious disposition, it might seem that irony were a
species of religious devotion.
   —Søren Kierkegaard, *The Concept of Irony* (1841)

In the age of irony even the most serious things were not
to be taken seriously.
   —Roger Rosenblatt, *Time*, September 20, 2001

You have a responsibility to the public discourse, and you
fail miserably.
   —Jon Stewart on *Crossfire* to Tucker Carlson, cohost (2004)

Nine days after the attacks of September 11, 2001, *Time* magazine
columnist Roger Rosenblatt declared "The Age of Irony Comes to An
End":

> One good thing could come from this horror: it could spell the
> end of the age of irony. For some 30 years—roughly as long as
> the Twin Towers were upright—the good folks in charge of
> America's intellectual life have insisted that nothing was to be
> believed in or taken seriously. Nothing was real. With a giggle
> and a smirk, our chattering classes—our columnists and pop cul-

ture makers—declared that detachment and personal whimsy were the necessary tools for an oh-so-cool life. . . . The ironists, seeing through everything, made it difficult for anyone to see anything. The consequence of thinking that nothing is real— apart from prancing around in an air of vain stupidity—is that one will not know the difference between a joke and a menace.[1]

Rosenblatt continued by unleashing a hefty amount of anger against "the vain stupidity of ironists" who try to see through everything. There will be no room in this new and chastened time for "columnists" and "pop-culture makers," people who think that they're "oh-so-cool."* Times now are serious, so the chatterers won't be around much longer. "In the age of irony," Rosenblatt offers, "even the most serious things were not to be taken seriously. . . .[even] death was not to be seen as real. If one doubted its reality before last week, that is unlikely to happen again."[2]

Rosenblatt's opinion of irony, it turns out, was shared by many. In an interview with the *Los Angeles Times* the esteemed civil rights historian Taylor Branch thought that the attacks on America had brought the nation to "a turning point against a generation of cynicism." Gerry Howard, editorial director of Broadway Books in New York, told *Entertainment Weekly,* "I think somebody should do a marker that says irony died on 9-11-01." The *Atlanta Journal-Constitution's* Phil Kloer reported that September 11 spelled the demise of a popular culture "drenched in irony and cynicism" that was "a playground for postmodern hipsters," wherein the "appropriate response to anything is the jaded, all-purpose 'whatever.'" James Pinkerton of *Newsday* went a triumphant step further and decreed a victory for "sincerity, patriotism, and earnestness" and, countering the Seinfeldian premise,

---

*Though I am sure Rosenblatt was aware, "oh-so-cool" is a nice turn of ironic phrasing. Though they think it is cool, it is not cool, by which he means, I am assuming, desirable. This fatwa on irony, with its inherent contradiction, is but a new rendition of Plato's eloquently written call for the ejection of the poets from the Republic.

announced that "there's more to life than *nothing*, that some things really matter."

Perhaps most famously and oft cited was Graydon Carter, editor of *Vanity Fair* and former editor of the defunct satirical *Spy* magazine, who predicted immediately after September 11 that "there's going to be a seismic change. I think it's the end of the age of irony." His pronouncements went rippling out into newspaper opinion-pages and websites across the nation. "Things that were considered fringe and frivolous," Carter claimed, "are going to disappear."

This reaction against frivolity is entirely understandable. Blogs and web pages of places like *Reason*, *Salon*, and *Slate* buzzed with commentary for and against Carter's and Rosenblatt's statements. Finally, a free-for-all topic. Everyone had something to say about attacks on irony, in part because, for those who use it regularly, it seemed so personal. More broadly, however, the logic of the cautionary tales seemed to hint at something bigger: a Marx-like alchemy at work: all that is ironic melts into air. The literal dissolution of the Twin Towers heralded a new day, a dispersal of irony into the ether. Patriotism and earnest engagement would rise like so many phoenixes from the flame. Earnestness regained.

Karl Marx as Talk-Show Host

Even on television! In a wise move, the Fox Network, which operates one of the most enthusiastically and self-consciously "pro-American" cable news channels, pulled the movie *Independence Day*—the defining image of which is an exploding White House—from its Sunday, September 15 airdate.

Likewise, the Family Channel yanked the movie *Earthquake in New York*, scheduled for September 18. Television comedians were faced with similar dilemmas. David Letterman, Conan O'Brien, and Jay Leno, showing great tact and public remorse, did not deliver their normal comedy routines. Outted by the tragedy of September 11, ironists and the postmodern hipsters who populated advertising firms, magazine editorial offices, and sitcom writing rooms were being seen for the plague on the land that they were. In this "new and chastened time," they would have to shape up or ship out. Somehow irony and terrorism became, in some more ethereal realms and for abstract reasons, conceptually interrelated: both were against holding society together.

But: popular culture to the rescue again—with irony, warts and all. New York City mayor Rudolph Giuliani went on *Saturday Night Live* three weeks after the attacks of September 11 to tell the country that it was okay to laugh again, that New York was "open for business," that life could get back to normal. Emanating from the hallowed portals of satire, the city's mayor avowed that the work of the nation could continue.

September 11's concrete horror, its piercing reality and unrelenting moral weight, in total effect, its *seriousness*, was supposed to have spelled the end of ironic disengagement in America. Pundits like those above argued that a whole generation of Americans, most notably so-called Generation X, having never felt truly threatened, would now have to shed their cynicism and take life seriously, as had their grandparents of the Greatest Generation. The morning of September 11 was supposed to have shorn Americans of their moral relativism and leniency, reignited earnestness and civic union. It was supposed to have summoned another, sustained, Great Awakening.*

*Times of unimaginable tragedy always call for deep, slate-cleaning renewal so that historical causalities of the present do not happen again. Anecdotally: in a reaction to the French Revolution that could easily be transposed to the reaction to September 11, the German Romantic philosopher and classicist Friedrich Schlegel wrote that it was "the most frightful grotesque of the age, where the most profound prejudices and their most brutal punishments are

It did not do that. American popular culture now and the sensibility necessary for the consumption and understanding of that popular culture is even more satiric-critical than before September 11. Though the political discourse (and corresponding political reality) has become more serious—grave, even—very little in pop culture has changed. The youthful taste for the ironic, sarcastic, and biting—especially as utilized in the critique of power— is perhaps now even more widespread on cable television, print publications, and the Web than before that fateful moment in American history.

The morning of September 11 was supposed to have summoned another Great Awakening of seriousness. It did not do that.

Perhaps most interestingly over the past few years is that the most strikingly truthful and enlightening points about society and politics are being highlighted by the most ironic among us. As the real news becomes more like a blockbuster movie filled with loud noises, PlayStation-like graphics, theme music, shiny things, and exhausted clichés, the most surprisingly truthful criticism of political leaders, culture, and social realities is coming from fake-news sources and satire. And some of the many places that summon and continue the satirical tradition—wherein irony serves to liberate thinking from deadening social forces, old clichés and stereotypes, stupid biases, hypocrisy, and oppressive public mores—are various television shows on Comedy Central, *The Colbert Report, Chappelle's Show, Adult Swim,*

---

mixed up in a fearful chaos and woven as bizarrely as possible into a monstrous human tragicomedy. . . . There is no greater need of the age than the need for a spiritual counterweight to the Revolution and to the despotism which the Revolution exercises over people by means of its concentration on the most desirable worldly interests." Of relevancy is that like the critics of irony immediately post-9/11, irony as an interest slowly faded from Schlegel's interest, and his politics turned increasingly conservative and religious.

and *South Park*, and on *The Simpsons, Curb Your Enthusiasm, Family Guy, American Dad!, Da Ali-G Show* (now exclusively *Borat*), *The Office, Extras;* magazines and websites like *Harper's, Gawker, Jest, McSweeney's, Salon*, and *The Believer;* and satirical newspapers like *The Onion*, about which the über-earnest Ken Burns has written, "Unlike any other entity in our media culture, [*The Onion*] offers a refreshingly *honest* look at our complicated life."[3] In a culture seen as having false values, honesty speaks most loudly under the cover of outlets posing as the real.

Television-news journalists and reporters were shocked in early fall 2004—particularly Bill O'Reilly of *The O'Reilly Factor*, who swiped at Stewart's "dopey show" for speaking primarily to "stoned slackers" (that was *Half-Baked*, holmes)—to learn that among nineteen thousand surveyed young adults in their twenties, 16 percent trusted Comedy Central's Jon Stewart, host of *The Daily Show*, more than they trusted two of the three major network news anchors. Moreover, "viewers of late-night comedy programs, especially *The Daily Show* with Jon Stewart on Comedy Central, are more likely to know the issue positions and backgrounds of presidential candidates than people who do not watch late-night comedy."*

---

*The results of the survey, conducted by Global Strategy Group and Luntz Research,were Tom Brokaw (NBC) 17 percent; Jon Stewart 16 percent; Peter Jennings (ABC) 15 percent; and Dan Rather (CBS) 10 percent. Each of the major network anchors has over two decades of reporting the news to their credit. Subsequent to these numbers the Annenberg Public Policy Center 2004 Election Survey, polling between July 15 and September 16, 2004, released a report that included information about young people who regularly watched *The Daily Show:* "People who watch *The Daily Show* are more interested in the presidential campaign, more educated, younger, and more liberal than the average American or than Leno or Letterman viewers." The study revealed also that the average correct score on a series of current political questions of eighteen- to twenty-nine-year-olds was only slightly behind sixty-five-and-over voters. Additionally, *Daily Show* viewers aged eighteen to twenty-nine scored as high as the same group that regularly watches at least four days of cable news a week and higher than those who read newspapers

Stewart and the writers at *The Daily Show,* as well as at *The Colbert Report* (both created by Stewart's Busboy Productions) deliver the news in spotlessly wry fashion, utilize irony, sarcasm, and general bubble-bursting to report on major events of the day from the perspective of the secretly-still-idealistic-but-presently-disappointed-in-everything observer. Colbert's entire show takes place under the cover of irony, from the cheesy patriotic graphics, theme music, bold typography, to the part he plays of the ultraconservative, vigorously pro-American talk-show host, mocking *en extremis* Bill O'Reilly or Sean Hannity of *Hannity & Colmes.* But it is crucial to note that *The Daily Show,* in particular—being the far more serious of the two—also repeatedly and rigorously holds politicians and other official figures accountable for their past public statements, which are, ideally, consistent and not duplicitous.*

Highlighted, of course, is the radical inconsistency and blatant contradiction at the highest levels of government and authority. At this point the show trades satire for brutal, bleak reality, accentuating the hard fact that this is, ultimately, no joke. In this sense *The Daily Show* values logical and moral consistency by using select video clips and actual quotations to do what many other talking-head shows do not (save Sunday mornings, Mr. Russert): actual analysis and setting standards for condemnation or praise. For these reasons—for both satire and bleak truth—the show's following is enormous (over 1.1 million each night), and Stewart's book, *America: The Book* was number one on the *New York Times* best-seller list for several weeks and a worldwide best-selling book in winter 2004–5. The host's appearance at the 2006 Oscars ceremony—impressive in itself for someone not yet a house-

---

one-to-three days a week. A helpful collation and analysis of both the Annenberg and Pew studies can be found in a master's thesis, "The Daily Show Effect: Humor, News, Knowledge, and Viewers" by Rachel Joy Larris of Georgetown University. Well, formerly of; I'm assuming she passed.

*When O'Reilly actually appeared on *The Colbert Report* and "jokingly" revealed his on-screen persona was "all an act," the more serious question—given that O'Reilly's viewers don't see him as acting—is what Colbert is actually mocking, if the person targeted doesn't really exist?

hold name—received mixed reviews, many saying that Stewart simply floundered. It must be hard to parody something that is already unwittingly parodying itself.

Nonetheless, when Stewart satirically reports the news, he is perceived as more honest and credible not because his *words* are more honest, that is, literal, matching directly word for meaning—for they mostly mean something other than what they say—but because his audience is interpreting the subject and sentiments that are *behind* those words: a melancholic yet searingly truthful account of how citizens feel about what is going on in the world as reported on network news. Through satire (not *fake* news, as the stories are always pegged to real events) *The Daily Show*, at the same time it mimics the format of serious news, also shows the artifice of other "unbiased," or "objective" news networks by highlighting the clichés and mechanisms by which they function. Through ironic posturing, that is, Stewart and the writing staff at *The Daily Show* and *The Colbert Report* are paradoxically communicating authenticity, sincerity, and honesty—legitimacy. Comedy keeps watch on journalism now; it is the Fifth Estate, so to speak—especially when journalism all around seems to be exhibiting increasing degrees of shoddiness, feigned objectivity, and an ability to be swayed by political "inducements."

The interesting and important conflict between the figure of the ironist and the television pundit was brought to a head in a now well-known spat between Jon Stewart and conservative talk-show host Tucker Carlson, along with cohost Paul Begala, on CNN's *Crossfire* in fall 2004.* In the conversation, it is Stewart-the-ironist, the satirist,

---

*Televised trauma dies hard: In an interview in the July 2006 *Texas Monthly*, two years after the event, Begala tells readers that when "Jon Stewart came on *Crossfire* and said the show was hurting America, I literally was reaching into my pocket to call my wife—live, while we were on the air—to tell her to watch. But 'hurting America'? I mean, come on. Even if the show's harshest critics were right, thirty minutes of a couple of knuckleheads shouting at each other wasn't hurting America" (30). Knuckleheads. On a channel calling itself "the most trusted name in news." Precisely the problem.

who tells the "serious" host that his program is not helpful to American culture, that *Crossfire* is not doing debate, it's doing theater; it's "hurting America." Stewart reaches a point of credible earnestness and concern for the public good; Carlson seems like the pundit who is not actually concerned with the public good, but rather, his television show and public persona (bow tie and all). Here's an excerpt from the official CNN transcript:

STEWART: You know, the interesting thing I have is . . . You have a responsibility to the public discourse, and you fail miserably.

CARLSON: You need to get a job at a journalism school, I think.

STEWART: You need to go to one. The thing that I want to say is, when you have people on for just knee-jerk, reactionary talk . . .

CARLSON: Wait. I thought you were going to be funny. Come on, be funny.

STEWART: No. No. I'm not going to be your monkey.

(Laughter)

BEGALA: Go ahead. Go ahead.

STEWART: I watch your show every day. And it kills me.

CARLSON: I can tell you love it.

STEWART: It's so—oh, it's so painful to watch.

(Laughter)

STEWART: You know, because we need what you do. This is such a great opportunity you have here to actually get politicians off of their marketing and strategy.

CARLSON: Is this really Jon Stewart? What is this, anyway?

STEWART: Yes, it's someone who watches your show and cannot take it anymore.

(Laughter)

STEWART: I just can't.

CARLSON: What's it like to have dinner with you? It must be excruciating. Do you, like, lecture people like this, or do you come over to their house and sit and lecture them? [Do you tell them] they're not doing the right thing, that they're missing their opportunities, evading their responsibilities?

STEWART: If I think they are.

So it is Stewart who, in the end, has the last word on civic responsibility on a program that boldly exists to foster civic responsibility through debate. "If your idea of confronting me is to say that I don't ask hard-hitting enough questions," said Stewart, whose show at the time was preceded by *Crank Yankers*, where foul-mouthed puppets make crank phone calls, "then we're in pretty bad shape, fellas." Shortly thereafter, deliciously, Carlson was fired from *Crossfire*.

For the reason of Carlson's release, CNN's then-new president, Jonathan Klein, "specifically cited the criticism that the comedian Jon Stewart leveled at *Crossfire* when he was a guest on the program during the presidential campaign," wrote *New York Times'* Bill Carter.[4] And when, shortly thereafter, *Crossfire* itself was canceled, Klein said he agreed "wholeheartedly with Jon Stewart's overall premise." Especially after the terror attacks on September 11, Klein believed, viewers were less interested in opinion, more in actual information.

To be fair, though, Carlson, who went to MSNBC in February 2005, said he had actually quit *Crossfire* prior to Stewart's appearance. He had agreed to stay on until his contract was over and said he actually had a deal as the host of a nightly program on MSNBC. (Either more or less embarrassingly, he was then eliminated from *Dancing with the Stars* in September 2006. No further comment is necessary.)

Meanwhile, back at the ranch, a bit over a year later, Leslie Moonves, co–chief executive of Viacom, owner of CBS and Comedy Central, speculated in January 2005 that Jon Stewart might take over for outgoing *CBS News* anchor Dan Rather. Moonves then let the conjecture slide, but even that this option was *considered* evidences the bizarre equivalence of real and satirical news and, moreso, how Stewart's *credibility* trumped that of other potential candidates—that is, actual journalists.

This begs an interesting question: Is *The Daily Show* just doing really good news, or is the real news becoming more like sketch comedy? Without a doubt, and more scarily, it is the latter; but it is in part because *The Daily Show* is highlighting the operational strategies, false sentiments, and techno-aesthetics of major-network and cable news programs, undercutting them as sources of trustable information. Of course, they make it easy: many segments are created simply to fill airtime. Stewart himself denies that his audience is getting their news from his show, per se; jokes on his half-hour show require preknowledge of political and historical events to comprehend. Apparently he's right: the Annenberg and Pew Studies (there you go) both confirm that young political sophisticates come to *The Daily Show* more for a sense of like-mindedness than to get the news.*

An additional and now-famed moment important to highlight this conceptual slippage, this friction between the serious and the satirical—something that is occurring with an absurd frequency†—happened on Saturday, April 29, 2006, when Stephen Colbert was the featured entertainer for the 2006 White House Correspondents' Association Dinner. His twenty-four-minute speech (and short film auditioning for the recently filled position of press secretary, which

---

*Dannagal Goldthwaite Young, the head researcher of the Annenberg Public Policy Center 2004 Election Survey, noted that the findings "do not show that *The Daily Show* is itself responsible for the higher knowledge among its viewers . . . [the program] assumes a fairly high level of political knowledge on the part of its audiences—more so than Leno or Letterman. At the same time, because *The Daily Show* does deal with campaign events and issues, viewers might certainly pick up information while watching."

†Beyond the confusion between what is real and what is a joke, even in realms that blend bleak humor with real facts there is confusion on occasion. *Harper's Weekly*, an email newsletter featuring a wrap-up of the world's ills and absurdities, sent a follow-up email to their April 3, 2007 release: "The statement 'in New York City, someone stole the penis of a chocolate Jesus' is not true; the source was a satire website that was mistakenly thought to be a genuine news source. *Harper's Weekly* apologizes for the error." Satire doesn't even have to work at its job; jokes now seem to make themselves. *Veritas* backwards, after all, spells satire (plus an extra V-thingy).

was introduced by the line: "You really should have hired me, Sir. I have nothing but contempt for these people") was broadcast on both C-SPAN and MSNBC. Throughout his presentation Colbert unremittingly lampooned the Bush administration and the White House press corps:

> I stand by this man. I stand by this man because he stands for things. Not only for things, he stands on things. Things like aircraft carriers and rubble and recently flooded city squares. And that sends a strong message, that no matter what happens to America, she will always rebound—with the most powerfully staged photo ops in the world.

And then this, among a litany of direct relentless affronts:

> I believe the government that governs best is the government that governs least. And by these standards, we have set up a fabulous government in Iraq.

And it kept on going:

> Let's review the rules. Here's how it works: the president makes decisions. He's The Decider. The press secretary announces those decisions, and you people of the press type those decisions down. Make, announce, type. Just put 'em through a spell-check and go home. Get to know your family again. Make love to your wife. Write that novel you got kicking around in your head. You know, the one about the intrepid Washington reporter with the courage to stand up to the administration. You know—fiction!

Perhaps predictably, the performance garnered only a lukewarm response from the confused and disbelieving audience of business professionals, decorated military folk, the press corps themselves, Pentagon officials, and whoever else goes to that dinner. Major media out-

lets—ABC, NBC, CBS, CNN, FOX—paid little attention to the broadcast. On MSNBC's *Hardball* host Chris Matthews pooh-poohed the
performance as "bad." Many opined that Colbert had "crossed the line,"
and *Washington Post* columnist Richard Cohen wrote that it was completely unfunny. To many, it seemed as though Colbert had bombed.
Unlike some others in the room, though, only metaphorically.

But the video of Colbert's speech jet-propelled into an overnight
Internet sensation, becoming the
most massively downloaded file on
Apple's iTunes within hours. Rat-
ings for *The Colbert Report* sky-
rocket an incredible 37 percent by
week's end, and the press slowly,
perhaps resentfully, began to recognize Colbert's speech as an
important event—even if unsure
why.

These episodes are telling, not
least because they speak to a "silent
majority" of people who understand what Colbert and Stewart
(and their writer-producers, like
Ben Karlin from *The Onion*) have
been doing: finding a way to credi-
bly and legitimately critique in an
age where serious critique is often   Stephen Colbert with Heart
incredulous or clearly partisan,
where political cynicism in the minds of millions is always and already
prepared to disbelieve anything thrown at it directly. They are and
have been rediscovering a method of critique that had long been
cheapened or discarded because it had not taken itself, yes, seriously
enough.

True, *Saturday Night Live, Politically Incorrect with Bill Maher, Mad
TV, Not Necessarily The News* (remember that!? Oh, Stuart Pankin and

Rich Hall, where are you now? Sniglets.), *This Hour Has 22 Minutes* (Canadian), and many others have been doing social, cultural, and political critique for decades. The formats vary, the personalities, too. But it is perhaps, beyond the humor, the moral vision and intellectual rigor of *The Daily Show* and *The Colbert Report* that have garnered them with legitimacy and credibility that are often seen to be lacking in nonironic news channels. Former co–executive producer of *The Daily Show* Karlin says it more succinctly. The targets are simply "hypocrisy . . . people who know better saying things that you know they don't believe." And Stewart, addressing the lack of overt partisanship of *The Daily Show*, declares: "We're passionately opposed to bullshit. . . . Is that liberal or conservative?"[5]

This has resonance because it touches on a mentality of frustration, on a recognition of political cynicism now so bare, so open to observation, so brutally real it verges on the totally boring. Yet all the while this political cynicism thinks itself hidden. Because it is no longer, this kind of critique succeeds because the interpretive schema of irony is so widely shared, such an informal and comfortable part of everyday life. "The cynical citizen is a mass figure, not an eccentric outsider," writes the political scientist William Chaloupka, author of *Everybody Knows: Cynicism in America* (1999). "Citizen-cynics are as easily found in rural Montana as in cosmopolitan New York."[6] The attitude of wry social distancing is no longer roped off in an exclusive literary enclave. "Irony," for the literary critic Andrew Delbanco, "has become the normative style of contemporary life."[7]

Colbert's speech resonated throughout the world. South Park *'s tenth anniversary took up the whole half-hour on* Nightline. Jeopardy! *now has a category from* The Onion. *The Discovery Channel held a satire competition. The serious have been subdued.*

And apparently now normatively celebrated. *South Park's* tenth anniversary took up the whole half-hour on *Nightline*. There is now a category on *Jeopardy!* from *The Onion*. The Discovery Channel held a satire competition. The serious *Spiegel* magazine in Germany now has a satire component on its site. The *Economist* ran an entire "Lexington" essay on *The Colbert Report* (March 31–April 6, 2007). The U.S. Mint unveiled an advertisement for coins that mocked a prescription-drug commercial; sufferers had numismatism. Satire is again serious business. The serious have been subdued.

The Ironist Sensibility: A Poorly Drawn Sketch

For all the political talk of seriousness and purpose coming back on one side, the use and comprehension of increasingly complex ironic language and situations on the other continues to be the key indicator of the "new," the insightful, young, and intellectually and politically astute. It is still how you tell if someone "gets it" or not. And this "getting it," that is, getting these shared assumptions about the nature of self and world, must be done with *immediacy*; irony cancels out the moment a word of interpretation is added. But as the ironic tone has come to dominate our structures of conversation, this "adding a word of interpretation" no longer suffices, for adding interpretation to an ironic situation has now itself become ironizing of those who would.* Ironic thinking is lightning fast, and it always reconstitutes itself behind attempts to name it directly.

This kind of "getting it," then, often entails a remorseful, frustrated default reaction to the Machiavellian realities of politics and social life and the attempt at distraction from these realities by American mid-

---

*Ironic awareness *always* supersedes attempts to "read it," even when a clear rule of "no interpretation of irony" is laid down. A nonimmediate interpretation of an ironic remark or situation can be done ironically, as if one does not get it. The ironist plays the fool—only to a fellow ironist, the one initially remarking—who does not know that the original remark *was* ironic. "Hey, wait a minute; you're not being serious, are you?" It's hilarious. Seriously.

dlebrow culture, which the ironist sees as hokey, false, uninspiring, uncreative, stupid, cheap, lazy, pandering, and ubiquitous. Beyond the political realm, there is an unspoken understanding within this ironic sensibility that mainstream American culture fundamentally perpetuates an *illusion* of suburban tranquility, beneath the surface of which lies turmoil, misery, and despair.* For the ironist, the one assumption that goes without questioning is that the mass of "Middle America" lives with its own delusions of life, that it does not "get" what is going on in the world, that it is complacent, that its moral rhetoric carries no weight. Much popular culture, particularly television, contributes to this attitude of seeing beneath the placidity of everyday life, featuring as it does a hefty amount of programming about murder, divorce, betrayal, addiction, sadness, and dysfunction of all flavors. Increasingly, these shows are, indicatively, "reality" shows. This assumption of seeing beneath the realities of normal living has taken hold particularly because the idea of the noble public has lost the ability to puncture with moral momentum into the private sphere.[8]

The division over what counts as humor and whether irony is divisive, particularly when it comes to large media events with corporate sponsors, was seen clearly in a debate over the song selection by Robin Williams at the 2005 Oscars, when executives at ABC told the comedian to drop a song because of its tone and content. Playing on the dark underbelly of cartoons, Williams was to recite lyrics such as "Pinocchio's had his nose done; Sleeping Beauty is popping pills; Fred Flintstone is dyslexic; Olive Oyl is anorexic," and so on. After being told to ditch the song, Williams said, "For a while you get mad, then you get over it. They're afraid of saying Olive Oyl is anorexic. It tells you about the state of humor. . . . We thought that they got the irony of it. I guess not."[9]

Evidenced here, this "getting it" also implies a sense of cultural, moral, or aesthetic superiority for those not liking the imperialism of

---

*This is the Cheever-esque basis of the incredibly popular television series *Desperate Housewives*, which began in summer 2004.

Wal-Mart, Starbuckification, "You're fired!" and Celine Dion. (Returning from commercial break during the Stewart *Crossfire* appearance,
Tucker Carlson blurted, "Back to *Crossfire*, where Jon Stewart was just
lecturing us on our moral inferiority"; "I'm a martyred moralist,"
Eggers confides.) On the ironist's hit list, then, seen in any number of
shows on VH1, are the sort of stupid, lounge-y, mawkish, falsely intimate, saccharine, feel-good products and emanations of middlebrow
American culture. This includes mostly cultural products that are also
lucrative, that become "culture" because they are such. There are, of
course, many specific incarnations, such as (take a deep breath): the
movies *Pretty Woman, Titanic, Bridges of Madison County, AI, Independence Day*, films that make New York City the backdrop for romantic
comedy, especially when starring the theatrics of actors such as Meg
Ryan or Tom Hanks; practically any film produced by Jerry Bruck-
heimer or James Cameron;* movies or television programs with an

---

*Locating cheesy (somehow always intertwined with things overtly uplifting
or pedantic) is always fun sport in popular American culture if you're an ironist (or a cheeky Brit), particularly if it contains the characteristics listed. On
December 6, 2004, Baker Warburtons in Great Britain—with typical drye-
mocke—released the top-ten list of the cheesiest lines in American film as
determined by British moviegoers. They are as follows: (1) *Titanic:* Leonardo
DiCaprio's "I'm the king of the world!" [*Author note:* this line was even worse
when repeated by director Cameron at the Oscars, for it reified in reality what
as fiction was bad enough—read: overly and inappropriately self-inflated,
showing a lack of tact and excess of teenager misperception of awesomeness.]
(2) *Dirty Dancing:* Patrick Swayze's "Nobody puts Baby in the corner." (3)
Four Weddings and A Funeral: Andie McDowell's "Is it still raining? I hadn't
noticed." (4) *Ghost:* Demi Moore's "Ditto" to Patrick Swayze's "I love you." (5)
Top Gun: Val Kilmer to Tom Cruise: "You can be my wingman anytime." (6)
Notting Hill: Julia Roberts' "I'm just a girl . . . standing in front of a boy . . .
asking him to love her." (7) *Independence Day:* Bill Pullman's "Today we cele-
brate our Independence Day!" (8) *Braveheart:* Mel Gibson's "They may take
our lives, but they will not take our freedom!" (9) *Jerry Maguire:* Renee Zell-
weger to Tom Cruise: "You had me at hello."(10) *The Postman:* A blind woman
says to Kevin Costner: "You're a godsend, a savior." He replies: "No, I'm a
postman." See http://www.warburtons.co.uk. Additionally, VH1 runs a

overt message of patriotism, positive thinking, Yes-I-Can-ism, or of a pedagogically uplifting spirit, books like the *Celestine Prophecy*, or *Chicken Soup for the Soul*,* angel statues, overt religious symbolism (especially in cheap plastic objects, glow-in-the-dark devotional statues, rosaries, and holy cards), the invocation of Jesus in any conversations—or T-shirts asking what he would do—the music of Yanni (and Public Television's surreal, confusing special, "Yanni: A Year of Excellence"), the Boston Pops, the singers Andrea Bocelli, Josh Grobin, and John Tesh; compact disc collections of the "Greatest Composers" with images of a snow-covered house with candlelit windows on the front, such as those mass-produced by the painter Thomas Kinkade ("Painter of Light"®,✝ the most highly sold artist in America‡), featuring pieces like "Pachelbel's Greatest Hit" (Canon in D); masterpieces of Western art reproduced on mugs, key chains, or dinner plates; sweatshirts or T-shirts with phrases like "So Many Books . . . So Little Time," "The World is My Ashtray," or "My Other Car is a Ferrari"; Dockers (too symptomatically plain); pleats (too distractingly decorative); channels dedicated to suburban home-decorating, the PAX network and its programming, especially ones such as *Miracle Pets*; the *Family Circus* cartoon or *Garfield* (bad as cartoon, worse as computer-enhanced feature-length movie); restaurants that attempt historical or ethnic authenticity through mass-produced faux elements, such as "rustic" walls, waxed decorative breads, old wine bottles, posters of kittens or babies

---

series on the "101 Cheesiest Moments" among other shows that highlight the worst (best) moments in popular culture over the past two decades. The comedian-hosts excel at commentary on why these moments are so great because so embarrassing/gladly reforgotten. You go, Mo Rocca.

*A book that was subsequently satirized by the newspaper *The Onion* with the title *Chicken Soup for the Publisher's Bank Account*. Again, this points to satire's energy and humor coming from the ultimate reduction of something "hopeful" or "inspirational" to something at root based on greed and self-interest. Thus, *again*, "It's funny because it's true."

✝The registered trademark on "Painter of Light" is not a joke.

‡Neither is this.

dressed as peapods or flowers (see photographer Anne Geddes and Celine Dion's lovely joint efforts in the 2005 book *Miracle*, which comes with its own CD of Dion's lullaby songs), faux-faded sepia tone photographs depicting "how things used to be," "distressed" furniture, paintings of "old Italy" or "Olde Tyme" Ireland. (In short, places and objects that replace authenticity and actual time with economics-of-scale production, that erase the violence and grit of getting food to the table at a reasonable price.) These restaurants would include the chains Olive Garden, TGI Friday's, Houlihan's, Chili's, Ruby Tuesday, or Cracker Barrel. This is especially compounded by these restaurants' location in a major urban setting, such as Times Square or the sprawling center of Los Angeles. The examples are endless. This is arrogant. It must be said.

This very small sampling pits dominant American culture against a more refined (read: educated, authenticity-obsessed) version of what counts as real culture. It holds middlebrow commercialism at arm's length because it does not want to accept it as the same caliber or quality of what counts as honest and authentic culture. It subsumes the moral under the guise of the aesthetic, the performative—but it does so wittingly and with announcement. Importantly, ironic sensibility does not negate moral concerns; it just devalues their presence in aesthetic production—which, when done, is known as "instructional art" or, forced to its logical extreme, social realism. These cultural items are despised and made fun of because they are things that contain no element of surprise or intellectual adventure. (Importantly, the cultural objects and works are deemed *kitsch* if they are not collected by ironists, *camp* if they are.)* They are repeated forms and predictable

---

*The reappropriation of the garden gnome by Travelocity is a good example of a company using camp to sell airfare and travel packages. The use of the "travel gnome" displays hipness and humor (and thus appeals to a target audience) by boldly placing the figure front and center as a mascot. Such a move counters the gnome's normal meaning as basically unseen kitschy decoration. To the consumer who ambivalently regrets the state of mainstream culture, when the past rises up to remind him of better days, it also thereby justifies

content. They accentuate and encourage rampant consumerism without cause. They operate by clichéd mechanisms that are as pandering as they are predictable and profitable. In short, they are all products of the "culture industry," having no real inventiveness or authenticity—exactly what the ironist wants from his culture and from himself. He sees the major thrust of mainstream culture as an embarrassing problem for his national identity because it perpetuates illusions, faux moral authority, obvious "moral lessons," and bad taste. Reactionary distancing—aestheticizing, ironizing—helps ironists to view these places, items, and products as something not a part of themselves. They are strangers in a strange land. They view them ironically or anthropologically, askew or from above—in either case, from internally afar.

But beyond the description of the ironist public character seen in the figures of Colbert, Stewart, Borat, et al., and beyond the sort of things he loves to hate, what, exactly, is this ironist character in social criticism of late? It would be helpful to draw a more detailed drawing before delving into more abstract ruminations based upon it. The qualities of this abstracted character come from a conflation of conversations, observations, television shows, advertisements, movies, and, of course, a lot of books.

[A warning for the Academics: As a matter of expediency and my own gender, I will be using the masculine pronoun to describe this aggregate character. This is because it is now a scientifically verifiable fact that all ironists are men. Relax. Sarah Silverman and Amy Sedaris, just for starters, would eat me alive. PLEASE, eat me alive!]

---

the present state of it, recontextualizing the past as merely marketable nostalgia. After all, it's "progress." Of course, for *the* landmark essays on camp and kitsch as sensibilities, see Susan Sontag, "Notes on Camp," *Against Interpretation* (New York: Anchor Books, 1966) and Clement Greenberg, "Avant-Garde and Kitsch," *Art and Culture: Critical Essays* (Boston: Beacon Press, 1961), 3–21.

Two Manifestations of a Social Character: Ironic and Cool

In everyday speech, the ironist often makes bantery caveats that point to an awareness of the socially constructed nature of his current performance; for him the social role, if not performed ironically, is false and dishonest. He senses clearly the distinction between the bourgeois ego in himself (his private self) and the social identity he "performs" (his role, oftentimes related to one's job or to expectations put upon him by having a certain title). The latter he does not see as fitting or necessary. Sociologists Stanley Cohen and Laurie Taylor write in *Escape Attempts* (1992) of young suburban couples basking in the illusion of their social roles:

> When the door is shut at night, and the two children are safely in bed, husband and wife turn to each other and laugh. They are subscribers to the new self-consciousness, apostles of awareness. Cynically they deride those who share bourgeois arrangements with them, but who do not see the joke . . . of their apparent suburbanity.[10]

That is to say, roles for the ironist, for the person who sees in this instance the contingency of identity, are "fake," or, to use the Salingerism, "phony." They represent for the ironist an outmoded way of being in the social world. The real way of being, of "being oneself," is a way that has divested the self as something that has un-self-consciously adopted a social mask, but rather, as someone who reveals his or her true innerness, that is, one's "deep-seated" self-interest and vulnerability. Every constructed image of heroism or perfection is "hiding" some flaw or insecurity.

The ironist is occasionally deeply self-conscious and, as Jedediah Purdy has observed, "debilitatingly self-aware." And sometimes paranoid, as in the case of Lenny Bruce slipping from the high mountain of cool into a mumbling hill of fear; the dawning of an acute awareness that the gap between "me" and "them" was no longer bridgeable. The contemporary ironist thus senses that his own words and performances are insufficient to express the totality of his experience. He senses somewhere in himself that all the most important and intimate things are somehow now derivative and contrived from Hollywood, preceded by known expectations or Kodak commercials; but he does not know quite how to escape the weighty banality of cliché. His life therefore seems at moments to him merely a copy of another life; ironic distancing, deliberate performance, and reflexive self-consciousness helps him to dissociate himself from this sense.

Strings of disclaimers, deprecations, and self-observations are all caveats that attempt to show that consciousness can always get behind itself, to show all as contingent.

He expresses this very personal awareness of derivativeness through strings of disclaimers, deprecations, and self-observations—all caveats that attempt to tell the people he talks to that his consciousness is always able to get behind itself, to see as contingent that which was presented as absolute, which is a cardinal sin for the (culturally astute, cosmopolitan, educated) ironist. As Dave Eggers, revealing the mind-set of a generation, writes in the preface to *A.H.W.O.S.G.* (which is still not described as an ironic book but rather a good example of a social character and familiar rumination),

> While the author is self-conscious about being self-referential, he is also knowing about that self-conscious self-referentiality. Further, if you're one of those people who can tell what is going to happen before it actually happens, you've predicted the next element here: he also plans to be clearly, obviously aware of his knowingness about his self-consciousness of self-referentiality. Further, he is fully cognizant, way ahead of you, in terms of knowing about and fully admitting the gimmickry inherent in all of this.[11]

The mind can run ahead of interpretation to guide it into conclusions it wants to convey, or away from those it doesn't. It wants to avoid "large" terms of finality or moral assessment—and disclaimers like this (and other emanations of metafiction) attempt to run from being captured in interpretive finality (this process is infinite). Absolute moral claims are evidence of one's naïve understanding of a multifaceted world. There are as many "valid" perspectives as there are sets of human eyes. To be morally stringent is the kiss of death, for it means one's mind is parochial, hidebound, premodern.

Richard Rorty with Sticker Album

These self-reflexive caveats are supposed to short-circuit or head off the interpretation of his comments or behaviors by others. In doing so, the ironist attempts to control both sides of communicative act, to overreach the delivery of his intentions, like throwing a ball to himself. While self-consciously aware of the absence or impossibility of a "correct" interpretation of the world or reality—and his knowledge of the knowledge that there is none—the ironist yearns to control the ultimate outcome of the communicative situation. He longs for the paradoxical respite of the metaphysical certainty that there is "no metaphysical certainty." Dealing with someone without such a consciousness is grounds for stopping the discussion. As such, the ironist lives the predicament of the postmetaphysical individual:

aware of the constructedness of social (and other) identities, which, by extension, includes his own.

Importantly, however, the consciousness of his derivativeness and attempts at ultimate conveyance of clarity of *intention* are simultaneously efforts to express sincerity, a declension of being that still holds value because it is an alignment of his inner life with itself and is thus a marker of integrity, of wholeness, the ironist's chief intrapersonal concern. He attempts to get around the confines of language. While discrediting belief and attempts by others at faith, he holds very deeply the belief that he can come home to himself, that he can arrive at a stopping point. He desperately wishes to arrive at a place where he need not pull the rug out from under himself because of an intellectual protocol ("political" or "postmodern" correctness, literary or artistic style, a nod to this or that precursor or influence), an unceasing and *de rigueur* recognition of the contingency of everything in order to show that one knows intellectually "what is up" in the world, what a contemporary intelligence requires. It is this respite for which he secretly strives, for he is, at heart, a person of tremendous feeling who wishes simply to rest.*

If the ironist character were a less intellectually and psychologically honest figure, there would be a way to rest. But for him "final vocabularies" (to borrow Richard Rorty's term)—references to a rationale for doing things: God, Country, History, the Church—are never *final* things, but just another group of words or justifications for behavior. Simultaneously, though, ironists attempt to gain individual autonomy in the move away from ultimate stopping points or rationales (mostly because they seem old, outdated, predictable, for the weak of heart). They wish ultimately to control the standards by which they are

---

*More simply, as the originally Louisianan, now Kansan bluegrass duo Truckstop Honeymoon put it: "I am tired / Yeah, I'm tired / Tired of red necks, white bread, and blue jeans. TNN Stars / And strip-mall bars / And all that my-country-'tis-of-thee-bullshit they shovel me / straight from Capitol Hill." From the song "Capitol Girl," on the album *Christmas in Ocala*, 2004.

judged, instead of being held to a metaphysical template that they don't believe exists, or a social template they see as unwarranted. Or just boring.

Enthusiastic dreams and liberal visions of a better future, or dictatorial statements about the Nation or the Church or the Party, then, seem to the ironist like silly ramblings, unnecessary optimism, hippie banter, political stumping, and impossible achievements, because they would require sacrifice of his inner measures for authenticity and individualism. And this threshold dare not be crossed. One need only recall the "Dean Scream" during the 2004 presidential campaign for resulting excoriation. When democratic contender Governor Howard Dean of Vermont became noticeably enthusiastic about his campaign doing well, his Internet fund-raising base increasing, and his desperately wanting to beat the Republicans at a crowded Midwestern political rally, letting out a thunderous yelp of excitement, he was consequently—and relentlessly—and satirically—upbraided in the media, on *SNL*, by Republicans, and elsewhere for being "crazy," "out of control," or "too much of a loose cannon."* Too much emotion and enthusiasm in political contexts is no longer an indicator of passionate involvement or commitment to cause (call up a mental image of Samuel Gompers, Vladimir Lenin, or Zel Miller), but rather, as a loss

---

*Of interesting note is that on December 15, 2005, Jon Stewart aped the Dean scream, making fun of the head of the DNC for a recent comment. But the audience's reaction was confused. For Stewart, the satirist, to make fun of Dean was in essence for him to take up the stance of Dean's Republican jeerers, canceling out Stewart's regularly liberal charge. Doing so put Stewart, just for a moment, in the awkward role of someone whose irony had fleetingly failed: while meaning to express frustration with the Democrat for saying something disagreeable, Stewart inadvertently mirrored the Republican response to the Dean Scream (intimating that political enthusiasm was a sign of being nuts), putting the audience in an odd space where they did not know how to interpret Stewart—was it okay to make fun of Dean the exact same way the Republicans had? Are we supposed to agree with that? Of course, as a failsafe, they (and I) laughed. After all, this is satire. Right?

of composure—and dangerous. Democrats were wild, Republicans civilized.

Yet emotional outbursts apparently do not choose sides. A similar incident in July 2005 was repeatedly played in the media when conservative columnist Robert Novak became so heatedly angry in a discussion with Democratic strategist James Carville that he tore off his lapel-microphone and walked off the set of CNN's *Crossfire.* Novak was said, thereafter, to be "under a lot of stress." The Plame investigation had begun in earnest.

> *A culture* falsely *enthusiastic over the trivial is ironically expressing the dead energy of loftier political ideology.*

Oppositely, to be *falsely* enthusiastic over the *trivial* is to ironically express the dead energy of loftier political goals.* It is to stick out one's tongue at goals that used to be worthy of enthusiasm, to signal the death of political hopes, the emptiness of ideology, which is now predictable on all accounts.† In this political mode the ironist most closely resembles the cynic. He doubts the possibility of political or social dreams' realization in the world by dint of human effort alone. Yet he cannot help being inspired—yes, there are heroes, mostly those who quietly use power to help those without any advantage—by pub-

---

*Recall the ironic protests "for" Communist regimes in Hungary, Romania, East Germany, and Poland, where the reality of opposition to the Party slowly dawned on vigorous, enthusiastic, sign-waving supporters of the Party.

†Of dead political hopes on the grand (rather than local) scale: some garner kudos for capturing this sense exactly. A blurb by the *Guardian* on the back of political cartoonist David Rees's *Get Your War On II* (New York: Penguin, 2005) states of the book's desperately bleak hilarity: "The most eloquent commentary by far on the mood of black humor, fear, panic, and bitter cynicism pervading life in the era of the War on Terrorism." Bleak satire and dark irony speak most truthfully in a culture saturated with cynics in power. This is the humor that cascades into crying. Or maybe "star-wipes" into it?

lic historical figures who have changed the world by their own deep wells of persistence and moral tenacity. This creates an inward tension between belief and suspicion that is with him at all times; his view of human nature is, in the end, deeply ambivalent.

As large political- or group-*joining* seems like a compromise to someone who is self-deprecating ("I wouldn't want to belong to a group that would have someone like me as a member"), the ironist often finds himself distracted by the dramas played out in his immediate circle of friends and in the passing of time with entertainment, often viewed with an ironic eye, or "anthropologically." As the novelist David Foster Wallace has written, television is an agent of "great despair and stasis in U.S. culture. . . . [so we] try to disinfect [our]selves . . . by watching TV with weary irony."[12] In the short term, however, survivalist scenarios (indicatively, again, "reality" television) or dark comedic situations confirm the ironist's beliefs in the near fruitlessness of all endeavor and the ruthlessness of everyday life, whether in a remote jungle or, importantly, in the urban environment, where the ideas for these types of programming emerge, and mostly where the ironist lives.

The wildly popular program *The Apprentice*, for example, featuring billionaire real-estate mogul and 1980s poster boy Donald Trump, reveals the rules and personality traits "necessary" to succeed in a hypercompetitive business environment. As a dominant concern in today's America, survivalism's apotheosis—a genre that emphasizes the need of seriousness and the dark arts for continued living—has found comfy residence not only in terror alerts, Hummers, fatigues, and sculpted bodies ready to chase down antelope or wrestle pythons, but forcefully in prime-time television slots offering life-instruction through other programs such as *American Idol, America's Next Top Model, The Amazing Race, The Contender, Next, Survivor, The Mole, Temptation Island, The Bachelor, Weakest Link, Dog Eat Dog, Deal or No Deal, Fear Factor, Survival of the Richest,* and many more, such as *Lost.* These shows do their part to lay bare the personalities required of one to construct if one is to "survive" the "reality" of any given situation.

Mostly the values and behaviors adopted are thoroughly Machiavellian in nature; the programs highlight the aspects of lying, plotting, strategy, and sneaky one-upmanship as the determining factors for survival in any of their environments, be they urban or island. Any attempts to abide by a set of moral standards (like not being an asshole) are quickly quashed, can lead to being fired, or touted out as an inability to "adjust." But, of course, in the end, it's "never personal." This is not because it isn't meant as such, but because it's convenient to denounce when the game is over. The real game for the winner—on *The Apprentice*, life in corporate America—is, of course, just beginning. The pathos of composure justifies the world that makes it necessary.*

Because of these shows' seriousness-as-entertainment factor, the ironist is too smart for reality television; he knows it is all constructed, and this is perhaps what is most real to him—the truth of that construction rather than the truth of survival scenarios. Various shows on VH1—*I Love the '90s, Worst Week Ever, 100 Cheesiest Moments*—or reality-show clip reviews on late-night comedy shows ripping them apart, both feature counterattacking commentary by comedians and pop culture critics dedicated to the practice of "unmasking" these shows, telling audiences what is "really" going on behind programs that pretend to represent without tricks or gimmicks. It is certainly this practice that makes the ironist feel as though he "sees through" the illusion by which so many are taken in. "How I hunger for that knowing tone!" wrote translator Wyatt Mason in the *New York Times Magazine*.[13] The ironist views these reality programs from afar, as survivalist American middlebrow, as a sort of propaganda for self-armament, though he is, nonetheless and indicatively, "guiltily" drawn in. He knows better.

Socially, then, as he needs the world to interact, to ground his iden-

---

*This line appears in chapter 2 ("The Culture Industry") of Theodor W. Adorno and Max Horkheimer's *Dialectic of Enlightenment* (New York: Continuum, 1994), 151.

tity in the not-me of cultural others, the ironist scans social cues for behavioral adjustments—rank, race, intelligence, like-sensibility. In yet another *Simpsons* example, nerdish-leaning eight-year-old Lisa meets some new kids at a beach resort; the small group is portrayed as laidback and cool. They begin to talk with Lisa and comment on her clothing: "Nice hat," the girl in the group says. Lisa's internal voice immediately starts in analyzing the comment: "Scanning for sarcasm . . . and . . . wait . . . (gasp) . . . none found!" At this point, knowing she is safe from a barrage of esteem-destroying criticism, Lisa answers the girl and begins talking to the group. This searching, reading mentality is part of the ironist's mental equipment that assesses the relative harshness—and comedic tolerance—of the social environment.

The contemporary ironist is thus on constant alert for the difference between his guarded interior life and the world around, which makes him, though a perceptive critic, vigorously self-aware. When he listens, he is suspicious that there is always "something else" going on, usually some sort of an ulterior motive or judgment. His perception exists within a kind of "skeptical closedness," a "holding" of himself back. Comedian Jerry Seinfeld's TV persona is often seen as the quintessential ironist—the wisecracking, emotionally detached, sarcastic, invulnerable, urbane, and affable yet frequently disgusted bachelor living in New York City. To draw again on an earlier reviewer of the ironic personality, Elise Harris:*

"The ironist" is a stock character in contemporary culture: the smartass, the snarky guy (or gal) who goes beyond funny to bilious and bitter, arrogant, sarcastic, making fun of people who aren't in the club. Someone who found in high school that intelli-

---

* *Seinfeld* was arguably the most popular sitcom in American television history, undoubtedly so in the 1990s, before it ended on May 14, 1998. Reruns of the show remain immensely popular, and the DVD set of all seasons was released for the holiday season in 2004 to great media fanfare.

gence couldn't bring popularity. Someone who thinks pointing out stupidity constitutes humor.*

The stock ironist character (always based on an amalgam of real characteristics, usually of their creators) makes fun, judges, and disdains—often noted by the (now-stereotyped) raised eyebrow or the mouth pulled back on one side†—because, ultimately, the world does not measure up to his ideas about how it should be; it does not measure up to the standards he has set both for himself and the society in which he lives. This character, wishing to see the world different than it is, all the while socially visible and entertaining, has been living for some period, privately, in an "inner somewhere-else."

---

*Elise Harris, "Infinite Jest," *The Nation*, week of March 2, 2000. The sort of characterization of the ironist as someone who is getting back at the in-groups is an interesting observation. The spate of irony-laden movies about high school in recent years by Hollywood producers and New York writers eerily confirms the resentment Harris identifies. *American Pie, American Pie 2, Mean Girls, Bring It On, Legally Blonde*, and a host of others revisit high-school years (or shortly thereafter) in a triumphant spirit where the nerds and geeks and outcasts take their revenge on the popular cliques of students. The gist of these films is that if you stick to you inner conscience and ignore the teasing and unpopularity, everything works out for the best and your enemies will learn something from you that will turn out to be a valuable life lesson. It's important to note that the writers and directors of these films were often the geeks and outcasts several decade ago. Revenge, particularly on the big screen and accompanied by buckets of money, is sweet. Also, pointing out stupidity does constitute humor. See, in short: humor.
†This has become, for some completely unknown reason, the trademark look of the Rock (I don't know his real name). As an action-movie actor, a genre that takes itself seriously (and whose cheesy tricks are revealed by Todd Phillips and friends in *Starsky & Hutch*, etc.), the Rock has a self-congratulatory public persona that expresses a sort of wry irony or cosmopolitan disdain. His roles actually do not express this sentiment, making him seem out of touch and self-inflated, particularly when the real, not fictional, Rock does it.

Cool

Through detachment and distancing, keeping separate the inner and the outer, via disidentification, the ironist hopes for both a feeling of control and freedom from externalities. In a *60 Minutes* interview, Stephen Colbert (the actual person) presented this distinction between inner feeling and external performance clearly. Paraphrased, Colbert said that he does not let his children watch *The Colbert Report* because often young people can't tell the difference between an ironic performance and a sincere one; he didn't want his kids looking at him skeptically when he puts them to sleep and says, "Yeah, I love you, too."

Satire attacking cool makes for tension. But it always wins.

This same psychological move of keeping inner and outer distinct can also be seen in the attitude of *cool*, which is, in addition to satirical attack, a variety of irony expressed outwardly. It somehow comes off most convincingly in America.* To be sure, cool as an emanation of the detached self is not morally concerned like the satirist, and is less defensible; moreover, as cool has spread all over, it has become utterly predictable. Borat asking a group of teenage black guys how to be like them ("Show me: how I be like you?") results in bagged-out underwear, pants dragging, and in addressing the white hotel worker,

---

*Having lived in Germany now and again over the past eight years, I can attest to the sheer oddity of cool there. German youths trying to be cool always seem like very poor imitations of their American brethren. It is an awkward aping of the "look" of cool—meaning, it looks like kids pretending to be Fiddy or Lil' Kim or Eminem or Jay-Z, but it does not emanate from inside them. When white suburban American kids ape the look they take from rap, you think, "Although you look ridiculous, there is some element of cool just because you are an American—a tough society to navigate." In the German case, one is simply too embarrassed to watch. Cushy social systems, as long as they are not totalitarian, don't require cool.

"What's up, vanilla face?" Its awkwardness is hilarious, but it also results in satire that pushes the boundaries; satire attacking cool makes for tension. But it always wins.

Yet cool as an often-necessary attitude, albeit one tinged with vacuous performance, itself defends to short-circuit expectations of response, and it projects slight disdain, evident in some emanations in a Bogart-like upturn of the lip or a smirk. "Wipe that smirk off your face," says the parent or authority to the young adult beginning his journey into American cool—and simultaneously into "himself." To journey into cool is to open up the self's space through social distancing; it is to awaken to the *freedom* of subjectivity.* As the art historian and critic Robert Storr has said about the American painter Alex Katz, whose flat images of beachgoers and Hampton parties exude a blasé, stylish distance:

> Cool is an essentially American characteristic. . . . You don't have to be rich, pedigreed, or exquisitely dandified to be cool. Quite the opposite, too obvious a display of class isn't classy at all; the aristocracy of cool is wholly self-made. Cool is an impeccable

---

*It is no mistake that as adolescents notoriously begin to become "distant" from their parents during their teenage years, that they are simultaneously learning how to be "cool." In a culture obsessed with this sort of social distance, influences from televised instances of cool—of the afterimages of Romantic remove seen in so many famous faces and scenarios of social antagonism, rebellion—permeate the consciousness and form models of social character. They are nearly impossible to resist not solely because they are so alluring, but often because they are necessary to adorn. They stir the self's desire for autonomy from all exterior determinations, for ironic remove from the mundane. The anthropologists James Fernandez and Mary Taylor Huber remark that irony, as it had for Kierkegaard, signals an "awakening of subjectivity, that is an awakening of the conception of oneself as a subject, something separate from, and undetermined by, a certain immediately given historical entity." *Irony in Action: Anthropology, Practice, and the Moral Imagination* (Chicago: University of Chicago Press), 4. Freedom from history is cool; doing homework is not.

street-smart formality in a country where . . . you might bump
into anybody.[14]

That is, you might go from being a stranger to not being one quite
unexpectedly, might shift from private to public in an instant. As an
attitude, then, cool is the resolute ability to maintain a certain cosmopolitan detachment, to be unruffled, unmoved; to be cool is to be
poised. It is to keep hold of oneself and to have the ego introjected as a
monitoring tool that at once keeps tabs on responses and disassembles
exteriorities. Think of cool Jack Black's character in *High Fidelity*. His
bitterness is driven by the idea that the father shopping for a Stevie
Wonder CD for his daughter isn't ironizing enough to deserve the
item he wants to buy.

The cool attitude, with all its contemporary marketability (and,
more depressingly, lack of feeling for living), became a more
omnipresent emotional style during the 1960s. Yet historian Peter N.
Stearns maintains that it took thirty to forty years for this emotional
style to manifest, having its inception in American culture of the 1920s
to the early 1940s, during the slow erasure of Victorian values. The
emotional culture of the Victorian era was coming to a close during the
years following the First World War, and in its place came new norms
of emotional expression and valuation, norms that led to, paradoxically, more restraint on the emotional life of citizens:

> Victorians valued emotions as motivators, as the sources of
> energy in work and politics and as a crucial cement for family life.
> The twentieth-century emotional style tolerated certain emo-
> tional interests as part of leisure . . . but urged overall restraint as
> part of the need to present a pleasing, unobtrusive front to oth-
> ers. Emotions [are] seen as more risky than useful.[15]

The attitude of cool has since enabled the self-management of emotional life; cool thus negotiates a dual situation: on the outside is the
need to relate to others, and on the inside is the need to maintain con-

trol over emotions so they conform to accepted standards of expression. Some of the emotions now kept under wraps—jealousy, guilt, anger—that once found acceptable outlets within everyday life, now must be managed, creating an individual that is "impersonal, but friendly." Well, when necessary. Nice is not cool; cool is cool. And proudly uninspired. As Mark Edmundson observed in *Harper's* of his always cool, detached, University of Virginia students: "Their *Weltbild* ... [is] a despondent place, whose sad denizens drift from coffee bar to Prozac dispensary, unfired by ideals and the glowing image of what one might become."*

Being cool, composed, and enacting social distance renders the other person, in essence, disposable. It fosters the sense of total autonomy and attempts to make the subject feel free. As such, cool is an appearance, a social performance, a strategy of social being, a role that is projecting a nonrole. It attempts through nonchalance or verbal disdain to rise above. From James Dean to Snoop Dog, the personality of cool is detectable by both its unflappability and its antagonism toward authority.✝ Moving into a regular life—giving in to social demands—

---

*Mark Edmundson, "On the Uses of A Liberal Education," *Harper's*, September 1997, 48. Slightly earlier, Edward Gibbon, in chapter 2 of *History of the Decline and Fall of the Roman Empire* (1776–88), writes: "The minds of men were gradually reduced to the same level, the fire of genius was extinguished. . . . A cloud of critics, of compilers, of commentators, darkened the face of learning, and the decline of genius was soon followed by a corruption of taste." Cool and commentary killed the empire.

✝Or, alternately, a radicalized Mischa Barton. An advertisement for Keds in *Vogue* (September 2006) announces that "COOL IS LESS MATERIALISM, MORE MATERIAL. It used to be that more, more, more meant everything. More bling, less content. More stuff, less space. More of everything, but less satisfaction with anything. But the tide has turned, and big isn't always better. Now it's about quality, not just quantity. Cool is the stuff that lasts for years, like Keds. The things you fall in love with repeatedly, like Keds. The kind of material that never, ever ends up in the Regret pile. Wanna see material worth coveting? You got it at www.keds.com/mischabarton." The next advertisement is for Jones New York, featuring Amber Valetta sitting in a silver convertible wearing a full-length leather coat.

is to sell out, to give over one's inward freedom. Cool flirts with illegality, but not in a way that would make it passionately rebellious, for, as mentioned at the outset, too much emotion and drive are patently not cool. The harsh world is confronted with ease.

It is this disjunction, this necessity of diligently maintaining the separation of private sphere and social mask, that places cool squarely (no, wait, coolly) in the modern era—it enacts a mask precisely so it can attempt to project that it is not a mask. For cool as a social attitude has the near-algorithmic function of showing the opposite of what it feels or experiences—hence its association with the ironic character. Most often this takes the form of nonchalance or dispassion when a subject is being humiliated or offended; such a response disarms and defuses aggressors. "Whatever" is never actually whatever, but rather, "I am disappointed." But to express actual disappointment is to express need or lack. As cool wishes for its complete autonomy, this expression is taboo.

> *Cool has the near-algorithmic function of showing the opposite of what it feels—hence its association with the ironic character.*

This stance can be seen playing out among youth confronted with grave economic and social disadvantage, as a means of maintaining integrity. One strain of cool comes from rappers who grew up having to enact cool to survive psychologically—and for real. The investigations in *Cool Pose* (1993), by sociologists Richard Majors and Janet Mancini Billson, look at the ways in which the psychological function of cool helped to protect the psyches of young black urban males in the 1990s. Majors and Billson write that the

> cool pose represents a fundamental structuring of the psyche—
> the cool mask belies the rage held in check beneath the surface.
> . . . Black males have learned to use posing and posturing to communicate power, toughness, detachment, and style-self. They

have adopted a "third eye" that reads interpersonal situations with a special acuity. They have cultivated a keen sense of what to say, and how and when to say it, in order to avoid punishment and pain.[16]

They observed games like "The Dozens," where children taunt each other with increasingly harsh insults. This is training for the maintenance of composure in an offensive and abusive situation, particularly if it involves the vitriol and subtle ubiquity of racism. The game

Norman Mailer Frontin'

teaches children to hide their innermost feelings, to display an exteriority of strength and stoic resolve. They are taught not to "crack"; the inside is fragile and must be protected. You can now find regular training for this on *Nick Cannon Presents Wild n' Out* and Wilmer Valerrama's *Yo Momma*, both on MTV. Practice in the arts of psychic self-defense has proved big business for Viacom. (Is it any mistake that all participants are all dressed in competitive sports-gear?)

A protective, dissembling response to an insult to one's abilities or character is therefore to display the opposite of what one feels. It is, in effect, to perform an internal ironic reversal of meaning. Ironic detachment is here a *psycho-strategy* for hiding one's feelings by suggesting their opposite—pretending to be bored in the face of danger, being amused at insult. It permits one to be unruffled while one is actually deeply offended or hurt. Like the irony used as a rhetorical device that sees sentences and words meaning their opposite of what one means, the attitude of cool frequently projects the opposite of—or serves as a counterbalance to—what one feels. The subject reverses or disguises the actual feelings he or she has in order to do something more immediately socially useful.

Cool's primary objective in all of this, importantly, is not to *provoke* anger or social rejection, but to feel free internally, to feel self-possessed, to reprieve itself of having to respond to interpersonal expectation. The goal of cool is to create an impenetrable core, total autonomy, freedom from need. This kind of distancing allows the subject to gain partial perspective on an otherwise overwhelming social world, which in turn permits a totalizing view in order to attempt control of that world, a feeling of freedom from the complexity and aggression within it.* This leads to a radical simplification and conceptual level-

---

*A cultural emanation of such a desire to return from cool, to "get in touch" with the more primal regions of feeling and surmount forced, oppressive composure is the movie *Fight Club* (1999), which sees a clandestine group of young men—professional and skilled laborers—who meet in secret locations to beat the crap out of each other because it makes them feel more alive. Slavoj Žižek writes of the film and its culminating moment: "In our alienated society only physical violence can bring us into direct contact with each other. . . . The ultimate scene for me is around the middle of the film, when Edward Norton goes to his boss and beats himself up. It's a terrible scene. But the way I see it . . . it's the necessary first step towards liberation. . . . The hypothesis of the film is right in the sense that you can't come directly to genuine political awareness. You need—to use a piece of terminology—those 'vanishing mediators,' that interim stage of uncontrolled violence, that perhaps, though also perhaps not, will help your transformation to political awareness. . . . I think it's the first Hollywood film to show the dark side of liberation." Quoted in "MP>TV," *Spector cut + paste*, June 2002, 68–69. It is also interesting to note that the main character, the businessman played by Norton, who one believes is led into the fight-club culture by a rough outsider-type played by Brad Pitt, is in fact schizophrenic; he led himself into the culture of fighting and out of the stultifying life of his previous existence. Such a figure can be read to be recapitulating the psychic structure of the contemporary cynical personality: living in his everyday life, but deeply not of it; and if so, not of himself.

ing of complex situations, which transforms the world into simplified forms and types.* For the ironist not in an advantageous situation, in a position of power, because he feels thrown around by social forces and decisions that he has not autonomously made or that necessity or survival require, this inward turn is an attempt at an escape to subjective freedom, to the locus of control. It is in these sorts of situations where, as Kierkegaard noted over a century ago, "the subject emancipates himself from the constraint imposed on him by the continuity of life, whence it must be said of the ironist that he 'cuts loose.'"†

Recent Talk about Contemporary Irony

In addition to these cultural emanations of the sensibility, and more abstractly, in some recent philosophical writing, the ironist is seen to

---

*It is the nature of this simplification that makes some recent animated cartoons already hilarious even before any jokes are sounded. *The Simpsons, South Park, Drawn Together, American Dad, Family Guy, Futurama,* and others all contain an inherent paradoxical tension between the utter simplicity of form (particularly *South Park,* which started as construction-paper cutouts and then moved to CAD graphics, allowing for greater speed of response to current events) and the complexity of the social issues with which they grapple, such as immigration, terrorism, war, commodification of public space, the pressures of modern work, rampant consumerism, and peer pressure. The jokes—as Freud would remind—allow release from this tension. Then again—as W. C. Fields or Dorothy Parker would—so does whiskey.

†Kierkegaard, *Concept of Irony,* 272–73. When Kierkegaard uses the phrase "cuts loose," he was undoubtedly portending the American actor Kevin Bacon, whose ability to "cut loose" in the 1984 movie *Footloose* was aided by the soundtrack title-song by Kenny Loggins, which contains the lyrics "Now I gotta cut loose / footloose / kick off your Sunday shoes." The reader who hit preteenhood in the 1980s will recognize this as an oddly welcome digression. They will also now try to remember the rest of the lyrics. They will not remember anything but the chorus. "Been workin', so hard . . . obeyin' ev-e-r-y rule." That's all I got.

have enacted a lived strategy for an entrenched and persistent critique of the present, particularly of the elements in social life that are perceived to threaten the integrity and sacredness of the self. For the philosopher Ernst Behler, in his compact *Irony and the Discourse of Modernity* (1990), ironic strategy as a mode of personality and social life, appearing with modernity itself, is phrased in a

> performative, self-referential contradiction necessarily implied in any totalized critique of reason and philosophy: one cannot criticize [them] without pulling away the basis from underneath this critique . . . itself an expression of reason and rationality. . . . Characteristically enough, the ironic discourse . . . because of its highly self-reflective character, practices critical, deprecating observations of a self-referential nature as a constantly recurring technique.[17]

That's chokingly syllabic. But still, as far more than simply a willful choice, as Behler purports, irony is a social strategy for a generalized critique of reason characteristic of cultural modernity, as well as a trait of the postmodern.*

---

*It is important to note that I will not be entering into the debate about postmodernity, post-postmodernity, and the like, in this essay—whether it is the age we are in, when it started, or if it exists at all, etc. Suffice it to say that Jürgen Habermas's arguments about the persistence of social modernity—meaning there is not yet reason to believe there is an all-inclusive "post-" to this term, are clearly accurate accounts of the behavior of nations, laws, and peoples in present-day industrialized nations. I find little practical evidence to believe that social modernity is over. As conceived by Habermas as Kant's shared Enlightenment goals for—and progress toward—more freedom for more people, individual liberties and fostering self-determination, transparency of government practices, and the good-faith efforts for the alleviation of poverty and humiliation, social modernity seems to persist quite healthily. We'd be in deep trouble if not. Cultural modernity, of course, is a different story altogether. Our current philosophical situation seems to stem from this disjunction.

Frequently cited "postmodern" characteristics or elements—the discrediting of metanarratives (big stories), media influence on one's sense of individual authenticity, commodification of human relations, loss of a credible and broadly shared moral vision, and the exteriorization of identity (fashion/glamour), threats to subjectivity—if *not* disengaged from or looked upon in askance, the same way cool does, would imperil the sacredness of the self and gnaw at the foundations of personal identity.*

Seeing the ironic mode in a less positive critical light, the American historian and social critic Christopher Lasch—undoubtedly an early figure on the horizon in the larger debate about civic responsibility to come—has called ironic detachment an "everyday survival strategy." In *The Minimal Self* (1984), an extension of his concerns with the effects of modern American life (media, advertising, bureaucracy, marketing, governmental expansion) on the psychology of citizens, Lasch writes convincingly that in America "everyday life begins to take on some of the more undesirable and ominous characteristics of behavior in extreme situations: restriction of perspective to the immediate demands of survival; ironic self-observation; protean selfhood; emo-

---

*Oh, Fashion, you're never far behind. The September 2006 issue of *Men's Health* features a spread and back cover of Joseph Fiennes with the subtitle "The inner man, his outward style." It is fitting that Fiennes actually played the role of Martin Luther in the 2003 film, eh, *Luther*. And in another fashion note that reveals much more than it should: in an increasingly disturbing phenomenon, teenagers are having plastic surgery to look more like celebrities they admire, and without any consideration that it is disturbing. MTV airs a show called *I Want A Famous Face*, which sees teenagers bringing photos of their favorite celebrities (as templates) to "aesthetic surgeons" for plastic surgery on their noses, cheekbones, breasts, calves, and, in general, for allover liposuction. Often the teens will explain that they are undergoing the surgery in order to gain self-esteem or self-confidence. The display of the body and approval by peers equals the attempt at securing identity inwardly. Yet this is exteriorization of identity willfully entered into, the radical reversal of Protestant inwardness, the triumph of fashion.

tional anesthesia."* Drawing from literature of survival in extreme situations (such as "lessons" from the Holocaust), Lasch includes ironic
detachment as a mode of "psychic survival in troubled times"
specifically because "[the] feeling of being acted on by uncontrollable
external forces prompts another mode of moral armament, a withdrawal from the beleaguered self into the person of a detached,
bemused, ironic observer. The sense that it isn't happening to *me* helps
to protect me against pain and also to control expressions of outrage
or rebellion."[18]

This defensive tactic is no individual phenomenon, nor is it confined
to the United States, nor is it at all new. The idea of survival of externalities and faltering metaphysics, dealt with by a recourse to subjective irony, has become for some commentators—usually from the
realms of philosophy and the other humanities—the talisman of the
postmodern age; and for the critics of the liberal, secular mind—a
social corrosive. As literary historian Alan Wilde precipitously wrote
in 1981,

---

*Christopher Lasch, *The Minimal Self: Psychic Survival in Troubled Times*
(New York: W. W. Norton, 1984), 94–96. With the onslaught of wildly popular reality television shows involving survivalist and extreme scenarios,
such an interpretation of the character of everyday life and the apotheosis of
the "survivor" makes the connection entirely simple and convincing. Yet this
is its allure. What is the need to dig further for a meaning that exposes base,
self-interested motivations and the relating of contemporary life to that of
extreme survival, when the base meaning is already showing? Nakedness
(both metaphorical and literal, which is often the case on reality shows) reifies
the situation that all is already "unmasked," and the motivation to dig beyond
the image one sees, to get to the "reality behind" the spectacle, is now itself
the illusion to get beyond. If power is nakedly presenting itself to the understanding, when the wizard is out from behind the curtain, what is the impetus
to uncover? Our postmodernist habits to uncover and unmask are forced to
turn back on themselves in neurotic fascination when they cease to be relevant to the public's desire for their use. Out of this cultural boredom comes
the urge no longer to uncover, but to destroy.

Irony . . . is this century's response to the problematics of an increasingly recessive and dissolving self and an increasingly randomized world. [It] strives, by constantly reconstituting itself, to achieve the simultaneous acceptance and creation of a world that is both indeterminate and, at the same time, available to consciousness.[19]

Irony as a beleaguered response to the present, in other words, is a means by which the subject attempts to cohere a lived experience, a lived morality (or entire lack thereof) that is not externally coherent or widely shared, that assails the self with contradiction and a feeling of invasion. Ironic detachment is a way to fend off that which is felt to be invading the self. It is a way to cohere the tumult of the modern experience, to ground the increasing dislocations of time and space. It is, in short, one of

Ironic detachment is a practical way to fend off that which is felt to be invading the self, a subjective recourse from a faltering metaphysics.

chief defenses of the modern, secular, agnostic mind. "Irony in its own right," writes David Worcester in his history of satire, "has expanded from a minute verbal phenomenon to a philosophy, a way of facing the cosmos."[20]

Many theorists and historians, lightly treading the trail of Hegel and Kierkegaard, have held that the ironic mentality is *the* defining characteristic of the late modern age and the postmodern mind. This position ranges from Georg Simmel's early twentieth-century observation that the stance of ironic/aesthetic detachment ("the blasé attitude") was the principal characteristics of modern urban existence,[21] to Hayden White's framing of irony as a major trope of historiographic representation in the nineteenth century, to Peter Sloterdijk's brilliant analysis of the cynical mentality in the Weimar Republic and in contemporary social life; Slavoj Žižek's conviction that cynicism has become the new dominant ideology; Ernst Behler's conviction that "postmodernity reveals itself as an ironic notion communicating indirectly, by way of circumlocution, configuration, and bafflement";[22] Andrew Delbanco's positing of the notion that irony is the mode that arises in America where a sense of evil has vanished; Walter Truett Anderson's conception of the postmodern ironist as the leading mentality of the educated West, seen in figures such as Richard Rorty and Thomas Kuhn. The political scientist John Seery, in his book about irony in politics and theory, *Political Returns* (1990), understands irony as "primarily an outlook, a worldview, a mode of consciousness, a way of thinking. . . . 'Irony' is not even a *thing* but is a complex, interactive process. . . . The term in noun form belies its elusive nature."[23] Linda Hutcheon's *Irony's Edge: The Theory and Politics of Irony* (1995) addresses irony's many psychological motivations, among them defensiveness, arrogance, humor, evasiveness, duplicity, hypocrisy, subversiveness, transgression, exclusion, and aggression, and maintains that irony is employed by various social communities and speakers and is always contingent on a specific locus of power.[24] Lastly, although there are plenty more, the literary critic Samuel Hynes contended in 1961 that contemporary irony was "a view of life which recognized that experience is open to multiple interpretations, of which no one is simply right, and that the coexistence of incongruities is part of the structure of existence."[25]

A recent and specific example might help elucidate this last point: *The Economist* ran a lengthy article on irony in December 1999, shortly after and in response to the publication of several books on irony in the United States. It observes that irony as a means of social engagement is the only way to appropriately deal with the world in a postcolonial era. When there is recognition of all types of value systems, one cannot but takes one's own value system as just another one among them. The attitude this entails—and which the author wholeheartedly recommends—is that of irony. Commenting on an article in *Prospect* by Robert Cooper, Britain's head of the Asia Department of the Foreign Office, *The Economist* writes that this is one reason why irony is a particular favourite among British diplomats. It allows them to tease foreigners, without the foreigners realising they are being teased. All the diplomatic proprieties can be observed—but the Brits can still feel quietly superior. In days of yore British superiority was proven by force of arms. Now the point is made with a joke, and a quiet, knowing smile. . . . Irony is a distinctly post-imperial quality. While irony aimed at foreigners may seem unpleasantly supercilious . . . it is particularly good at puncturing pretension [of Brits themselves] . . . at exposing the gap between appearance and reality.[26]

Where it is gauche to reveal a sense of superiority of any sort, irony communicates without having to show its beliefs directly. It reveals itself as a secret wrapped within acceptable expression. It is the sublimation of a sense of moral, corporal, or intellectual dominance, or, at least, echoes of its past. (Of course, it hardly makes any sense to attack your opponent if they don't know you are attacking them. At best, that's empty protest.)

As some of the critics above attest, this attitude now roams free. When listening to a speech of this-or-that politician claiming to have the answers to a social problem, listeners from Manhattan to Omaha may utter, "I'm sure they'll do that immediately." These utterances are not mere tools of facile sarcastic disagreement, but rather reveal a now deeply entrenched view of political and social life, especially as a view that is concerned with the world outside one's immediate purview. While lending evidence of this inner rebelliousness toward authority or claims to noble ideals, ironic insight can provide a muscular counterweight to the dominant culture and politics of an age; it challenges power assumed natural, or, more poignantly, that overreaches its authority. Most importantly, the ironic mentality is rooted in a belief that *individuals* have the *legitimacy* to challenge those structures of power.

Yet it is here important to recall that while it does lend itself more readily to the progressive minded (because it is often critical of power, which always needs the force and symbols of history to stay afloat),

irony as an antagonistic mechanism is empty, tautological, algorith-
mic; it can go either way. It has no built-in politics. All that is needed
for irony to function is some kind of social fuel, a moral situation, a
charged existential moment—and a knowing audience. Thus, contrary
to the example above, one can equally imagine words from a caricatured magnate in a smoky backroom lair saying that he will "immediately donate fifty percent of profits to a local charity," pausing momentarily to look at his chums and then laughing heartily; a big slimy cigar
wedged in at the corner of his jowls. Irony in this sense is amoral, even
cynical. Either side of a power relationship can use irony to skewer
nearly any aspect of life on Earth.

To reiterate, then, on the one hand, ironic *disengagement* signals an
individual strategy for maintenance of the self's integrity in the face of
threatening elements of a cultural or social situation—the attacks on
and challenges to the maintenance of personal integrity. On the other
hand, when irony as a form enters into cultural production through
various means (as cool, through advertising, television, high art, film,
literature, satire of all sorts), it is both an active *social* strategy for the
critique of those elements, as well as, though far less often, a force for
maintenance of the power relations of the present.* That is to say,
because as a form irony is empty, it can only do something "political"
in the hands of its users. It depends upon who picks up its ammunition.

Irony and Cynicism

At last, as these two terms have been conflated both by me and in
much writing, and complained about because so treated, it's helpful
here to spell out some differences, however much the words partake in
one another and remain blurry as two widely shared attitudes.

---

*The political scientist William Chaloupka has written that "strategy inter-
venes everywhere in the social world, disrupting the connection between
style and intention." Letter from Chaloupka to author, January 17, 2005.

Defined briefly, modern cynicism is the "condition of lost belief,"[27] as "enlightened false consciousness . . . a modernized, unhappy consciousness, on which enlightenment has labored both successfully and in vain."* A kind of detachment results from this worldview, but one that has digested the realities of brute power to affect change. The ironist, on the other hand, retains a nervous charm about his alienation; he does so because he holds on to an entrenched hope that the cynic has long since disavowed. *Might* magazine, which attempted to give voice to a young generation caught between cynical leanings and social hope, wrote in its last issue that to admit that "night only grows darker and hope lies crushed under the jackboots of the wicked" would be, in essence, to give up—regardless of the knowledge that "no matter how good our deeds and truest wishes . . . evil will run roughshod over the earth, and the planet will be left a playground in ruins, fit only for cockroaches and vermin."† The ironist, in the presence of this knowledge at all times, seems to flit about with efforts to the contrary. The cynic maintains openly a wry and resolute realism of these

---

*Peter Sloterdijk, *The Critique of Cynical Reason* (Minneapolis: University of Minnesota Press, 1987), 5. The term "unhappy consciousness," notes the *Critique's* translator, Michael Eldred, refers to an important subchapter of Hegel's *Phenomenology of Spirit*, trans. A. V. Miller (New York: Oxford University Press, 1977), wherein the unhappy consciousness is "the consciousness of self as a dual-natured, merely contradictory being" (introduction, B. Self-Consciousness, IV, p. 126).

†*Might* no. 16, the "Are Black People Cooler Than White People?" issue, 1997. A worthwhile note on the extent to which *Might* captured something: on the blog www.lindsayism.com, the New York–based comedy writer attests: "I only had a few short years with *Might*, but I read each issue at least 20 times, most memorably reading aloud the whole way to a packed car on a road trip to Atlanta to see a Luna show. When I got the last issue and found an essay on 'Death' in the front and the words 'At least we tried' and realized that *Might* was over, I cried. Then, I called the subscription line and left a long message about how *Might* had changed my life and I just wanted them to know that." The author, now a writer at Comedy Central, was raised in the Jesus movement. In Florida. Salvation is possible.

gloomy facts, tinged with a taste of defeat. The cynic is a failed opti-mist.

He has given up entirely on performing a social role and on hope in general. Where the ironist remarks, the cynic disregards. In this sense, because he says what he feels and thinks and is not confined by the whisperings of the superego, the cynic is perceived as more *honest* than the ironist. He speaks truths more directly, because he has less at stake at their disbelief. He sees himself on the side of reality. But his honesty is almost always painful because his assumptions about the operating principles of the social world are brutish. He likewise conceives of him-self as the most *authentic* kind of person because he expresses truths that others are either too ignorant to know or are timid to reveal. He knows because he sees things "realistically," a favorite word of the cynic, because it assures him of the nonideological nature of his obser-vations and opinions. Cynicism thus counts as positively unspoken (but commonly known) political wisdom. *Realpolitik* is life.

"Unveiling" this logic was interestingly on display for *New Yorker* investigative journalist Seymour Hersh when writing about the Pen-tagon's "plans" for going after Iran already in the summer of 2005. Appearing on various talk shows the prior winter, the seasoned Hersh repeated phrases such as "Look, they have a plan. They are going to do this; it's just a matter of when. They mean business. These guys aren't joking around." Translation: they did not hide. Cynicism, when joined with power, doesn't need to. Watching Hersh, one had the feel-ing that his "discovery" of the Pentagon's forethoughts did not matter much to the Pentagon itself, nor the Bush administration—however much they did some obligatory damage-control to pacify the media and masses. When power is naked, *noblesse oblige* becomes far less con-vincing—or necessary.

When power is naked, noblesse oblige *becomes far less convinc-ing—or necessary.*

Thanks to neoconservative doctrine (and its politicized rhetoric, which massages the brutal, crushing honesty of its ideas—such as "full-spectrum dominance"—into more civilization-friendly phrases, like "encouraging helpfulness through suggestion" [file under: speech-writers]), physical power is again a dominant value, as in the Roman or Ottoman empires or in any other superpower that aspired to more.* "The United States is now totally frank about putting its cards on the table," Harold Pinter said in his Nobel speech in 2005. "That is the case. Its official declared policy is now defined as 'full-spectrum domi-nance.' That is not my term, it is theirs. 'Full-spectrum dominance' means control of land, sea, air and space and all attendant resources." As it is clear by now to everyone awake, Power is the renewed meta-narrative. We know this better today than we have in some time. It is truly no wonder at all that survivalism in pop culture has become so, er, popular. Not only have some political narratives in America for several decades been trying to create a nation of strident individuals, but the accompanying corollary to this idea has of late been accentu-ated: if there are only individuals, they must be bound in a state of con-stant competition, toiling against each other under the frightful vision that everyone else is out to beat them. There is no rest, no consolation.

In part reacting to this tense cultural predicament, there is more of a performative aspect to the ironist's "sensibility" in social situations, for not only is power slightly embarrassing to him—for it evidences what for sociability should be hidden—but, more importantly, he still faintly believes in the benevolent public. Moreover, he needs it. Where the cynic is perceptibly finished with trying to be coy, witty, or insightful, the ironist has partially interiorized his disgust (introjected it on himself, resulting in melancholy) and re-presented it with a smile; he frequently elicits the best joke of the party, before going home alone. As the young and ironic Kierkegaard wrote in his *Journals*, "I have just returned from a party of which I was the life and soul; wit

---

*All of this, in the DOD's "Joint Vision 2020," can be read at www.dtic.mil/futurejointwarfare. See the Defense Advanced Research Pro-jects Agency (DARPA) for other delightful developments.

poured from my lips, everyone laughed and admired me—but I went away—and the dash should be as long as the earth's orbit———————and wanted to shoot myself."[28]

The ironist, therefore, though he shares many of the cynic's assumptions about social reality, is a somewhat lighter, more effete character. He is more publicly bubbly than morose, more skittish than weighty—indeed, a charming depressive. He holds secret melancholy about the world hidden behind a facade of joviality and sarcasm. The ironist realizes the necessity of roles, though he is pained by their awkward contingency, particularly if taken to be real. Oppositely, the cynic avoids playing a social role, and he avoids the party equally as much as he avoids introspection about "serious matters," because the world's just not worth it; and those at the party, he believes, are all somehow guided by illusions, particularly that being among others can provide some measure of fulfillment.

More broadly, cynicism is not as secretly morose as the ironic stance because it has fully abandoned a belief in the Enlightenment's promise of increasing returns on broad social investments, such as public education, the alleviation of poverty, the redistribution of wealth, charity, and freedom through technological rationality. If not part of politics already, the cynic is alienated from political life and broader social aspirations because he does not see any alternative to fill the social space left empty by failed political hopes, by failed promises of Enlightenment progress. He therefore has nothing to lament when social ills confirm his worldview. The Nietzschean "death of God" was a welcomed event, because it finally revealed things as they are: a Hobbesian nightmare of competition and survival concealed by "manners" and mores, blood-soaked lessons cloaked in the garb of morality and "dignity," the most stalwart kernel of the privileged bourgeois concepts.[29] Taken further, there was no "death of God," as that concept was *always* just a ruse by the powerful scheming to keep power. There are no more illusions. "Everybody knows."

These views and character types did not spring from nothing. Real-world events made them appear on the broader social stage and qualify as verification of one's terrestrial knowledge. Some of the motivations behind the appearance of cynicism and irony on the postmodern stage are a widespread mistrust of politicians and a broad loss of faith in the political institutions they engender, a persistent suspicion toward Enlightenment discourses about rationality and "progress," particularly due to their dehumanizing and totalizing effects on actual humans they have transpired, the renewed fascination with mystical or religious accounts of the world, and a nostalgia for lost innocence. These broad characteristics of the postmodern age, as an age conscious of the selfish political nature of social promises, gave rise to the everyday cynical personality. This description fits today's mass figure who is disillusioned, who sees clearly with Nietzsche and the plethora of business managers or political advisors the Machiavellian workings of power. The ends justify the means, at all costs and regardless. Nothing less than absolute implementation of the will, and ideally in plain sight, is accepted.

The cynical mentality is thus one "of strategy and tactics, suspicion and disinhibition, pragmatics and instrumentalism—all this in the hands of a political ego that thinks first and foremost about itself, an ego that is inwardly adroit and outwardly armored," writes Peter Sloterdijk, continuing, "The metaphysical illusions of God, Universe, Theory, Object, Subject, History, Spirit, Nothingness are for the cynic 'nouns for young people'."* The cynic knows that these concepts

---

*Sloterdijk, *Critique of Cynical Reason*, xxvi, xxix. If television advertisements have anything to say about the Zeitgeist, then a recent Nike commercial says it all. Flashing to different sports stars in a totally black room lit by a stark overhead light, each player, in slow motion, goes from helmetless to helmeted, unmasked to masked, each version of which is increasingly and violently defensive: spikes, barbs, some in the shapes intimating armor or monsters. Indeed, this is defense of the head, of the seat of the Western self, against the violence perceived to be done against it. Importantly, there is not one other sports object—a ball or otherwise, save one blip of a baseball bat—in the advertisement to say that the Nike accoutrements should actually be used for "play." No, this is serious business. Sports metaphors have always been with American culture, but in recent years, as American life (in both for

merely decorate the way the world works—fictions that have lost all credibility because of an Enlightenment that, after erecting them, also inspired their destruction. So the subject shifts from generalized and default social trust, from a faith in "intersubjective communicative rationality," to a individually oriented, survivalist mode of existence. Present-day cynics are "borderline melancholics," who keep their depression under wraps to remain able to work. And

> indeed, this is the essential point in modern cynicism: the ability of its bearers to work—in spite of anything that may happen, and especially, after anything might happen. . . . A certain chic bitterness provides an undertone to its activity. . . . For cynics are not dumb, and every now and then they see the nothingness to which everything leads.[30]

In this sense the cynic is the progeny of a modernity that, having lost belief in an afterlife and a religious view of the world and his own life, faces the abyss and must go on nonetheless. Though young people are far from dead, it is oddly a gallows humor we share.

The most useful distinction I want to make between these two declensions of character, because it has the most effect, because it casts the two modes into higher relief, is that the ironist harbors a desire for trust and a "return" to something better than what is. His cultural references to the immediately preceding decades, currently seen in the form of trucker hats, retro fashion, and massive 1960s Jackie O sunglasses, are a readily available cultural expression of nostalgic longing, a longing for a time, like most all nostalgia, that was far more imperfect than we remember it, if we do at all.* It's a false longing that is motivated more by a compulsion to escape the present than a heartfelt

---

eign and domestic policy, too) increasingly resembles an extreme game of survival, those metaphors are all the more ubiquitous—and apt.

*A personal note on the shock of nonironic, non-nostalgic moustaches: at a party recently, someone I had met before, around my same age, had on aviator glasses and a moustache, just like a character from some retro film, like

desire for a past we hardly knew. Both irony and nostalgia are the ironist's public methods of retaining hope; they operate by playing with
past forms that, skipping over the present, will enable a way to a better future* (* = *An extended note on nostalgia* at the end of this chapter).

In retaining some measure of optimism, then, the ironist is oriented
toward this future, which is why any current incivility he displays is
justified to him by the ends of a more honest society. "What you do is
not honest!" Stewart, the satirist, accused *Crossfire*. Protecting the
vision of a better society and culture within himself, he utilizes irony
and sarcasm to cajole honesty out of what he perceives to be a
repressed or dishonest bourgeois mentality, a forest of masks, an
implicit and eternal hypocrisy of values, an infinite jest. In this sense,
irony holds "a conviction so deep . . . an emotion so strong, as to be able
to command itself, and to suppress its natural tone, in order to vent
itself with greater force."[31] Though he often avoids speaking directly
what he means, the ironist is a sworn enemy of hypocrisy—of doing
the opposite of what one says. Ironists have acquired an "inverse
knowledge"; knowing well what words mean, they are even more
aware of how meanings can be and are manipulated.

The ironist, behind his mask of "selfishness and diffidence," is an
incorruptible moralist.[32] Thus his psychological and social resonances
of maintaining this distant hope play out in the character formation
and life choices he makes. The cynic, who has given up, and for whom
self-reflection or social reflection is hardly worth the effort, has abandoned believing that things will ever change for the better—for society or for himself as an isolated unit of that society. The only way to

---

Anchorman. It looked like a disguise or camp but was not. Quickly realizing
the realness of the moustache, I did not make a knee-jerk comment about the
moustache. But for that split moment between, in that unclear interim, in the
not-knowing of what the meaning of the moustache was, the person before me
transformed into a more self-aware, stylized, "contemporary" individual than
I had known before. What had happened to him? It was weird. I had to try
hard not to stare at the nonironic moustache. No, sir, that moustache was real,
which made the man who had it, just for a split second, not.

win is to play by the unspoken or cloaked Machiavellian rules, which, depending on the comparative power of the cynic, he will either perform in politics or live out in everyday life—each with equal vindictiveness, sometimes with a coy smirk to those who share in his knowledge.

When cynicism is found on the side of power, in a public role, these coy smirks are more easily visible to a public well habituated to descrying them. "This smile defends a bad status quo," writes Sloterdijk,

> as one corner of the mouth, often the left corner, is drawn upward; while the other half knows there is nothing to laugh about. The worldly realism of the master cynic comes from the wish to save face while getting his hands dirty. This face often goes together with polished manners. . . . [It] is the smile of high officials, politicians, editors.[33]

There has been an increase in these insider smiles—or, at least there are media that are more ever present, more microphones that have been unintentionally left to capture the whisperings of cynics in power. These whispers and smirks go hand in hand with nods and winks, particularly to an audience filled with peers.

Peter Sloterdijk at a *Kneipe*

But this kind of personality is no longer quite so cliquish. As they have come to dominate the urban social landscape, for both the haves and the have-nots, cynicism and irony have come to act as private bulwarks against the state of the public—always a relative determination, always defined with relation to who's defining it—in which they find themselves. These attitudes have been at it, for better and worse, for some time. And like nearly everything else—civil engineering, democracy, Twinkies—they have their origins in ancient Greece.

* *An extended note on nostalgia:* Interestingly, current nostalgia for sixties, seventies, and eighties' fashion and culture seems to confirm that those eras are definitely dead, not returning. Popular culture began heaping nostalgia upon Americans in the 1970s with the television shows *Happy Days, Laverne & Shirley, Grease,* and *Sha-Na-Na;* each in its own special way reminded citizens of the recently bygone 1950s. With greaser haircuts, leather jackets, a stable nuclear family, and poodle skirts, the shows helped to see a generation through contemporary social strife and to remember when things were orderly and right in the world, a place where Fonzie's hitting the jukebox always worked. The immediate past in popular culture appears as an idealized afterimage: nostalgia.

But over the past several years the nostalgic turn has varied wildly from the 1920s (Gap swing ads) to the 1980s (return of eighties star Jason Bateman, pastels, upturned collars, Donald Trump, overpriced Lacoste, world tours of Van Halen, The Police, Genesis, Kylie Minogue; the sound and dress of The Killers and Scissor Sisters; a recent commercial with Lee Majors as *The Fall Guy;* the return of stripes vis á vis Paris Hilton, a child of the eighties).

A small sampling of American obsession in entertainment with things recently obsolete reveals *That '70s Show; Spiderman 1, 2 , and 3; Scooby Doo; Laverne and Shirley Reunion; Old Sitcom Stars—Where Are They? Childhood Stars—Where Are They?; That Eighties Show; NBC Celebrates Seventy-five Years; Mary Tyler Moore Reunion; M*A*S*H* Reunion; Cosby Show Reunion; Brady Bunch* appearance on (now itself nostalgic) *X-Files; Undercover Brother; Starsky & Hutch; The Nick & Jessica Variety Show,* featuring the Muppets and Mr. T; *Good Times* skit on *Saturday Night Live,* Britney Spears as Marilyn Monroe in a fifties diner or on a sixties Malibu beach as Gidget; eighties break-dance moves in Mitsubishi car commercial; the return of break-dancing in general; a Mercedes-Benz advertisement as a 1940s heartland TV show, the remake of

The Dukes of Hazard, and VH1's *I Love the 70s/80s/90s* (and every year therein), just to name a few. In advertisements, Budweiser in 2005 ran its original television commercials from the early 1950s, offering a "limited-time only offer" of the Budweiser six-pack with its original 1936 design. Reebok posted billboards featuring the actress Lucy Liu as an adult, juxtaposed to her image as a child. The text read, "I want to go back to the feeling of being a child, when the heart told you all you needed to know." (And don't forget: she's a painter.) Additionally, companies with young execs have been advertising with groups of cartoon mascots and superheroes from products that many thirtysomethings consumed as children: the Jolly Green Giant, Puff 'n Fresh, Boo-Berry, and Count Chocula. This will make you want to get the new Visa card with Rewards.

The nineties, remember, were filled with sixties nostalgia (Lollapalooza, Nirvana, Lenny Kravitz, bell-bottoms), but America remains mainly smitten (aside from the surfacing of eighties girl boots, mesh stockings, and Don Johnson jackets) with the 1970s (thigh-faded jeans, OutKast funk, Grammy performance by George Clinton, Scissor Sisters [who combine both irony and nostalgia in "I Don't Feel Like Dancing," where everyone is, in seventies disco attire], moustaches, two-tone shades, pimp hats à la Britney Spears). And for that early 1970s feel, Penguin and its graphic singularity came back in the late nineties. Not to mention the ubiquitous fishing hats (Henry Fonda, J. Crew ads, L.L. Cool J, and Cypress Hill).

Popular culture likes referring back to fashions, characters, movies, television shows, and the general feel of decades that have recently passed so much so that it's increasingly difficult to see anything in popular culture that does not refer to something that came shortly before. What would the look be of, say, 2005–6 if not for historical pastiche? What would we do without mesh trucker-hats, Jackie O sunglasses, T-shirts featuring ads for rodeos, Tron, local swim-clubs, all in intentionally dated typography? What would be considered "edgy," plunging headlong into the future, if not for the revival of the moustache, exaggeratedly nerdy eyeglasses, or feathered hair?

Just what is it about those times or places that we want back so badly? Happier times remembered by the mnemonic icons from our past? That's depressing but true. What are we trying to fix, relive, forget, or redo?* It certainly can't just be the bygone clothes or footwear—Keds, Hush Puppies, Wranglers. Authentic living un-mediated by celebrity culture? Suburban living more deliciously remembered because it's economically more difficult to achieve? Urge for pre-Watergate, pre-Lewinsky political belief? Or is it a true lust for Tab soda and Lite Brite? These things alone cannot have had marketing gurus, television producers, fashion editors, and product designers gainfully employed and harping for the bygone days for well over a decade.

What would we do without trucker-hats or T-shirts featuring intentionally dated typography? What would be considered edgy, plunging headlong into the hip future, if not for the ironic revival of the moustache, exaggeratedly nerdy eyeglasses vis-à-vis Marc Jacobs, or feathered hair?

No, in our reach back to the three decades prior to our own, what we miss is not the objects, design, typefaces, and clothing in themselves, but the defining characteristic of those decades, when we were younger and things were easier. There is something bittersweet about the recent past, something we project as more innocent and less demanding than the present. Because those things are no longer possible, nostalgia helps us along. There are some theories about this somewhere.

---

*Again with Marc Jacobs, a designer partially responsible for peddling retro: *The Guardian Monthly* writes, "His clothes still betray those late 70s, early 80s influences from the time he was growing up, with their tight T-shirts, vaguely retro prints and pastel trousers. He always wants, he says, 'to keep it in that 70s look, which I so love,' which is a little surprising because his childhood wasn't particularly happy: his father died when he was seven, his mother used to dress up as a prostitute character . . . Jacobs, an unsporty, shy little boy, was raised by his grandmother." Jacobs has recreated his boyhood self in the look of nerd hip, now so indicative of retro-cool.

But nostalgia for an era is evidence of a small death of that era's inner ethos. Like smoke from an extinguished match, visual references to past styles are a sign that the energy of that era has gone out. The ethos of unobstructed individualism seen in the call of the youth of the Beat fifties, the sixties, and the early seventies (freedom from social rules, antiorder, antiauthority and antideference, obsession with youth, the celebration of immediate personal desires over the collective good, instant gratification, fun, sex, apotheosis of the present) has become—as people such as Daniel Bell, Tom Wolfe, and Thomas Frank have long held—a form devoid of content, have become the center. Jeans, *Vogue* photo shoots, computer sales-pitches, and hip-hop soda commercials now claim the radical message; but these values don't dominate our practical lives or public culture in any meaningful way. And when an era becomes style, it enters the pantomime of history, shedding its redemptive value. As Christopher Lasch wrote already in 1979, "Having trivialized the past by equating it with outmoded styles of consumption, discarded fashions and attitudes, people today resent anyone who draws on the past in serious discussions of contemporary conditions or attempts to use the past as a standard by which to judge the present" (*Culture of Narcissism*, p. xvii).

And this is exactly why we now see abundant references to 1960s, 1970s, and now (ugh) 1980s: in a bizarre reversal, it's our way of saying those eras are dead, our way of showing that we know they are dead. It took Mel Brooks's nostalgic *Springtime for Hitler* to show that we know *he* is dead. The irony that hangs around with stylistic nostalgia thus behaves as a ghostly reminder: *Look at this fashion or idea that walks around, though I know it is now only a remnant of something once living.* Irony here distances the content of the nostalgic object or situation, turning it into something "interesting" or "campy" or just plain not there any more. By presenting nostalgia through fashion, graphic design, and entertainment, we're saying that we live in a culture where the cherished values of those decades no longer have a grip on us, that though we can see the shell of what the values once lived in, that shell is now empty. Entertaining, not really meaningful.

We also present recent history perhaps also to remind ourselves of the contingency of our own present: that it too will become a time relegated to fashion, caricatured by its obsession with nostalgia. For T. S. Eliot, things had been going downhill since Dante. Homer had thought the golden age passed with Hesiod. Contemporary American popular culture takes the lower-brow version: all that was good passed away with polyester slacks, Connect Four, aviator glasses, PBR, and Atari. All "slumming" is a kind of remembering. And reclaiming.

CHAPTER TWO

Excursus on the Genesis of Irony as a Worldview

> Irony in the eminent sense directs itself not against this or that particular existence, but against the whole given actuality of a certain time and situation.
> —Søren Kierkegaard, *The Concept of Irony* (1841)

> Confronted with a randomized world, irony enacts suspensiveness, which implies tolerance of fundamental uncertainty about the meanings and relations of things in the world and in the universe.
> —Alan Wilde, *Horizons of Assent* (1987)

> Enjoy Uncertainty. Give Chance A Chance. Life Is Random.
> —Advertisement for Apple iPod Shuffle, 2005

Nostalgia often plays a role in how we relate to the present, how we identify the present's outstanding characteristics, even as one of relentless appropriation. But this extended note is a sidetrack: irony is also a way that we are relating to the present—a way that keeps some unpleasant realities at bay.[1]

And of course, the history of irony is long, complex, and debatable. Yet this much is clear: what begins as a rhetorical trope and a vague character trait transforms in romanticism into an entire worldview. From there, irony, while retaining all of its garnered linguistic, dramatic, and situational meanings, comes as well to describe an entire personality type inhabiting advanced industrial nations. Let's get this party started.

From its earliest days, in preclassical Greece, irony (*eirōneia*) was a part of the field of rhetoric; it was deployed as a technique of verbal communication.[2] For the playwright Aristophanes, irony was, simply, lying. The fox, deceptive and sly, was its quintessential caricature. Demosthenes and Theophrastus used the term to mean deceptive self-deprecation, a "vicious dissimulation of one's political and social powers."[3] In Theophrastus, the ironist was someone "who could never be got to do anything, or to commit himself in speech so that he was forced to take sides in an active discussion. This is irony which has become a social vice."[4]

Socrates with Gameboy™

Eirōneia acquired its first noticeable significance in the dialogues of Plato (BCE 428–347), referring to the discursive methods employed by Socrates: praise-by-blame, blame-by-praise, sarcastic commendation, and disingenuous self-deprecation. Irony was for Plato "mocking pretense and deception." In the various Platonic dialogues, Socrates would feign innocence or naïveté when questioning someone in order to draw the truth out of him, in order to show that he *did know* answers he believed he did not

know. Oppositely, Socrates would use the technique of feigning ignorance to show a speaker that he *did not know* what he claimed to know,
thereby dispelling the speaker's proclaimed wisdom or expertise. In
this sense, Plato deployed the tactic as a method of showing ignorance
where there was previously hubris, or showing that knowledge was
merely "forgotten." It is with Socrates that irony first comes to be as
an entire mode of engaging the public—especially for engaging the
public. Aptly, this would be fittingly described in the late eighteenth
century as Socratic irony.

In his *Rhetoric* and *Nicomachean Ethics*, Aristotle (BCE 384–322)
referred to irony with distaste. Playing down one's virtues and intelligence—as in Socratic irony—was its primary characteristic. But Aristotle did not regard this sort of personality as pernicious *or* ideal;
eirōneia—often translated as a "self-depreciator"—was more subtle
because it was context-dependent, not absolute.* Yet it was definitely
not a virtue and was interpreted ultimately by Aristotle as a form of
dishonesty in civic life. The virtuous citizen avoided both boastfulness
and understatement, instead presenting himself forthrightly; he was
engaged, forward, generous, modest, and unself-conscious in his dealings with others: "When an individual has no ulterior motive, he
speaks, acts, and lives his real character. . . . [The self-depreciator] dis-
claims especially those qualities which are highly valued by others, as
Socrates used to do."[5] Aristotle's description undoubtedly moves irony
into the moral arena, conflating a rhetorical technique with a charac-

---

*Aristotle, *Nicomachean Ethics*, 4.7.3–5., trans. Martin Ostwald (New York:
Macmillan/Library of Liberal Arts, 1962), 104. Aristotle's use is translated as
"depreciator," and not "deprecator." Ostwald notes, "'Self-depreciation' is perhaps the least inaccurate rendering of *eirōneia*. The best description of the
quality is found here: it is the exact opposite of boastfulness and involves
qualities such as understatement, pretending ignorance, mock modesty and
the like, but sometimes has overtones of slyness. Self-depreciation, in the
form of feigned ignorance, was frequently attributed to Socrates" (e.g. Plato,
Apology 38a; *Republic* I.337a; *Symposium* 216e).

ter-type defined as having ulterior motives, being sneaky, immodest, and overly self-concerned. This moral association will remain with irony.

The Roman orator and statesman Marcus Tullius Cicero (BCE 106–43), influenced by Aristotle's writings but not his subtle disdain for the ironic man, made reference to irony, particularly in *De Oratore* (BCE 55) and *De Inventione* (BCE 99), as it was used by Socrates. It was

in Cicero that irony first attained a sort of positive dignity, a trait to be cultivated. He was flattered to be thought an ironist of a Socratic caliber, and for the first time, in Cicero, there is a distinction between irony as a mere *figure of speech* and that of a pervasive manner of behavior. Nonetheless, Cicero does not imply anything approaching a philosophical worldview, as would happen later, when the world would warrant it.

The mode of ironic satire in Juvenal (CE 60–130) found home in sixteen biting essays that ridiculed Roman extravagance, corruption, and immorality, of which, apparently, there was plenty. Juvenal (Decimus Junius Juvenalis) believed that society should be run by men like himself: the old upper class of Italian birth.

Cicero with Cheeseburger

(He also, like a Talibanized Lou Dobbs, hated the success of foreigners and a burgeoning freedom for women.) Juvenal's third and tenth satires are his best known; the third attacks Rome because it is noisy, uncomfortable, dangerous, and full of thieves and immigrants, much as, I've read in my *Lonely Planet* guide, it is today. Juvenal's voice seems so contemporary when he writes, "It is harder *not* to write satire. For who could endure this monstrous city, however callous at heart, and swallow his wrath?" Slightly milder, the tenth satire is more philosophical in tone, lamenting the consequences of seeking beauty, power, fame, and material success. It urges the reader instead to desire a healthy and simple life, like that of the athletic Stoic. Or Paris Hilton. "Artful ridicule," wrote the satirist Horace (BCE 65–8; *né* Quintus Horatius Flaccus—son of a slave, soldier under Brutus, and receiver of an "estate so you can just write" from a wealthy arts patron), "can address contentious issues more competently and vigorously than can severity alone."

Cicero's definition of a behavioral kind of irony was honed by the influential Roman orator Quintilian (Marcus Fabius Quintilianus, ca. CE 40–95). In his *Institutio Oratorica* (CE 93), Quintilian refers to irony as three distinct moments: "(1) a brief figure of speech embedded in a straightforward context ('trope'); (2) an entire speech or case presented in language and a tone of voice which conflict with the true situation ('schema'); and (3) a man's whole life as colored with irony, as in Socrates, who assumed the role of the innocent man lost in wonder at the wisdom of others."[6] In this last case, patently for the first time, irony is conceived of as an ethos, as a type of social character whose personality was ironic, an entire mode of existential engagement.

Yet still, irony's general definition, beyond this, remained relatively stagnant for the next fifteen centuries, all the way to sixteenth-century Britain, where it retained the meaning that Quintilian had lain down in the *Institutio Oratorica*, as a simple mode of speech, and how we still popularly conceive of the term: "a moment in which something contrary to what is said is to be understood."[7] Even during the English classical age the word continued to be a technique of cultured speech, reserved mainly for wordsmiths, not something eminently present in everyday life; certainly not something that could be described as capturing the imagination of an entire era or conceived of as a mode of interpretation among everyday citizens.

This is clearly not at all to say that prominent writers did not *utilize* irony in their literary works in earlier eras, particularly during the age of Reformation and the northern and English Renaissance: Martin Luther, Desiderius Erasmus, Sebastian Brant, Johann Pauli, François Rabelais, Thomas More, Francis Bacon, Christopher Marlowe, and William Shakespeare all obviously and effectively deployed irony as a trope. Alexander Pope's *Dunciad* later bitterly satirizes the deterioration of culture, especially by atrocious literature and ill-considered education. Yet confined to use by intellectuals and literary types, irony was not widespread as a means of apprehending broader social life, not a word that used to describe a general popular mind-set. As literary historian Norman Knox notes, "[While] the contribution of the English classical period was to introduce certain Classical concepts of irony into the main stream of English literary culture and to develop these older concepts in small ways . . . it did not stimulate anyone to extend irony into startlingly new realms."[8]

The third earl of Shaftesbury (Anthony Ashley Cooper, 1671–1713), however, described a "soft irony" that "spread alike through a whole character and life." This kind of ironic view was both a sign of goodness and the expression of a perfected way of living. Irony's ethical implications here see a reversal of those held by Aristotle and his followers: irony was something to be cultivated, something toward which one should aspire. As such, Shaftesbury was seeing irony in a "modern" way (officially eighty years premature), from the subjective, existential angle of individualism rather than from Aristotle's attempt at a politically and sociologically objective one. That is, Shaftesbury's emphasis was on the ironic *attitude*; an ironic manner of speaking was only the external expression of a broader apprehension of reality.

Actually, the Earl described the degree of opposition between praise and blame as something that should be kept to a minimum, for one should avoid "satiric virulence or comic buffoonery" and instead cultivate a grand ethical fusion of "modest self-abnegation, gentle gravity, and a general tolerance of all things"—all the while hiding one's actual reservations. This would, of course, later come true in the throbbing genius of Bob Newhart and nearly everything British, from *Monty Python* to *Faulty Towers* to *The Office* and *Extras*. This kind of reserve evidenced in the real social world an increased valuation of the individual, the human spirit triumphing over the externalities without. Holding back centered the subject so that he was not disturbed by the "immediate changes and incessant eternal conversions, revolutions of the world."[9] As long as the ironist lived "disinterested and unconcerned" (stoic countenance with a twist), he would become increasingly independent of the world, could accommodate all appearances into his purview, which put "everything in its due light."

This is a thoroughly modern political and social attitude insofar as it implicitly recognizes a pluralistic world, even if aristocratically inspired. (I mean, come on, the guy *was an Earl*.) For Shaftesbury, Socrates had obtained this high-water mark of cultured disengagement. The Greek gadfly was

> a perfect Character; yet . . . veiled, chiefly by Reason of a certain exquisite and refined Raillery which belonged to his Manner, and by Virtue of which he could treat the highest Subjects, and those of commonest Capacity . . . together, . . . both the heroic and the simple, the Tragic and the Comic.[10]

For Shaftesbury, then, irony was a goal of human being, a strategy to be implemented in all of life in order to acquire the distance necessary for happiness and, importantly, a sense of freedom. It allowed the subject to soar above the social world and the mass of opinion. It allowed him to feel superior, to be free from constraint.

This increasing flair for the ironic mode of speech and writing continued in the eighteenth century, coinciding with the rattle of social and cultural modernity and the increasing attention paid to the burgeoning concept of rights of the individual. Consequently, irony began to acquire more widespread popular mention and use. In addition to Shaftesbury, the satires of Defoe and Swift during the 1720s, concomitant with the plethora of pamphlets and periodicals—*Tatler, Scots Magazine, Courant*—and the general increase in literacy, saw rapid consumption of the popular witty, daily journal *The Spectator* of Joseph Addison and Richard Steele.[11] The proliferation of parody and satire became an increasingly common means of expressing both ambivalence and raillery at political and social events and figures—that is, at power, as critique—in both literary production and in common usage. Irony as distanced attitude allowed an individual the self-controlled delimitation of his private conscience as set against political foibles. The increase in irony's use coincides with the positive self-regard that individuals have for themselves, as well as the sociopolitical arrangements that make such self-cultivation possible.

Jonathan Swift Using a Mouse

Swift's time-tested exemplar of satirical writing, *A Modest Proposal* (1729), written about exhaustively, thankfully, suggests that the suffering Irish poor should simply sell their children to the English for "not above the value of two shillings" for income to stave off famine: "A young healthy child well nursed is at a year old a most delicious, nourishing, and wholesome food, whether stewed, roasted, baked, or boiled; and I make no doubt that it will equally serve in a fricassee or ragout."[12] This method of blame-by-absurd-recommendation was utilized to draw attention to the blatant social negligence—and parliamentary tax-plundering—that the English were displaying toward their desperate Catholic neighbors in the 1720s. In one of earliest deployments of irony as a general social and moral corrective, Swift combines the unfit combination of logical clarity, compassion, and total naïveté in relaying his enormous plan for fixing a social ailment. Irony is deployed in the spirit of Christian charity in order to highlight the *hypocrisy* of avowedly Christian neighbors. It works because of sharp intelligence masking as idiocy. "I Profess, in the Sincerity of my Heart," Swift writes, "that I have . . . no other motive than the publick Good of my Country, by advancing our Trade, providing for Infants, relieving the Poor, and giving some Pleasure to the Rich."[13]

After 1755 irony began to intone several new meanings, particularly in Germany, less so in England: Dr. Johnson's *Dictionary* had retained irony's definition as Quintilian had offered nearly 1700 years earlier, as "a mode of speech in which the meaning is contrary to the words."

Irony in an Early American Vein:
Two Figures Every American Ought to Know

Not to be neglected, of course, is the use of literary irony in America early on, when pamphleteers and almanac-makers were arguing either side (though mostly on the Whiggish one) of colonial independence. Though the literature of the time—whether political philosophy or sermons—does not approach irony as an attitude whatsoever, as it does in Shaftesbury—those using satire, for example, Nathanial Ames of Massachusetts, Hugh Henry Brackenridge of Pennsylvania, the Connecticut Wits, and Philip Freneau of New Jersey did so in order to goad an uncertain mass of individuals to (or in the case of the Connecticut Wits in Hartford, against or dismissing of) the revolutionary cause.

Drawing on British, Scottish, and Irish influences, the works of Philip Freneau (1752–1832), born and raised in Monmouth, New Jersey, and America's first homegrown poet-satirist, were of tremendous importance in gathering strength for the revolutionary and then anti-Federalist causes. "Like a disgruntled Daumier with a bad spleen," writes biographer Jacob Axelrad, "Philip Freneau caricatures the so-called leaders, the elite of society, whose one concern is, now as always, with themselves, their own pleasures and profits."[14] Freneau was likely influenced politically in this direction early on: his roommate at Princeton was James Madison, who would later call on Freneau, at the behest of Secretary of State Thomas Jefferson, to come to Philadelphia to edit *The National Gazette*, the publishing arm of the young government. Can you imagine Lewis Black being offered a job by Condi?

Having studied theology, the fractioned reason for The College of New Jersey's existence, Freneau became disquieted with the field, writing in his college notebook: "Farewell to the study of Divinity—which is, in fact, the Study of Nothing!—and the profession of a priest is little better than that of a slothful Blockhead."[15] Raised French Protestant, Freneau grew into a populist, deist, and secularist, to be sure, and one who was against the vain seriousness of the clergy, wealthy merchants, businessmen, and politicians he believed had no interest in the larger cause of human liberty that was being waged in the hearts and souls of the citizenry. In this sense Freneau, who deemed himself, instead of A.M. or LL.D, an "O.M.S.: One of the Swinish Multitude," was ultimately a more serious person than the clergy he despised. Freneau was afraid of that "man who was never known to transgress the demands of strict sobriety in drinking. [They are] cold and unfeeling. . . . To be always serious is not true wisdom. Life should, in a certain degree, be chequered with folly."[16]

Freneau's satires appeared in many places throughout his life, including in the *United States Magazine*, and the *Freeman's Journal*, in essays called the "Pilgrim Papers," and under the general series *The Philosopher of the Forest*. Though his output throughout his manic career was immense, his modesty about it was apparent and abiding: "Fellow Citizens: After having debated the matter with myself at least twenty times," Freneau writes in his satirical *Letters on Various Inter-*

---

esting and Important Subjects (1800), "at last I have determined to publish all my letters . . . that may amuse the ignorant, whose brains, like my own, are not able to bear deep reasoning, because they have never learned Latin."[17]

Called in 1791 by Jefferson to edit *The National Gazette* in Philadelphia, Freneau took careful aim particularly at the editor of the politically adversarial *Gazette of the United States,* John Fenno. Freneau and Fenno—both in Philadelphia at that time—lashed out at each other in print, each claiming the other a pawn to larger political purposes. Freneau used sharp irony while going after the Federalists, claiming, like many believed, it was an ideology of the rich and powerful. Pretending to be writing the news of 1801 (instead of 1792), Freneau sardonically writes some "fake news," à la the *Onion:*

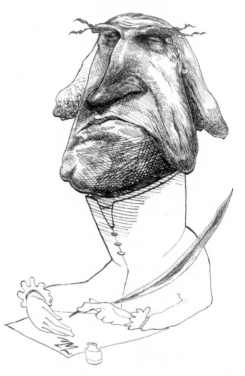

Thomas Jefferson Creating Nation

On Monday last arrived in this city in perfect health, his Most Serene Highness and Protector of the United States, who on Wednesday next will review the regular troops which compose the garrison. . . . Yesterday came on before the Circuit of the Protector, the trial of James Barefoot, laborer, for carelessly treading on the great toe of My Lord Ohio. [He was found guilty and] the court fined him only 100 pounds or ordered him to be imprisoned for six months. . . . A few copies of the act to restrain the freedom of the press may be had at this office.[18]

Importantly, from his years fighting in print and with arms, from sailing and seeing the frailty of human being and the greed of war profiteers, Freneau took this one lesson: no one could be trusted but the people themselves. All history was proof to the simple truth that no one else could be relied upon to guarantee freedom but the governed. Though his concerns grew more serious with age, Freneau remained a satirist of the utmost moral conviction.

He was friends at Princeton with Hugh Henry Brackenridge (1748–1816), the Pennsylvania author of the three-volume political satire *Modern Chivalry* (1792–93), a rambling satirical novel that jabbed at the pretentiousness of the east and the backwardness of the west in Pennsylvania, essentially embodying the tensions of the fragile union in its formative years. The first two volumes of the book were published in 1792 and the third in 1793, in Pittsburgh—the first book ever published west of the Allegheny Mountains. The book made him famous and was widely considered the first important work about the details, duties, and drudgeries along the American frontier. *Modern Chivalry* has been dubbed a work that is "to the west what *Don Quixote* was to Europe." And Henry Adams called it "a more thoroughly American book than any written before 1833."

Freneau and Brackenridge were already writing and publishing satires together against the Tories at Princeton, and both belonged to the Plain Dealing Society, a Whig-sympathetic organization set up to counter the Well-Meaning Society, which had overt loyalist affiliations. Satire played an influential role in their spirited public exchanges, and each was inspired as well by Princeton president John Witherspoon's pamphlet "Ecclesiastical Characteristics," which with biting satire (and a subsequent satirical "apology") hunted down the waning religious interests of the clergy of Witherspoon's native Scotland.* The two also composed the satirical "Father Bombo's Pilgrim-

---

*See John Witherspoon, *The Works of the Rev. John Witherspoon: Late President of the College at Princeton, New Jersey* (Montville, NJ: Sprinkle Publications, 2001). And, no joke, this is Reese Witherspoon's great-great-great grandfa-

age to Mecca in Arabia" (oh, is *that* title a prediction), often designated the first American short story, a satire based on a feud between rival clubs—Whigs and Tories—at Princeton.

Brackenridge's first draft of *Modern Chivalry* was the *Modern Chevelier*, composed as a long poem of thirty pages. Dissatisfied with the composition in verse form, he revised it in prose based on the voice of Swift and other Anglo-wits like Addison, Tillotson, and Bolingbroke. Brackenridge wrote that he formed the voice and composition of *Modern Chivalry* "on the model of Xenophon, and Swift's *Tale of a Tub* and *Gulliver's Travels*. It is simple, natural, various, and forcible."[19]

In using such force, Brackenridge composed a work that essentially pits an elite against the people—the environment in United States in the Federalist/anti-Federalist debates. Captain Farrago, the well-read farmer and militia officer of western Pennsylvania—Brackenridge's alter ego—is set against the fall-guy character of Teague O'Regan, an illiterate Irish servant encouraged that in America even simpletons can get rich. And how. He is the true butt of Brackenridge's satirical shots, though the author really stood somewhere in the middle. He disliked the arrogance of the Federalism of Hamilton, but also despised the homegrown, unreflecting acquisitiveness of the hardscrabble west.

The narrative of *Modern Chivalry*, then, America's first travelogue, sees Farrago and O'Regan move from the wilderness of the western frontier eastward to Philadelphia, illustrating throughout that this new land of "the people" also contained a lot of stupidity and ignorance. Neither respectable political culture nor the church was spared in Brackenridge's satire. When O'Regan barely escapes being proselytized, Brackenridge opines,

> I feel myself disposed to agree with those who reject human learning in religious matters altogether. More especially as sci-

---

ther. It's likely that everyone who goes/went to Princeton since *Legally Blonde* is required to know this.

ence is really not the fashion at the present time. For as has been before seen, even in the very province of science itself, it is dispensed with. . . . In state affairs, ignorance does very well, and why not in church? I am for having all things of a piece: ignorant statesmen, ignorant philosophers, and ignorant ecclesiastics.[20]

Not only are institutions and people being satirized, but all sorts of contemporary cultural practices, too: the duel, the Indian treaties, the aristocratic leanings of the Order of Cincinnati. And by now the journey has taken us to Philadelphia, where Brackenridge opens fire directly at the Federalists. When Farrago searches for the vanished O'Regan among the office seekers in the urban setting, Brackenridge narrates,

The candidates were all remarkably pot-bellied; and waddled in their gate. The captain, inquiring what were the pretensions of these men to be elected, was told that they had all stock in the funds, and lived in brick buildings; and some of them entertained fifty people at a time, and ate and drank abundantly; and living an easy life, and pampering their appetites, they had swollen to this size.[21]

The examples here given of Brackenridge's humor stand as precursors to the satire and irony deployed in service of social criticism seen so prevalently today. Yet as historian Walter A. McDougall writes, "[Brackenridge's] serrating satire had no echo in American letters until Artemus Ward and A. B. Longstreet. . . . Perhaps Americans were not ready to peer into the mirror he held."[22] Brackenridge's voice was one of enlightened social criticism during a time when light was being shone into the darkness of daring parliamentary overreach. In Europe at the same time, as so often, things looked even more dark.

CHAPTER THREE

European Romanticism Ushers in New Meanings of Irony

In irony everything should be all jest and all seriousness, everything guilelessly open and deeply hidden. . . . It contains and
arouses a sense of the indissoluble antagonism between the
absolute and the relative, between the impossibility and the necessity of complete communication. It is the freest of all licenses,
because through it one transcends oneself, but at the same time it is
the most prescribed—because absolutely necessary.
   —Friedrich von Schlegel, *Fragments* (1797)

Irony is not only the evil, that is, the entirely general evil in itself,
but also adds the form of evil, subjectivity, vanity, by proclaiming
to know itself as the vanity of all content, and to know itself in
this knowledge as the Absolute.
   —G. W. F. Hegel, *Philosophy of Law* (1821)

When I use the expressions: irony and the ironist . . . I could just as
easily say: romanticism and the romanticist. Both expressions des-
ignate the same thing.
   —Søren Kierkegaard, *Concept of Irony* (1841)

Incidentally, the habit of irony, like that of sarcasm, ruins the
character; eventually, it lends the quality of a gloating superiority;
finally, one is like a snapping dog, who, besides biting, has also
learned to laugh.*
   —Friedrich Nietzsche, aphorism 372, *Human, All Too Human* (1878)

---

*An alternative translation of this aphorism is: "In the end one comes to
resemble a snapping dog that has learned how to laugh but forgotten how to

Entirely new, overarching implications of irony that escaped the confines of unreflective, if very effective, usage were ushered in with the unraveling of some Enlightenment hopes in Europe. Continuing religious conflicts and persecution, political fragmentation, and Napoleonic sorties contributed to the faint sounds of European romanticism, a broad movement of cultural and intellectual activity from 1780 to 1830. This, at least, is what it says when I Googled the term.

Entirely new, overarching implications of irony were ushered in with the unraveling of some Enlightenment hopes in Europe.

In the Germanic case, writers and philosophers found irony to be a crucial outlook of the modern mind, one we are, in part, still thinking with. German Romanticism was a cultural moment caught between a longing for the simplicity of the past via nostalgic projections (among conservative thinkers) and the enticements of a politically brighter future (loudly cheered by progressives). Living in splintered states not bound by a political union, German Romantics nourished the ideal of democratic republic advocated by the French revolutionists but did not support violent upheaval. In its place they supported, vis-à-vis Schiller and German *Aufklärung*, the role of culture, art, poetry, and

---

bite." The interesting difference is this: in the one, the dog has also learned how to laugh in addition to his regular activity of biting. This suggests that irony has added to the dog's life insofar as he now has respite from his regular activities, that he is somehow more human. In the other, the dog has "forgotten how to bite," suggesting that the habit of irony somehow ameliorates the need to. For Nietzsche, this forgetting how to bite would most likely be construed as something bad, for it suggests that irony has "civilized" the person out of more fundamentally violent and dominating instincts. Indicatively, Nietzsche also wrote in the same aphorism: "Where there is no relation as between teacher and pupil, irony is impolite, a base emotion. All ironic writers are counting on that silly category of men who want to feel, along with the author, superior to all other men, and regard the author as the spokesperson for their arrogance." Yes, *this*, coming from Friedrich Nietzsche.

philosophy as *Bildung:* as an education for people to become the future citizens of the ideal republic.

Of course, it is a hilarious understatement to say that much has occurred between the time of German romanticism and today's American Universe. Yet there are broad similarities shared by both the German Romantic ironist and the one who has been described as inhabiting the contemporary American social and cultural landscape: someone who recognizes the contingency of vocabularies and the inability of everyday language to capture experience fully, the teeming ineffability and ambivalence of the universe, dubiousness toward claims of moral authority, a lack of clear moral standards, doubt toward objective notions of truth, beauty, and morality, and the valuation of, above all else, personal authenticity of identity and in culture.

The ironist character of romanticism and of the contemporary West each stands internally afar from the world around him yet longs for the immediacy and primacy of experience that would dissolve his self-consciousness and alienation. Each uses ironic engagement to shield the inward self from a world seeming to encroach too far upon subjectivity. It is this similarity that brings me to romanticism's propelling irony forward as a worldview, deeply into the present.

Romanticism

Having perceptible cultural beginnings around the year 1780, European romanticism was motivated in part by the subtle belief in the indeterminacy of *all* language, as well as by language's specific inability to capture the complexity and mystery of the inner self, particularly as opposed to the growing scientific comprehension of the natural world. To be sure, romanticism itself is, of course, like all -isms, a broad cultural description rife with complication and lack of consensus about its meaning.* Yet there is agreement that this originally Euro-

---

*For a helpful discussion of romanticism's complications and contradictions, see, among others, Jacques Barzun, *From Dawn to Decadence: 500 Years of*

pean phenomenon remained a dominant mode of cultural consciousness both in Europe and in the United States until about 1850.[1]

Essential to this new Romantic view was that the mind did *not* have
direct access to reality, whether through God's revelation, moral
insight, or scientific inquiry.[2] Rather, Romantics, influenced by the

powerful and far-reaching idealist
philosophy of Immanuel Kant,
particularly his *Critique of Pure
Reason* (1781), assumed that learning about "reality" said more about
the mind and how it structures the
raw material of reality and nature
than it did about nature itself.
Inquiry was always firstly
reflexive.

As such, romanticism—an
extenuated form of idealist philosophy insofar as the mind was conceived of as cut adrift, isolated—
assumed the absolute enormity of
nature and reality, and the feeble-
ness of the human mind to capture
and represent it, no matter the
power of logic and human motivation. Between the mind and the
world there was an insurmount-

Immanuel Kant with Bobble-Head Doll

able gulf that we can never know if we've traversed. The mind, ultimately, could not *know* nature. In this sense romanticism represents an
epistemological crisis.

Western Cultural Life: 1500 to the Present (New York: HarperCollins, 2000)
4–26. See also Erich Heller's *The Artist's Journey into the Interior and Other
Essays* (New York: Harcourt Brace, 1965); Paul Johnson's influential *The Birth
of the Modern: World Society, 1815–1830* (New York: HarperCollins, 1991);
Anne K. Mellor, *English Romantic Irony* (Cambridge: Harvard University

Whereas the Enlightenment impulse had posited the ultimate possibility of knowledge through the use of rational inquiry and the means of scientific reasoning (that is, active penetration *into* objects and phenomena and the deduction of real knowledge from true premises), the Romantic understanding saw the mind as, in part, a *receptacle* for the impressions of the world. In this passivity it sought, ultimately, a communion with the totality of nature, the inflow of a sense of the divine and pulsating dynamism of nature.

Press, 1980); Harold Bloom, *Romanticism and Consciousness* (New York: W. W. Norton, 1970); and Ernst Behler, *Irony and the Discourse of Modernity* (Seattle: University of Washington Press, 1990). Indeed, the influence of romanticism spans into twentieth-century political life; where some contend that it was the inspiration behind movements such as National Socialism and Fascism, others—because of irony's liberating quality—hold that it was the only way to fight against them. Romanticism is sometimes seen as the valuation of individuality, sometimes as the obliteration of it within the universal. Nonetheless, it will always be linked to the French Revolution insofar as it argued for the liberation and recognition of the individual: his sensibilities, his affections, his freedom of conscience inscribed in the very makeup of the state, the rights he has to stand against that state. Yet like other terms that claim an entire worldview under its definition, romanticism's divergent meanings vary, naturally, according to the age that defines them. I utilize the definition that leans toward the primary valuation of the individual's subjective experience. It is that image of the Romantic individual soul that stands against the wider social world. As romanticism holds the fundamental conviction that the world is ineffable, especially for those whose scientific or technological attempt to claim the opposite, it is a worldview fundamental to modern versions of mysticism and back-to-naturists. For one imaginative and additional definition of who today's Romantics are, see Walter Truett Anderson, *The Truth About The Truth* (New York: Tarcher/Putnam, 1995), 110–16, who describes them as the most nostalgic of today's social types, looking to the past, nature, or New Age spirituality to define and complete personal identity. For Anderson, the "romantic–back to nature" type of worldview is not the same as the "postmodernist-ironist"; they are even set at odds with one another insofar as, in Rortian fashion, the "romantic–back to nature" mind-set does not see itself as historicized or relativized, but rather as a natural type with "an original relation to the universe."

Ultimately this sort of reverence for nature and the unknown was a curative attempt, for the Romantic also felt that there was something about the present and himself that was in need of repair. They sought a new wholeness in nature, in the future, or in nostalgic longings for the past because they believed perfectibility was possible and the present had been corrupted. This yearning pressed into the Romantic mind an experience of loss, melancholy, irony, and regret, all the while going ahead into life, teeth bared, "in spite of." Metaphysical isolation and social alienation became paramount philosophical moods.

In order to attempt to cure this sense, the Romantic *imposed* on nature its meanings through artistic and poetic creation rather than scientific understanding. The Romantic also imposed order and roles on (or shed from) the individual self, which was free to construct its identity. The Romantic individual in society was surrounded by social roles seen as not experiencing the deeper reality that the true self did, as imposing an inauthentic role upon him. This imposition of social roles was felt by the Romantic as a sort of violation, a restriction of the self's inherent freedom and creativity. This sense of encroachment lies at the heart of the Romantics' alienation, because they possessed a "consciousness of the void *beneath* the conventional structures of reality."[3] The imposition of social roles on the individual compromised the sincerity of the inward self.

Having inherited the valuation of sincerity from the Protestant ethos, the Romantic mind was, to many Catholic observers, a secularized Protestantism: more than anything else it sought authenticity, sincerity, commitment, self-realization, and honesty to one's inner self above all. This valuation of the true self motivates the Romantic to go *around* the role, that is, society's imposition of identity—conceived of as inauthentic and performative—to connect *pure* nature to the inward self, thus restoring a particular kind of experiential mode, subjective *feeling*, as a source of value and assurance, as an attempt of being at home in the world.

From Rousseau's *Social Contract* (1762) and *Confessions* (1782) (the latter stemming from the spiritual autobiographies inspired by the

Reformation's accentuation of inward experience) comes the idea that by tuning in to the inner voice, the seat of right and moral conduct, the self can become moral without the aid of social instruction; the divine in nature is the sole necessary teacher. Man is innately good, a noble savage; it is society and its institutions that make him into an insincere, selfish beast.

The self, bound as it is to nature, then, was wholly inward, mysterious, and unique, something so ineffable it was impossible to communicate it in any direct way. This mysterious self can only speak its truths outside the realms of social life, conceived now as inauthentic and artificial. Yet, importantly, the Romantic mind yearned toward expression of self; expression of one's inner life, one's uniqueness, was essential to an individual sense of freedom; imaginative creation displayed the declension of spirit.

Alas: irony as a technique of communication became an important means for the self's presentation—how the invisible is made visible by pointing to other than itself, how sentiment and true feeling are divulged to others who understand you. The true expression of inner authenticity could only be done *indirectly;* that is to say, inner authenticity could only be revealed *ironically* or through the use of pseudonyms, characters, fictional constructions, and other mechanisms that allowed authors to reveal themselves in ways other than direct polemic or address.

Roman-tic, in fact, is derived from German philosopher and classicist Friedrich von Schlegel's use of the German noun *Roman,* or "novel," designating that literature was the "Socratic dialogue of our time," a means by which the individual could navigate the vague interstices between self and world while remaining an authentic being. This attitude has come to be known as Romantic irony, though only very sparingly did Schlegel use these terms in conjunction.[4] The conception of irony as an attitude toward communication whereby the self was both hidden and revealed, addressed "the indirect communication of the hidden truth of inwardness," something spiritually valuable, existentially necessary.[5] The technique allowed for the preservation, protection, and presentation of the authentic inner self that was under threat from ossified forms and langauge. The mystical inwardness of individuality could remain guarded. Writing and artistic creation were not primarily representation, but shield. As such, the realm of aesthetic and spiritual value was now *internal* to artists, as part of the now-deified *imagination*—which made artists and other creators god-like, rather than as tied to the objective standards by which artists had been judged in the past.[6]

This newfound uncertainty threw into doubt notions of objectivity and agreed-upon standards for aesthetics and moral behavior, which bothered some philosophers at the end of the eighteenth century because it meant that the basis of aesthetic criticism—particularly for a proponent of neoclassicism—was lost to the vagaries of subjective preference. For example, Schlegel after 1796 abandoned neoclassicism, asking himself the question: "How does criticism operate if there are no rules of taste?"* In brief, he responded with his theory of irony: a choice to move ahead in the absence of rules and standards.[7] Moreover, this loss of a center for aesthetic criticism was particularly worrisome with regards to morality. In this sense, the Romantic mind asserted its own independence by insisting that the only valid judgment of what it produced was a standard of its own making. It pulled back from the world of sociality; it reasserted itself as the standard of judgment with a resolute subjectivity.

---

*This, by the way, to art's unfortunate disadvantage, is the same confused attitude that anyone not deep into contemporary art has about . . . contemporary art. Meaning, nearly everyone. The efforts to explain a work's "meaning" or "relevance," are, in effect, attempts to justify artistic activity today as doing something at all rather than nothing, or not knowing exactly why. Narratives of artistic "expression" or "dematerialization" have become as passé as the narratives of "representation" they replaced. While art that forces thought into unseen corners is without doubt necessary, it now, in short, though far from over, unfortunately, has fallen into trouble. See *The End of Art* by Donald Kuspit (New York: Cambridge University Press, 2004).

Thus this new worldview ushered in by the critique of Enlightenment epistemology, while privileging an ironic distance, at the same time revaluated interiority, *furthering* its own perception of a gulf between self and world. Literary historian D. C. Muecke describes the spread of the ironic mentality during the Romantic era:

> Irony enlarged in [the] Romantic period beyond Instrumental Irony (someone being ironical) to include . . . Observable Irony (things seen or presented as ironic). These Observable Ironies— whether ironies of events, of character (self-ignorance, self-betrayal), of situation, or of ideas. . . . were all major developments, not least in the development of the concept of *Welt-Ironie*, Cosmic Irony, or General Irony, the irony of the universe with . . . the individual as the victim.[8]

And because the Romantics saw irony as "neither a technical rhetorical trope nor as a stylistic device, but as a metaphysical term which best embodied their epistemology, for some . . . irony was of cosmological significance."[9] So Romantic modernism ushers in the view of an ironic universe not only as an adopted stance and enacted through artistic creation, but also as an objective situation conspiring against man. Ultimately ironic consciousness recognizes the problematical nature of language itself; it points to the potential foolishness of "all linguistic descriptions of reality, to the absurdities of the beliefs it satirizes."[10]

This kind of totalizing irony we share with Romantics.

This is the kind of totalizing irony we share with Romantics: the solid knowledge of the malleability of language and its randomness at describing reality. History, luck, and weapons, not the discovery of objective forms, make names.

German Romantic Irony

Germany was particularly adept at theorizing the term. The Germans made it possible to think of irony as something *unintentional*, as organically generated in nature, as having no discernible author. D. C. Muecke, author of *The Compass of Irony* (1969), has written that "with minor exceptions. . . . the theory of irony has been in the hands of the Germans or of those with a German education, like Kierkegaard and the Swiss Amiel in the nineteenth century and Vladimir Jankelevitch in the twentieth."[11]

Freed from the restraints of authorship and intentionality, irony became something like a situation to apprehend for the German theorists, as well as something meant or injected into the world. Its fundamental characteristics combined a heightened self-consciousness, a recognition of epistemological tangles, an acknowledgment of the contradictoriness of the world, and, moreover, the human inescapability of facing up to that world. The historian Norman Knox has written:

> The German theorists of the new irony . . . found themselves in a situation that has become familiar to the modern mind. On the one hand, there seemed to be considerable evidence that human values are only subjective and sharply opposed to an external world that is chaotic, inhumanly mechanistic, or ultimately unknowable. . . . On the other hand, they could not relinquish their faith that the values of the human spirit must be substantiated somewhere.[12]

As a new subjectivism acquired lived evidence, Romantic irony in Germany was seen foremost by Friedrich von Schlegel, chief progenitor, as, among other things, "self-parody that enables one to regard jest as earnestness and earnestness as jest." Wit, humor, satire, and buffoonery were useful for Romantic irony because they upset normal logic and sense; but as forms they were entirely different from the larger sensibility of *Ironie*—something more serious, actually—and about which, Schlegel asserted, "irony the clear consciousness of eternal agility, of an infinitely teeming chaos." This was all achieved by a sort of self-imposed distancing, above the crowd, as "the need to raise oneself above humanity is humanity's prime characteristic."[13] The subsuming of the world as an object of thought was what made humanity fully itself. It was humanity's Apollonic ability. It was, however, primarily the purview of the aesthete for now, circumscribed within the fields of art and philosophy; these activities allowed for a feeling of freedom from the confines of the everyday, much the same as they had for Cicero.

Irony in German romanticism, then, shifts its meaning from that of a rhetorical strategy to that of a *strategy of being*, such that irony became the only true and, most importantly, *authentic*, style of existence. And to be authentic was to be attuned, sensitive to the times—characteristics that many Romantics from throughout Europe and America saw as threatened by the encroachment of industrialization, commercialism, and science upon the mysteries of human being. As such, the ironic perspective as a total worldview has in common with a religious sensibility its totalizing aspect, its subsuming of the subject into a coherent vision. Indeed, it replaced that vision. As the Scottish sociologist Harvie Ferguson has written, "Irony is essentially and inherently a spiritual phenomenon."[14] All of life is made anew under its gaze.

The developing relationship between the individual and society was clearly on the minds of many philosophers and politically oriented intellectuals in Germany, France, and the United States at the end of the eighteenth century. Speaking broadly, revolutionary feeling (in France and the United States), and then the conservative backlash against those revolutionary sentiments, dominated educated Western minds and tore apart old allegiances. As comprised of aesthetes and philosophers, German Romantic thought was caught between these polarized sentiments. It struggled to avoid the extremes of both liberalism and conservatism because individual liberty tended to wreck social bonds, and an overemphasis on community quashed personal liberty. Instead, it endorsed liberalism's defense of the individual, while it simultaneously criticized rampant self-interest.[15]

Early notions of this Romantic individualism have, at least in part, philosophical beginnings in German philosopher Johann Gottlieb Fichte (1762–1814), and in his supremely influential *Wissenschaftslehre* (or *Science of Knowledge*). Here Fichte was more concerned with the "I" that was doing the apprehending than the mental states or categories that Kant argued must exist internal to the mind (a priori) for experience to occur at all. In doing so, Fichte heightened the attention to the self as an apprehending entity, as the very *activity* of positing itself; it "exists" only by virtue of the fact that it is aware that it does. The "I" derives this self awareness from things that are "not-I."

Very, very long story short: Fichte's philosophy had the total effect of stressing the freedom of inward subjectivity, a significant influence on the incipient Romantic mode. Yet he also held that *total* freedom was practically impossible to achieve because the ego was always a relation of self to a nonself and, as such, was always bound in relation, producing only a *negative* freedom. Influenced by Fichte's conception of the self, Romantic irony took on the subjectivity that is a "concentration of the ego into itself, for which all bonds are snapped and which can live only in the bliss of self-enjoyment."[16] This was a sort of purifying inward remove most aptly characterized by Fichte as spiritual.*

Friedrich von Schlegel (1772–1829), the son of a Protestant minis-

---

*Fichte became employed as a professor of philosophy at the University of Jena in 1793, after his publisher revealed his name as the author of the anonymously published *Attempt at a Critique of All Revelation*, which many believed to have been penned by Kant. Six years later, in 1799, Fichte was stripped of his professorship owing to his belief that God was not, in fact, a person, but rather the moral force of the universe—a position that had him branded with the contemporarily unfortunate title of *atheist*. His position on this deistic conception was uncompromising, but what added to the dismay of his colleagues and those in the academic administration was Fichte's ardent support of the French Revolution a decade prior. Unable to secure a post nearby, he moved north, where he became the chair of philosophy at the University of Berlin.

ter, held that—in defense of his own stance against impending movements of English empiricism and materialism that were crass—"from the point of view of the consistent empiricist, everything divine, dignified, sacred, great, sublime, etc. is nonsense. All this is really mystical."[17] Like other incipient Romantics, Schlegel insisted upon the rejection of utilitarianism and scientific reasoning made dominant during the Enlightenment's push to total knowledge.*

Irony (*Ironie*) was first discussed by Schlegel in 1797, when he wrote in a fragment, "Philosophy is the homeland of irony, which one would like to describe as logical beauty."[18] And in another early fragment (fragments themselves being indicative of a new way of writing about a fracturing present): "Internally [irony is] the mood that surveys everything and rises infinitely above all limitations, even above its own art, virtue, or genius; externally, in its execution: the mimic style of a moderately gifted Italian *buffo*."[19] Irony was revealed in a perpetual "tension of opposites," such as in satiric and comic irony (in literature), when the apparent meaning begins to reveal the actual meaning. Schlegel was intrigued by the gradual slippage of avowal and content that give rise to two meanings at once.

Before the actual meaning is revealed, there is a moment when both meanings are present in an uncertain balance. Such a state, Schlegel contended, had always resolved in favor of the real meaning. But he didn't want to resolve the tension; that seemed too easy. More so, because in the concrete world in which the modern subject found himself, certainty seemed to be an illusion, all was relative to particularity. So irony became "an incessant . . . alternation of two contradictory

---

*Of note is that the big guns associated with German romanticism—Novalis, Goethe, Schiller, Herder, Fichte, Tieck, Hölderlin, Schlegel, Hegel, Schleiermacher, Solger—all were raised either Pietist, Calvinist, or otherwise Reformed Protestant. Even Heinrich Heine, who was born Jewish, converted. And Rousseau, who was born into a Calvinist family and who later converted to Catholicism, converted back again to Calvinism.

thoughts" that the modern subject wrestled with. The predicament of the modern person was to hover between these two spaces, between a world of vaguely sensed ideals and a reality that always fell short.*

At times Schlegel conceived this existential tension, this suspensiveness of being, as itself something stable. He wrote about it as a movement (a dialectic) from one thought to another, as in dramatic irony, where contextual tensions give way to another interpretive option. The author for Schlegel appears to engage himself fully with one meaning; he then appears to destroy that initial meaning by revealing and attaching himself to a contradictory one. But the author does not settle on this destruction. He destroys this as well, either by returning to the first meaning or progressing onto another; this process can be repeated indefinitely.

This was a methodology by which expectations were undercut and then surpassed, undercut again, and then surpassed again; new, surprising meanings were created in doing so. As such, irony lent credence to appearances that are only partially real. On all accounts, however, it was something serious, something permanently engaged. "No things are more unalike than satire, polemic, and irony," Schlegel wrote. "Irony in the *new sense* is self-criticism surmounted; it is never-ending satire."[20]

Schlegel wrote that irony in the new sense (1797) is "self-criticism surmounted; it is never-ending satire."

Schlegel's image of truth, a result of fascination with irony's role in life and interpretation, was rather confounding—or, for us, absolutely commonplace. In his influential essay "Über die Unver-

---

*Greil Marcus, in an interview on WNYC about his recent book *The Shapes of Things To Come: Prophecy and the American Voice* (New York: Farrar, Straus and Giroux, 2006), suggested that the American is particularly in this predicament, as "the tension between the betrayals and the ideals really becomes the engine of our history."

ständlichkeit" ("On Incomprehensibility"), he contends that "1) all truth is relative; 2) everything is self-contradictory; 3) the essential quality of actuality is eternal becoming; and 4) everything ought, therefore, to be organic."[21] The eighteenth-century Schlegel held the equivalent of some postmodern, postcolonial notions that remain present with us today as commonly accepted (though philosophically debated) assumptions: truth as relative, nature and reality as always changing, reality as contradictory and complex—incomprehensible, untotalizable—aptly: fragmentary.

These ideas predicate what is to come in Schlegel's later years, when irony was no longer an area of interest; he became someone who was increasingly *unironical* (again, not in the sense of humorous, ha-ha, irony, but in the sense of irony being the way in which expression *worked the best* in communicating true meanings). Politically, Schlegel was an early proponent of the French Revolution. But when the earnestness of military campaign overwhelmed the sensitive thinker during the War of 1806 (anti-irony tends to rear its head in times of crisis), when Napoleon came marching straight-backed into Jena—the most important city for Romantic ironic theory—Schlegel intimated an end to jest and irony in favor of sincere engagement and, more significantly, commitment to high-minded political causes.* He came to advocate an old pre-Revolution multinational state, under the control of an emperor and the pope. With consistency, Schlegel converted to Catholicism with his Jewish wife, Dorothea Veit, one of the gifted daughters of Moses Mendelssohn—and seven years Schlegel's

---

*A more contemporary German, Peter Hahne, a sort of Teutonic Bill O'Reilly, published in November 2004 *Schluss mit lustig: Das Ende der Spassgesellschaft* (more or less: *The End of Fun*) to a receptive audience of ferocious readers: "Hahne manages to be fully incorrect in nearly every one of his statements. . . . And the whole book is written in an offended and offending style barely surpassing the hell-in-a-handbasket level of a local bar." Thomas Berger, www.amazon.de, August 26, 2006; "What Germany does not need," writes another reader, "are self-declared apocalyptic prophets and their bad books."

senior—in 1808. It is significant that after this date, Muecke writes, "His work shows [none] of the brilliance and imaginative penetration of the *Fragments* and the early essays."[22] But Schlegel had already done the damage to the sensibilities of his older self: he isolated the ironic and propelled it as the aesthetic hallmark of his day.

This identification of the age with irony infuriated G. W. F. Hegel (1770–1831), who was equally as influenced by Napoleon's ride into Jena. He wrote to a friend, "I saw the Emperor, that World-Soul, riding through the city reconnoiter. It is in truth a strange feeling to see an individual before one, who here, from one point, as he rides on his horse, is reaching over the world, and remolding it."[23] Schlegel's ideas about irony and romanticism were seen by Hegel as having a negative character, specifically so in his *Aesthetics: Lectures on Fine Art* (pieced together by his students posthumously and published in 1835) and in the massive *Phenomenology of Spirit* (1807). In a phrase, irony is for Hegel "infinite absolute negativity," and is, much more condemningly, in his *Philosophy of Law* (1821), "not only the evil, that is, the entirely general evil in itself, but also adds the form of evil, subjectivity, vanity, by proclaiming to know itself as the vanity of all content, and to know itself in this knowledge as the Absolute."[24]

In the unfolding of spirit in the world, irony represented for Hegel the self-consciousness of self-consciousness. It was an *immature* mode of radical subjectivity, tinged with vanity and knowingness. It was immature because it was not a religious kind of subjectivity that opened itself up to the Absolute, where true human freedom and its connection to the divine is found, where the inner-directness of consciousness transcends itself. Subjective irony was instead an adolescent mode that provided only the illusion of freedom at the expense of realizing the truth of objective Spirit.

For Hegel only a philosophical Christianity could provide complete inward satisfaction. He vigorously attacked the ironists of romanticism, particularly Schlegel, because they lived under the illusion that freedom was the ego's projection of itself over the world, that the ego could provide its own escape and salvation. They had it backwards. Lee M. Capel writes in the introduction to Kierkegaard's *Concept of Irony* that in Hegel, "irony is treated as . . . a subjectivity [that] ultimately seeks to isolate itself and . . . degenerates into . . . 'the moral forms of evil,' with irony (romantic) assigned its place as the final phase in such an aberration, the furthest reach of subjectivity."[25]

Irony as negative and incomplete freedom can only negate that which already exists; it cannot create of its own. Negativity is thus irony's fundamental characteristic for Hegel, for "irony knows itself to be master of every possible content; it is serious about nothing, but plays with all forms . . . it is . . . infinite absolute negativity."[26] This negativity expressed the *distancing of consciousness from the world* and itself, self-alienation. By

Hegel with Slayer Pin

adopting this stance, the modern Romantic spirit becomes totally withdrawn, a situation that Hegel characterizes, clearly, as evil (*das Insichgehen des Bösen*, "the inward turning of evil upon itself"); irony *moves away from* the Absolute, denies the Absolute. This activity of consciousness seeks to preserve its freedom and extend its potentiality, though never fully engaging, never using its potentiality except in the actions of negation. Irony, then, with its uncommitted Schlegelian relativism and Hegel's characterization of it as evil, complicated the issue of being a Christian—earnest, forthright, sincere—exactly how

Aristotle characterized the proper mode of citizenship. This complication was one of the deepest concerns, persistent problems, and vulnerable targets for irony's lead nineteenth-century interrogator, Søren Kierkegaard.

Søren Kierkegaard

Irony for the Great Dane begins as the general solution to melancholy—that is, a heavy sadness without cause—which had plagued the philosopher since his youth. Irony as an attitude, as mocking superiority, relieved him by permitting a temporary feeling of freedom and lightness. Influenced by Fichte, romanticism, and Hegel, Kierkegaard's *Concept of Irony* (1841) interpreted the theory of irony as discussed by Schlegel, Karl Solger, Ludwig Tieck, Hegel, and others to be an attempt to talk about the relation of individual spirit to society in the modern age. Irony was partially the recognition of multiple, mutually valid worldviews. It abandoned the single perspective of events; it threw history into doubt. Nothing could be taken at face value, for there was no single reference, no single world, to which all language now referred. This aspect was the defining feature of modern life.

As early as 1835, six years before his dissertation on irony was completed, Kierkegaard noted in a journal entry that irony was "an irksome traveling companion that one must be free of to acquire repose and meaning."[27] In youth, though, one should cultivate the ironic perspective, for "Irony distances you from the world at the same time it allows the world to reappear more vivid but also more elusive and . . . [in] more disturbing guises than it does for a person preoccupied with the everyday."[28] Yet one "survived" this stage of irony in a "self-conquest." For Kierkegaard, irony presented itself as both a personal struggle and a moment in the movement of self-consciousness in the world.

He, like Hegel, whose Berlin lectures he attended, was upset with romanticism and how it disengaged the cosmopolitan subject from the world; both thinkers believed this attitude led to a spiritual poverty and distracted the individual from developing a fully spiritual life. Romantic irony is attacked early on in Kierkegaard's writings, years prior to his *Concept of Irony*, because it lacked any sort of "dialectical potential"; that is, for having no inner tension that would allow something positive to emerge from the stance. Irony was purely negative; it could only exist because of the existence of something else.

As irony so dominated the German Romantic worldview, Kierkegaard associated and interchanged the terms:

> When I use the expressions: *irony* and the *ironist* . . . I could just as easily say: *romanticism* and the *romanticist*. Both expressions designate the same thing. The one suggests more the name with which the movement christened itself, the other the name with which Hegel christened it.[29]

Irony as an attitude is inseparable from the rise of modernity. This equivocation futhers the understanding that irony shares with romanticism a worldview: the contingency of vocabularies, skepticism toward moral authority, social and epistemological doubt, the inauthenticity of society and roles, the romance of nature, and the apotheosis of subjective experience. Irony and romanticism are linked as a way of being-in-the-world.

Irony and romanticism are linked as a way of being-in-the-world.

Yet Kierkegaard, too, became frustrated with the Romantic version of irony because though it raised the individual above the world and distanced him from its everydayness, it did not, like Socratic irony, have an ethical principle in mind. Socratic irony was ultimately serious about its lack of seriousness, earnest about its ignorance, employing ironic tactics and acting the fool for the benefit of truth. Romantic irony had no such ethical impulse. It was empty. Where does it progress from its feeling of freedom? What is it *for*? By affording the subject with a distance and scorn for the world, Romantic irony was hermetic and caused a feeling of unreality in those who did not "outgrow" it. Carried to maturity, the stance caused a breakdown of the subject's psychological relationship to the world, where, for Kierkegaard, "the whole of existence becomes alien to the ironic subject, and the ironic subject in turn alien to existence. . . . As actuality has lost its validity . . . he himself has to a certain degree become unactual."[30]

For the Romantic ironist, in Kierkegaard, nothing can have weight or earnestness. Because he lends no weight to the world, his total tendency is toward total egoism. And this ironic ego is such that

its relation to the world is never at any moment to be in relation to the world, its relation is such that at the moment this about to commence, it draws back with a skeptical closedness. But this reserve is the reflex of personality into itself that is clearly abstract and void of content. The ironical personality is therefore merely the outline of a personality.[31]

Søren Kierkegaard on *American Idol,* 2007

Merely the outline of a personality. Kierkegaard, seeing the ironic personality as devoid of some crucial components of authentic personhood, developed this further in later works, such as *Either/Or* (1843), calling this sort of self-regarding irony an "aesthetic" mode of life. The aesthete is left having to create his own reality because by being intransigently ironical and skeptical toward everyday realities, he has negated all that was given. Such an attitude of constant rejection leads to despair and alienation. But the worldview of the aesthete, now for him a generalized character trait, fails to perform that last of skepticisms: the negation of itself. As Kierkegaard explains of this view's near total arch over existence, that irony is "infinite absolute negativity," as it was presented in Hegel:

> [It] is negativity because it negates; it is infinite, because it does negate this-or-that phenomenon; it is absolute, because that by virtue of which it negates is a higher something that still is not. The irony establishes nothing, because that which is to be established lies behind it.[32]

Ultimately, this is conceived as an intrapersonal "crisis of the higher life of the spirit" because, ultimately, the Romantic, pervasive ironic sense is *for* nothing—a rebel without a cause.

To the point: it is thus because of its endless negation, its failure to reach out into the moral sphere of the world, that Romantic irony was thus condemned as anticivic by Kierkegaard. By rejecting everyday commitments and the universe of social meanings in which he found himself, the ironist (the aesthete, the self-distancing subject), becomes the anticitizen; he will not enter into the precious balance of his individuality with the identity of the social whole. Society and its requirements have no weight for him. He does not take his role, his social obligation, "seriously." He does not join in shared history and the maintenance of public life. And, as such, as literary historian Gary Handwerk writes of Kierkegaard's ultimate rejection of this attitude:

> This detachment and negation of history and culture is essentially anti-civic, so that the Athenian state is seen as justified in its condemnation of Socrates, having recognized the absolute incongruity between their values. Socratic irony can finally be justified only by its momentary character. As a response to

Sophistic egoism it has its necessary role, but its reappearance in a Romantic guise is unhesitatingly condemned by Kierkegaard.[33]

Where Socratic irony for Kierkegaard was imbued with value because of its ethical impulse set against sophistry, its earnest desire for knowledge by means of ironic methodologies, Romantic irony negates the very value of the civic sense that Socratic irony attempts to *uncover* or *reveal* (recall that Socrates died rather than injure civic duty by escaping from prison). It is the destruction of the ethical impulse. Kierkegaard consequently finds himself confronted with the need for a muscular faith that embraces existence and transcendence, that allows for both the individual conscience and the trust of community to coexist. While the attuned individual searched for this sort of commitment, he adopted the ersatz freedom of detachment and irony as a placeholder. There was eventually no middle ground: the choice was either/or.

Modernism Redux

Kierkegaard himself belongs to a modernism that was prompted by anxiety to rediscover its lost wholeness. He represents for us a social character that was involved in this sort of attempted recovery: longing, wistful, melancholic, searching, self-conscious, without home. And romanticism is frequently cited as a good jumping-off point for modernity, messy as it may be: it integrated self-reflexivity and self-criticality in its very cultural forms. Irony is one philosophical result of this self-reflexivity. The tactics of irony and satire are quintessentially modern philosophical responses to the world. Irony was, for Schlegel, an "involuntary and yet completely deliberate dissimulation."[34]

Modernity, as such, yearns to overcome the estrangement that it helped to create. This is its motivating force. The aesthetic or ironic view of life generated throughout cultural modernity was later countered by a longing on the part of artists, writers, and the spiritually attuned to bridge the gap between the "hovering" self and the now-distant world, to get back to where they once belonged. At times this is evidenced in attempts to overcome irony with recourse to hyper-sincerity. The tension between the self-conscious outsider and the enrapt participant provides obsessive, relentless fascination.* The consequence of this detachment gives rise to both irony and melancholy.[35] In this sense, the character of Romantic irony is the character of modernity itself: it seeks wholeness and unity; it is skeptical of the rational appropriation of the world. It views social reality as violent and imposing upon the sacred self; nature as spiritual salvation, as diametrically opposed to the social; innocence as the circumvention of reason; life as chaotic and

Andy Warhol with Home Remedy

---

*This seems to be the operating logic of practically all documentary work—that quintessentially modern form of representation—particularly when it involves issues of class. However much he is well-meaning, the alienated, privileged documentary worker attempts to bridge his social distance from everyday life through connection with "regular" people. But because he or she is never them, this sort of operation ends in even worse umbrage to regular people and profoundly blind narcissism on the part of the documentary "worker." See the earth-scorching work by James Agee and Walker Evans, *Let Us Now Praise Famous Men* (Boston: Houghton Mifflin, 2001). The attempt to close the gap is also the reason for modern art's fascination with the insane, primitive, illegal, and otherwise antisocial. The more radically self-alienated the privileged artist, the more radically outside he must go to actual social alienation to attempt to heal himself through art.

random; art and the imagination as supreme for the comprehension of the cosmos and reality.

In terms of a *moral* assessment of irony in modernity, then—where today's meanings have in part come from—it survived German romanticism and Kierkegaard with the battle scars of condemnation. Specifically it represented a form of radical subjectivity as per Hegel. It represented relativism because it was uncommitted to one moral stance, as promoted by Schlegel. And because it was characterized as inwardly focused and uncommitted to an ethical impulse, it was also narcissistic and hollow, as Kierkegaard's critique proclaimed. Because it fled from the Absolute, irony was tinged with the scourge of atheism and, ultimately, hermetic moral evil, as Hegel's final evaluation pronounced. And because it attempted to soar above the everyday to see from afar, it was vain and elitist, as intimated by all.

Such a characterization of irony is not easy to overcome. And it is precisely this characterization that echoes into the present and creates problems for our own notions of civic trust.

CHAPTER FOUR

Irony and Civic Trust

Irony tends to dissolve all belief in the possibility of positive political actions. In its apprehension of the essential folly or absurdity of the human condition, it tends to engender belief in the "madness" of civilization itself and to inspire a Mandarin-like disdain for those seeking to grasp the nature of social reality in either science or art.
—HAYDEN WHITE, *Metahistory* (1973)

Oh heavens, irony! Guard yourself . . . from taking on this mental attitude. [It] makes for depravity, it becomes a drawback to civilization . . . a vice.
—THOMAS MANN, *The Magic Mountain* (1924)

The men believe not in the women, nor the women in the men . . . and the aim of the *litterateurs* is to find something to make fun of. . . . Genuine belief has left us.
—WALT WHITMAN, 1866

Since the inception in the late eighteenth century of serious dialogue about irony as a social attitude, it has been conceived of as corrosive to social life, seen as an ethical show-stopper, brandished as a poor—if not impossible—neighbor and confidante. This belief has often originated from the perspective of a religiously rooted moral commitment to public well-being. As the spiritually curious, seeking, Scottish

111

essayist and critic Thomas Carlyle wrote in 1833 in the autobiographical *Sartor Resartus:*

> Often, notwithstanding, was I blamed for my so-called Hardness, my Indifferentism towards men; and the seemingly ironic tone I had adopted, as my favorite dialect in conversation. Alas, the panoply of Sarcasm was but a buckram case, wherein I had striven to envelope myself; that so my own poor Person might live safe there, and in all friendliness, being no longer exasperated by wounds. Sarcasm I now see to be, in general, the language of the Devil; for which reason I have long since as good as renounced it. But how many individuals did I, in those days, provoke into some degree of hostility thereby! An ironic man, with his sly stillness, and ambuscading ways, more especially a young ironic man, from whom it is least expected, may be viewed as a pest to society.[1]

Speaking in part through the figure of Professor Dr. Herr Diogenes Teufelsdröckh,* and in part through Teufelsdröckh's "editor," Carlyle

---

Teufelsdröckh translates alliteratively and poignantly as "Devil's dung." The use of the name Diogenes references the figure of Diogenes of Sinope (ca. 412/403–324/321 BC), the ancient Greek philosopher-in-a-tub who remains, with Crates of Thebes (c. 368/365–288/285 BC), an oft-cited (and, in the modern period, obligatorily nodded to) figure of the Cynic (Gr. "dog-like") movement in philosophy. Its founder, however, Antisthenes (ca. 445–after 366 BC) was throughout antiquity held as the founder of the Cynics; he was also the only "member" present at Socrates' death—a figure and event that had important influence on the Cynical impulse and its rhetorical methods. Though not technically a school (there were no Cynic classes, for example, as there were with Stoics, Pythagoreans, or the Platonists in the Academy), the Cynic movement was influential by means of mimesis, by those wishing to espouse its principles copying the character of older Cynics. As with all things in antiquity, literary myth and parable have more solidly secured the figure of Diogenes as a staple of the Western philosophical repertoire. His actual teachings, however—like many contemporaneous Greek schools—

tells of his woes in love and confusions in religion. He was confronted with what he saw as an outdated Christian church that was out of touch with the moral and social complexities ushered in by modern social structure and industrialization. Carlyle—who had moved to a remote farm for six years to escape the city and his success within it, who translated Goethe and was friends with Emerson (his American

---

were primarily concerned with moral instruction for human happiness, or *eudaemonia* (εὐδαιμονία). Among the principles Diogenes espoused and promoted to this end were (1) that there was an observable ethical norm seen cross-culturally and among animals (2) that Greek society was at odds with nature and therefore produced false values (3) that human beings needed rigorous exercise and discipline (4) that the goal of this discipline was to promote a happy life, freedom, and self-sufficiency, and (5) that in order to help others to achieve this it might be necessary to deface and subvert existing authorities corrupting the way to true happiness. It was because of Diogenes' actual acts of social antagonism, which frequently overstepped accepted social mores, that Plato famously regarded him as "Socrates gone mad." Specifically—and now numismatically verifiable—it was Diogenes' defacing of public currency that was his coup de grace; he was exiled from Sinope for doing so.

The figure of Diogenes appears plentifully throughout the literature on modern cynicism and irony, given the explicit relevance of his ideas and actions of social resistance to mainstream values and to an individual interiority preciously guarded by the modern sensibility. Prior to the twentieth century, works such as Christoph Martin Weiland's *Socrates Mainomenos or, The Dialogues of Diogenes of Sinope* (1770), Denis Diderot's *Rameau's Nephew* (1805), and Friedrich Nietzsche's (first book) *The Birth of Tragedy* (1872), and *The Gay Science* (1887) featured the famed Cynic for his character of resistance. Most recently and noteworthy, it was German philosopher Peter Sloterdijk's magisterial *Critique of Cynical Reason* (originally published in German in 1983 as *Kritik der zynischen Vernunft* by Suhrkamp Verlag, Frankfurt am Main) that brought Diogenes center stage in the consideration of cynicism, kynicism, irony, and the philosophical justification for an active and generalized social resistance to contemporary social life, as well as an understanding of how the powerful can use cynicism to nefarious—if obvious—ends.

A valuable resource for the historical context and a thoroughgoing reading of the Greek Cynic movement in philosophy and literature, as well as its migration into modernity, is R. Bracht Branham and Marie-Odile Goulet-Cazé, *The Cynics: The Cynic Movement in Antiquity and Its Legacy* (Berkeley and

agent), even if critical of *The Dial,* telling Emerson of society and its messes, "Come back to it"——in the above passage, tells the reader how he had resorted to an attitude of mocking superiority, of ironic distance to shield his inward, private self. Carlyle posits the ironic tone as a defense, sarcasm as something in which he had aimed to "envelope" himself, so that he could "live safe" there.

These images paint a clear picture of irony as something with which one protects oneself from the outside, of an inner self that guards with outward remove. In the hindsight of this passage, this attitude for Carlyle—himself an aesthete and a skeptic, a vitalist who had experienced a sort of cleansing Christian rebirth—is a fundamentally anticivic stance. It made the habitual practitioner of irony a bad citizen, a pest to his fellows.

This view of the disengaged subject, of the ironist, has not changed much in the last 174 years. For those concerned with America's present-day social health, let alone for that of the nineteenth-century Scotsman, this sort of ironic or sarcastic attitude as a relationship toward the public—not taking seriously one's civic responsibilities or ethical responsibilities, a lack of commitment to principles, a focus on the self, a dismissal of others, a constant protection of oneself against them—has been accused of affecting our immediate relationships and the broader civic culture as well. If such a detached social stance— once relegated to philosophical skeptics, the literati, and aesthetes— migrated to the very center that it originally condemned or scoffed, the arguments presented by some philosophers and social scientists goes, it would provoke further alienation and social tension, become a knot of cultural contradiction.

According to these cultural theorists and philosophers, such an event, if we follow the philosophical narrative, is and has been occur-

---

Los Angeles: University of California Press, 1996) (with some translation by Michael Chase). The authors themselves recommend, as the best introduction in English to the Cynic tradition, D. R. Dudley, *A History of Cynicism from Diogenes to the Sixth Century A. D.* (London, 1937).

ring in the West; it was called cultural modernity, and it took particularly good root in America, with its massive cultural machine enabling the proliferation of the attitude of social outsiderness to migrate to the commoditized middle at a rapid gate. This appears in some places as the attitude of *cool*, of a style of being wherein the subject imagines himself as "outside" mainstream culture while very much a part of its reification through commodifying his dissent.* In other, more politicized contexts the attitude appears under names like "aesthete," "narcissist," "relativist," and, on occasion, "the liberal elite." A detached, wry view—*né* "disenchantment"—has become a default reaction toward politics and broader social hopes for the future for people in the West. The attitude is born of Enlightenment goals (and its concomitant metaphysics/stories) becoming less credible (particularly following the mass death of two world wars and the Holocaust), as fodder for inspirational posters and coffee mugs, but not for guiding one's choices or beliefs, not for illuminating a vision of a better world, not for accurately perceiving reality, certainly not for building private hopes about how one will contribute to that end or adjust to the world situation.

Irony Is Just Another Word for the Disintegration of Measurable Social Capital

Debate about irony as an injurious social attitude in the United States and Britain has been a resurgent theme over the past decade or so,

---

*This logic—made explicit in the social criticism of Theodor W. Adorno, Daniel Bell, Lionel Trilling, Mark Edmundson, and Thomas Frank—runs confidently through countless advertisements today, beginning earnestly in the early-1990s. The formula is simple: "Be different, not like everyone else. Be a rebel, an outsider, and buy [fill in product or service here] and [use one of these phrases: "Blaze your own path," "Think different," "Get out of the box," "Break the routine," etc.]. What are you waiting for? [Insert logo of giant, most likely global, corporate entity]." Done. Dissent from the mainstream brought to you by the center of mainstream commercialism. Cool achieved.

having begun in earnest in the early 1990s and culminating in the "end of irony" thesis following the terrorist attacks on the United States. In a way, outbursts calling for the end of irony immediately post-9/11 were predicated on a litany of complaints and social science metrics of citizen cynicism and ironic detachment that had been germinating for several decades. What had begun as a stance that negated other forms of life and sensibility had become throughout the latter decades of the twentieth century a default way of being for individuals inhabiting Western-style democracies—a normative first-world attitude. And if it continued to become an increasingly shared social posture, citizen cynicism would threaten the very idea of participatory democracy itself.*

Western democracies tout court at the end of the twentieth century were dealing to some degree with a shared problem of the "cynical" or "ironical" society.

Western democracies *tout court* at the end of the twentieth century were dealing to some degree with a shared problem of the "cynical" or "ironical" society insofar as those attitudes had been conceived as part of the broader problem of civic disengagement. The attitude was increasingly seen as intrinsically (and somewhat mysteriously) connected to the state of democracy.[2] Declining "social capital" revealed, in part, citizens' donning of a cynical attitude toward politics, government, and the common good.

Already evident in surveys beginning in the mid-1970s, the growing phenomenon (and from the perspective of governance, *problem*) of citizens' public dwindling *participation* in democratic process and public life was tackled by the first international Trilateral Commission on Democracy, whose core analysts were Michael J. Crozier, Samuel P. Huntington, and Joji Watanuki. The assembly convened in 1975 to discuss the governability of Western-style democracies and the role of

---

*Reverberations of this grave concern ripple into the very present; see Alan Wolfe's *Does American Democracy Still Work?* (Yale University Press, 2006).

civic trust—widely interpreted as the opposite of cynical disengagement—in the current state of successful democracies. Social demands were on the rise, they noticed, and an era of lagging economic growth slowed the mechanisms of the state from responding to them in an efficient and socially useful manner. Simultaneously, citizens' faith in political and moral authority was declining. After heavy analysis, the authors concluded in *The Crisis of Democracy* (1975) that the future of democracy itself seemed to be in trouble.

Shortly after the meeting of the Trilateral Commission, President Jimmy Carter gave his foreboding "national malaise" speech, on July 15, 1976—two centuries and eleven days after the birth of the independent American nation. After returning from an extended stay at Camp David, Maryland, where he had met with constituents from "almost every segment of our society—business and labor, teachers and preachers, Governors, mayors, and private citizens," Carter stood before a nation in the grips of a debilitating energy crisis and claimed that America had lost its spiritual way. His speech eventually addressed specific energy policy changes, but the primary impetus behind the televised appearance was to be a beacon for civic renewal, to boost Americans' confidence and faith in their special errand:

> So, I want to speak to you first tonight about a subject even more serious than energy or inflation. I want to talk to you right now about a fundamental threat to American democracy. . . . The threat is nearly invisible in ordinary ways. It is a crisis of confidence. It is a crisis that strikes at the very heart and soul and spirit of our national will. We can see this crisis in the growing doubt about the meaning of our own lives and in the loss of a unity of purpose for our Nation. . . . The erosion of our confidence in the future is threatening to destroy the social and the political fabric of America. . . . But just as we are losing our confidence in the future, we are also beginning to close the door on our past. . . . In a nation that was proud of hard work, strong families, close-knit communities, and our faith in God, too many of us now

tend to worship self-indulgence and consumption. Human identity is no longer defined by what one does, but by what one owns. But we've discovered that owning things and consuming things does not satisfy our longing for meaning. We've learned that piling up material goods cannot fill the emptiness of lives which have no confidence or purpose. . . . The symptoms of this crisis of the American spirit are all around us. For the first time in the history of our country a majority of our people believe that the next five years will be worse than the past five years. Two-thirds of our people do not even vote. The productivity of American workers is actually dropping, and the willingness of Americans to save for the future has fallen below that of all other people in the Western world.

As you know, there is a growing disrespect for government and for churches and for schools, the news media, and other institutions. This is not a message of happiness or reassurance, but it is the truth and it is a warning.

We were sure that ours was a nation of the ballot, not the bullet, until the murders of John Kennedy and Robert Kennedy and Martin Luther King, Jr. We were taught that our armies were always invincible and our causes were always just, only to suffer the agony of Vietnam. We respected the Presidency as a place of honor until the shock of Watergate.

First of all, we must face the truth, and then we can change our course. We simply must have faith in each other, faith in our ability to govern ourselves, and faith in the future of this Nation. Restoring that faith and that confidence to America is now the most important task we face. It is a true challenge of this generation of Americans.

In the midst of a global oil-crisis and rising inflation in the United States, Carter summoned the deepest concerns of social faith, summoned the ghosts of Kennedy and King, and reminded Americans of their earliest spiritual bearings, their deepest existential yearnings.

More serious than the current economic slowdown was the "invisible" threat to American democracy and the crisis of confidence, the loss of national will, the erosion of "meaning" in individual lives. But oddly, while loss of confidence in the future was occurring, Carter claimed, so was the deprecation of the past; America was becoming stuck in an eternal present—one rife with hedonistic consumption, turning its back on God and on the authority of institutions. More importantly, it was turning its back on the promise of Americans' expectations of themselves as citizens of the world's oldest and greatest constitutional democracy.

It is well known that while Carter was at Camp David during that week that he was reading the *New York Times* bestseller *The Culture of Narcissism* (1979) by the late University of Rochester historian and social critic Christopher Lasch, mentioned earlier for his take on ironic detachment as psychic survival "in troubled times." A searing indictment of American culture as one diminishing in its expectations of itself in all realms, from sports to public education to conceptions of character, Lasch's influential book claimed that Americans were increasingly focused on the present and had a waning interest in both the future and past. He protested that a therapeutic sensibility had overtaken public discourse; citizens had become concerned primarily with survival rather than loftier social goals. Simultaneously, the external world, including the state, had ingratiatingly penetrated into the private sphere of family and self—realms that the state and society were supposed to protect and nourish.

These trends in American society, Lasch claimed, were concomitant with the rise of the "liberated personality," characterized by manipulative charm, a pseudo-awareness of one's condition, love of sensuality, fascination with oral sex, hypochondria, protective emotional shallowness, avoidance of dependence, inability to mourn, and a dread of old age and death. This new personality type's pseudo-self-awareness and obsessive concern with therapy defended the subject against the besiegement of his inner life, causing people to feel distanced from work and everyday life—a social arena that had become objectively bureaucratized and devoid of existential meaning.

Significantly, Lasch saw "ironic detachment as an escape from routine," and removal from political and communal life as a strategy of psychic survival in contemporary American society because "as more and more people find themselves working at jobs that are in fact beneath their abilities, as leisure and sociability themselves take on the qualities of work, the posture of cynical detachment becomes the dominant style of everyday discourse."* Jokes, mockery, and cynicism are tools by which individuals adjusted to routine permit themselves to psychologically escape; by refusing to take seriously the various roles the modern subject performs, he dulls their potential to injure him.

---

*Christopher Lasch, *The Culture of Narcissism: American Life in An Age of Diminishing Expectations* (New York: W. W. Norton, 1979), 94. This thesis can hardly be doubted today, as advertising has made "the routine" into a self-aware marketing strategy that, luckily for the consumer, a multitude of products and services now offer to heal. An advertisement on television (January 2005) for the restaurant chain Chili's features a young affluent couple coming home from work at the same exact hour, putting separate plates of food into the microwave, asking each other obligatorily how their days were, simultaneously answering, "Good. How was yours? Good," and then, after a short walk to the couch, plopping, finally, each with a small folding table, in front of the television with a sigh of relief. The dubbed-over voice then asks, "Tired of routine? Live a little! Come to Chili's." The lighthearted and tongue-in-cheek tone simultaneously exaggerates the banality of contemporary living and thereby dissembles the oft-reported and statistically compelling accounts that daily living has become for many families a boring routine without purpose beyond survival. Moreover, the Chili's ad also uses the distancing effect of humor to imply that it's part of the solution to domestic ennui, and not, as may actually be the case, part of the problem (another night of going to the bland theme-restaurant because everyone's too tired to cook or wash dishes and just want something familiar and safe). Chili's, in fact, effectively combines two accoutrements—the microwave and the television—of the life that its ads pretend to relieve. In this sense, Lasch's observations seem even more astute for having been made 1979, as the ironic tone in many of today's commercials highlight themselves as artifice, making it easier for social critics to pick up on the self-consciousness of the therapeutic impulse of advertising, something Lasch would undoubtedly find curious, as, perhaps, hiding in plain sight.

However, this sort of distancing, too, "becomes a routine in its own right. Awareness commenting on awareness creates an escalating cycle of self-consciousness that inhibits spontaneity."[3] There was for Lasch "No Exit" from the reification of modern forms of labor, the intrusion of the political and cultural into the private sphere, and the violent banality of contemporary life that created within citizens a bemused yet sur-

Jokes, mockery, and cynicism are tools by which individuals adjusted to routine permit themselves to psychologically escape.

vivalist mentality, a resentful resignation to one's cultural fate.

To return with Lasch's critique in mind, the immediate gloomy economic forecasts of the first Trilateral Commission proved eventually to be accurate, echoed in President Carter's woes and in Lasch's premonitions about the loss of American confidence. But the social and political predictions made by the commission were, of course, completely wrong. The collapse of Communism and the successful spread of democracy to further corners of the globe—with American capitalistic optimism in tow—dramatically underestimated democracy's staying power. Still, even given the fall of democracy's then archnemesis in the winter of 1991, the question of democratic social health persisted.* Social statistics continued to point toward citizens' increasing alienation from the public sphere and their disengagement from the democratic process. Something had to be done.

So twenty years later the Trilateral Commission on Democracy met for a second time, in Cambridge, Massachusetts, in September 1994 in order to ask, "Why, in some of the world's oldest democracies, in an era in which democracy as a form of government has triumphed worldwide, is public confidence in leaders and the institutions of

---

*The official end of the Soviet Union and the formation of a Commonwealth of Independent States (CIS) took place on December 21, 1991; Gorbachev resigned as president of the Soviet Union on December 25.

democratic governance at or near an all-time low?"[4] This time the commission included intellectual luminaries such as Robert Putnam and Theda Skocpol of Harvard University, Peter B. Evans of the University of California at Berkeley, and Alan Brinkley, among eleven other accomplished academics.

Whereas the first commission met to discuss the very health of Western-style democracy and the governability of those democracies' peoples, the latter commission searched and found that the causes of the decline in confidence did not so much have their origins in an inherently fraying social fabric; the grid of democratic governance was found to be in good health. The decline had even less to do with general economic conditions, the end of the Cold War, or the media—three explanations that had been passed around as easy answers. The problem, the authors found, was instead with the specific people and actions in contemporary government and politics themselves; citizens did not feel connected to their elected representatives and were upset by the dealings and decisions those representatives had made on behalf of the public and, more deeply, on behalf of the national identity. A resultant disconnect and citizen cynicism had consequently taken root, leaving people feeling alienated from those who had claimed to have their best interests at heart, whom they claimed to represent.

The disconnect manifested itself in, among dozens of other quantifiers, a famed American public-opinion measurement, the Harris Poll. This questionnaire asks the responder to evaluate his or her agreement with the following five statements:

1. The people running the country don't really care what happens to you.
2. Most people in power try to take advantage of people like yourself.
3. You're left out of things going on around you.
4. The rich get richer and the poor get poorer.
5. What you think doesn't count very much anymore.

In the 1960s respondents to the Harris Poll showed only nominal agreement with these statements; barely one-third of respondents concurred. By the mid-1990s, however, over two-thirds of respondents found these statements to accurately describe their view of the political world.[5] It was clear that the American population had slowly adopted a rational skepticism toward American politics and governance. They distrusted their leaders and felt isolated from a national identity created in part by the actions their leaders were taking in the world and at home. The result was a psychological break and consequent delegitimizing of authority. The sure sign was an increasingly pervasive citizen-cynicism.

Sociologist Jeffrey C. Goldfarb's *The Cynical Society* (1991) had picked up on this earlier and reported with a patently clear iteration: "I believe that the single most pressing challenge facing American democracy today is widespread public cynicism. . . . Cynicism in our world is a form of legitimation through disbelief."[6] Likewise, as there were no signs of letup or ease in this seemingly mysterious growth of cynicism, Michael Lerner's broad-based *Politics of Meaning* (1996)—itself both a book and small social movement that included intellectual luminaries such as Naomi Wolf and Cornel West—begins with saying that

> we are caught within a web of cynicism that makes us question whether there could be any higher purpose besides material self-interest and looking out for number one. . . . The ethos of cynicism and selfishness plays through our personal lives, often in destructive ways.[7]

In 1995, Andrew Delbanco, frequent contributor to the nation's intellectual pages, noted, in an increasingly frequent conflation of cynicism and irony, that "the triumph of irony has never been as complete as it is today. We have reached a point where it is not only specific objects of belief that have been discredited but the very capacity to believe."[8]

Such attitudes were not limited to American borders. In Great Britain on January 14, 1994, Prime Minister John Major's chief secretary of the Treasury, Michael Portillo, delivered a speech in front of a conservative dinner gathering in London, stating that "national cynicism . . . [is] one of the greatest threats that has ever faced the British nation."[9] Portillo went on to condemn, as his conservative counterparts in the United States were also wont, the universities, intellectual elitism, cultural relativism, and the decadence of the 1960s for the current state of public apathy and civic disengagement. The 1980s and 90s were, of course, the era of the rise of a populist strain of conservatism, particularly on the religious Right in both America and Britian.

The dangers of the humanities and of irony's liberating possibilities at the expense of democratic procedure and, importantly, behavior, were at odds. Which is why, perhaps foreseeing the Portillo portent, in 1994 in Britain's (unfortunately, now-defunct) literary bimonthly the *Modern Review*, editors Toby Young and Tom Vanderbilt inquisitively asked, seven years prior to September 11, 2001, if it was the "end of the age of irony?"[10] For Young, he had hoped not; the only alternative in this age would be, he proclaimed, naive idealism, and that, for the intellectually honest, was not an option. Irony and detachment were a way of dealing authentically with the cultural situation in which he found himself.

As *The Economist* wrote of *A Heartbreaking Work of Staggering Genius* (2000) by Dave Eggers, founder of the magazines *Might*, *McSweeney's*, and *The Believer*, the supposed harbingers of all things ironic in literary expression and pop-culture commentary beginning in the mid-1990s, "It supposedly hailed a new narrator: the desultory, contemporary dilettante who uses irony as a counterweight to cliché and anything earnest. Savvy, satirical, and fluent in pop culture, this voice also uses self-deprecation to inoculate against criticism."* The

---

*"McSweeney's: Ironic Tendency," *The Economist*, January 8–14, 2005, 75. *McSweeney's*, as a cultural presence that aimed in some sense to counter the onslaught of sentimentalized or earnest middlebrow cultural expression, has performed the considerable accomplishment of maintaining a surprising and

New York Times Book Review wrote that Eggers's work was providing a "counterweight to what Ian Frazier once called 'the encroaching Hefty bag of death,' and [writing] about it, in our age of irony, with genuine, unsentimental poignancy." The *Christian Science Monitor* echoed the phrase, saying that *A.H.W.O.S.G.* may be "the bridge from the Age of Irony to Some Other As Yet Unnamed Age that we've been waiting for." And novelist Benjamin Anastas ironically concurred on the general age of irony pervading literary and cultural production in the late 1990s:

> If you are a regular consumer of cultural journalism you will already know about the fierce battle underway between the

---

idiosyncratic voice in the chorus of literary journals by steering from the tempting, hyperironic one-upmanship—though it undoubtedly popularized the tone initially—and cleverer-than-thou (and limiting) self-consciousness to which much young writing falls prey. Instead, *McSweeney's* can unsuspectingly promote poignant satire and volumes dedicated solely to comic art. This, among other outlets throughout the culture of hip understanding, fosters a consistent look of askance upon things middlebrow and parochial, mingled with a thoroughgoing knowledge—and ironic spicing—of both pop and high culture. The publication also has the ability to generate a sort of bizarre hostile jealousy in those not inside its covers; it ignites a high-school-like competition of hip insiderness. Commentator Ada Calhoun at www.nerve.com, in an article about unrequited love with a *McSweeney's* editor, writes that "*McSweeney's* smugly epitomized a culture with its own language (too smart for pop culture), style (too smart for fashion), and social schematic (too smart for anything remotely overwrought). On all scores, in fact, *McSweeney's* was underwrought, cold and pretentious (but affable about it). . . . [It is, a friend says] 'Inside-jokey, Ivy-Leaguey, casually bantery, but referencing every writer of the past three hundred years.' In order to participate, you have to have your eyebrow cocked twenty-four hours a day. Or, as another friend says, 'It's like they built a cool treehouse in the backyard but required everyone to invent their own cutesy conceit before they'd allow them up the ladder.'" Calhoun makes sure to let the reader know that she had recently been asked to submit a piece to *McSweeney's*, which she did not do. Touché!

scheming agents of irony—infidels all—and those honest souls in the arts who practice "earnestness." That is, a cultural war pitting the crusaders of Truth and Beauty versus the dark forces of Deconstruction and Moral Relativism.[11]

A clash of sophistications was raging. On one side were those attempting satirical commentary on the serious business of life, and, on the other, those trying in earnest to ferret out cynicism that was rampant and mysteriously acquired, like a disease floating through the social body. Irony in this sense during the 1990s was a resurgence of a kind of dandyism that attempted to critique culture through artifice and aristocratic remove.

In 1996 a momentous figure was reported by journalist and social critic Daniel Yankelovitch that solidified the sense of the gravity of the situation shared by both sides in the 1990s: "Public distress about the state of our social morality has reached nearly universal proportions: 87 percent of the public fear that something is fundamentally wrong with America's moral condition."[12] Conflated in this worry about moral condition were the state of incivility, the decline of civic trust, and the relaxing of "moral values." That view would so continue to obsess Americans that stressing "moral values"—however vague, political, and selective a term—became the surefire way to later win a presidential election. Well, sort of win.

Widespread social opinion metrics confirmed every worry over the state of Americans' public trust in the mid-1990s. Even among the other areas represented in the Trilateral Commission on Democracies—Japan and Europe—the authors of the second Trilateral were forced to admit that the "downtrend is longest and clearest in the United States, where polling has produced the most abundant systematic evidence."[13] Former Democratic U.S. senator from New Jersey and 2000 presidential candidate Bill Bradley quoted a "Mood of America" poll from 1995 that found "76% of those surveyed agreed that 'there is less concern for others than there once was.'"[14] Robert Putnam, coauthor of the Trilateral report and author of *Bowling Alone: The Collapse and Revival of American Community* (2000), about the decline of social trust in the United States, noted that during the two decades from 1974 to 1994 neighborly socializing—a trusted indicator of social cohesion—declined from 61% to 47%.[15] Further, taking the temperature of Americans' everyday behavior toward one another in public life, a *U.S. News and World Report* national survey from 1996, the same year in which Yankelovitch reported on the nation's shaky moral bearings, reported that "eighty-nine percent of Americans considered the nation's incivility to be a problem."[16]

Shortly thereafter, Harvard University's John F. Kennedy School of Government helped to sponsor the Saguaro Report, a lengthy brief on American civic health by a national research team spearheaded by Putnam and composed of academically illustrious sociologists, political scientists, demographers, and civic leaders. The final report, published in 2000, revealed that simple events like dinner parties had declined 25%

Robert Putnam as Irresistible Stereotype

since the mid-1960s; the number of people who served as club officers, attended school or community meetings, political events, or worked with political organizations had dropped by 35%; and the number of times friends got together during a typical week had dropped 45% since the mid-1970s. Disturbingly, the report showed that less than a third of Americans felt they could trust one another, and that Americans' perception of their fellow citizens as moral and honest individuals had fallen dramatically since the early 1950s. The picture was progressively more clear: Americans were spending more time alone and spending less energy either thinking about or being with others.

The decline in civic engagement—or in Putnam's use, "social capital"* —the Saguaro investigators claimed, was primarily the result of television having taken the place of social gatherings as a form of relaxation, a shift from a more civic-minded generation of adults to a less civic-minded generation of baby boomers, the expanding load of work hours, and the politically charged but statistically accurate observation that women's entry into the work world had sapped neighborhoods of once-vital civic leadership. Lastly, car-centered cities and insufficient amounts of communal space have had the effect of degrading and even preventing daily public interaction.

In a 1997 article on CNN's website, commentator William Schneider noted that polls taken in 1958 and 1964 showed that three-quarters of Americans believed they could trust the federal government "to do what was right." The percentage who said they trusted the government in Washington fell to 65% in 1966, 61% in 1968, and 53% in 1970. After Vietnam and Watergate, in 1974, 36% said they still trusted the government; this number rose to 44% in 1984. Thereafter, according to the same polls, in 1997, only 32% of United States citizens put their faith in the federal government to do the right thing. By yet another poll, quoted in a September 2004 article by *Harper's* then-editor Lewis Lapham, a survey of respondents about trust in govern-

---

*Though it's now most often associated with Putnam, the term *social capital* was used much earlier—at least in its English variation—by Jane Jacobs in her 1961 masterpiece, *The Death and Life of Great American Cities*, and then by sociologist James Coleman in chapter 5 of *Foundations of Social Theory* (Cambridge: Harvard University Press, 1990). Jacobs used the term to express the vibrant and organic matrix of social relations that gave rise to neighborhoods—as opposed to city planning. Coleman used the term to describe the social norms and expectations that form the base for economic activity but could not be grasped solely from an economic perspective. Putnam's later use (1995) popularized the term and introduced it to the general educated reader.

ment was at 62% in 1964; that number had sunk to 19% by 1994.[17] As well, a 2004 Reuters/DecisionQuest poll revealed that 61% of Americans had lost faith in both government and corporate leaders over the past four years, about which Philip Anthony, DecisionQuest's CEO said, "There is an epidemic level of lost trust here."[18]

The statistical evidence makes it patently clear that a concern for the state of Western democracies' social health and trust in their leaders was garnering much attention during the 1990s. So much so that we can say, without hyperbole, that Americans' trust in one another and in their government has fallen *drastically* over the past forty years. Whatever factors have contributed to this demise, it can be confidently stated that "ironic detachment" is closely *related* to civic disengagement—indeed in certain places synonymous with that disengagement—and that this attitude somehow coincides with the decline in "social capital." Insofar as irony proposes a skepticism toward or distance from social life, a guarding of private interiority and reflexive psychological remove, it is pitched as antagonistic and essentially anticivic.

Americans' trust in one another and in their government has fallen drastically *over the past forty years.*

For anyone who is remotely concerned about the state of social health in the United States, these are unsettling statistics. Regardless of how anyone may spin them, these data spell out the enormous loss of trust that citizens of the United States have in their elected officials, both national and local, the leaders of businesses—a crucial component to the financial and organizational support structures of civil society—and to other professions entrusted with maintaining public levels of truthfulness, such as judges, doctors, and lawyers. The legitimacy of democratic institutions was being shed in tow, and citizens gradually looked to private life as refuge, as, per Christopher Lasch, a "haven in a heartless world."[19]

Jeremiads: The Social Tonic

Conservative commentators like Bill Bennett, Ellen Goodman, Gertrude Himmelfarb, Paul Samuelson, Ken Bode, Charles Krauthammer, Mary Matalin, Bill Kristol, and, much further afield, Rush Limbaugh, all came to the discussion about renewing civility with a call for a rebuilding of traditional values and family life.* To varying degrees, these commentators believed that fundamental, Christian institutions—family, church, nation—were being eroded by a liberal, secularist culture and media bent on selling their version of anti-American relativism and a moral free-for-allism, and that such attitudes—accelerated by the decadent days of the 1960s—were having corrosive effects on the culture at large, raising, in the following two decades, the rates of crime, drug use, and illegitimate births. The solutions to these statistically corroborated social problems came in a variety of flavors; nearly all of them contained some version of a renewed respect for moral authority and social hierarchy, seriousness of purpose, renewed civic and religious belief, and patriotism.

For intellectuals of a conservative bent, the media had come to be known as the spawning grounds for the social detachment and moral decay that was haunting the land. Working within the broader metaphor of disease, neoconservatives and those standing for family values argued that pop culture—through television, radio, rap music, and magazines—was releasing a morally degenerating influenza upon

---

*Following the Jeff Gannon/James D. Guckert episode, the reporter/stalwart Republican/military-porn blogger that surfaced on various sites in 2005 (which CNN covered, without pictures, of course), *The Daily Show* made sure to note, in typical home-run fashion, that at least this is increasingly clear: if you're looking for discrete hookups (now all the more relevant after Mark Foley's career-ending page fiasco, Bill Bennett's gambling, Limbaugh's drug addiction, any variety of clergy coverups, Newt Gingrich's affair-causing-divorce-turned-marriage-turned-annulment with a congressional employee episode), just go to any site promoting family values or back-to-basics to start your search.

the nation's youth. Alas, this most recent round of target practice at pop culture arguably started with what has come to be known as the "Murphy Brown" incident, a public comment made in 1992 by George Herbert Walker Bush's vice president, Dan Quayle.

In response to then-recent studies about the rise of illegitimate births in the United States, Quayle brought the topic of moral values and civility further into public discourse by pinning it to the television show *Murphy Brown*, the title character of which was played by Candice Bergen, for having portrayed a woman conceiving a child out of wedlock. Though many of Quayle's fellow social conservatives publicly voiced their agreement, the comment was just as equally met with laughter at the vice president's indignation at a fictional woman on a half-hour sitcom for being a harbinger to society's decline. He said, in August 1992:

> It doesn't help matters when prime time TV has Murphy Brown—a character who supposedly epitomizes today's intelligent, highly paid, professional woman—mocking the importance of a father, by bearing a child alone, and calling it just another "lifestyle choice." I know it is not fashionable to talk about moral values, but we need to do it. Even though our cultural leaders in Hollywood, network TV, the national newspapers routinely jeer at them, I think that most of us in this room know that some things are good, and other things are wrong. Now it's time to make the discussion public. It's time to talk again about family, hard work, integrity and personal responsibility. We cannot be embarrassed out of the belief that two parents, married to each other, are better in most cases for children than one. That honest work is better than hand-outs—or crime. That we are our brother's keepers. That it's worth making an effort, even when rewards aren't immediate. So I think the time has come to renew our public commitment to our Judeo-Christian values—in our churches and synagogues, our civic organizations and our schools. We are, as our children recite each morning, "one nation

under God." That's a useful framework for acknowledging a duty and an authority higher than our own pleasures and personal ambitions.

Quayle's sentiments were part of a growing political shift to the right in the concern for Americans' private morality, as well as in the concentrated critique of the academic Left by conservative think tanks. The 1980s and 1990s saw a huge influx of funding to these think tanks, foundations, and publications aimed at "correcting" the perceived ubiquity of liberalism's influence in America, from television to the courts.* The critique of academia was brought on by frustration with flagging standards, tolerance for a lack of rigorous academic discipline, and the collective dislike of French literary theory, perceived as helping to further relativize and destabilize the dominant Protes-

---

*For a specific first-person narrative of observing the beginnings of this communication program on behalf of the conservative agenda, see Lewis Lapham's "Tentacles of Rage." The article was subsequently debated in the libertarian magazine *Reason*, as well as on Slate.com and on the Accuracy in Media website ("Liberal Editor is Disgraced" by Cliff Kincaid on September 24, 2004, at www.aim.org/media_monitor/1965_0_2_0_C/), specifically for Lapham's hasty "reporting" on characteristics of the Republican National Convention in New York City before the convention had actually taken place. In the *Reason* article from September 3, 2004, "Higher Goals: Republicans learn to stop worrying and love Leviathan" (www.reason.com/sullum/090304.shtml) senior editor Jacob Sullum writes, "When *Harper's* editor Lewis Lapham described his thoughts as he listened to the speeches at the Republican National Convention, the problem was not just that the convention had not occurred yet. It was also that the Republican Party he imagined does not exist. Writing in the September issue of *Harper's*, which subscribers received in early August, Lapham said 'the speeches in Madison Square Garden affirmed the great truths now routinely preached from the pulpits of Fox News and the *Wall Street Journal*—government the problem, not the solution; the social contract a dead letter; the free market the answer to every maiden's prayer.' Even as a caricature, that list bears little resemblance to the main themes of the actual convention, where calls for cutting government and praise of the free market were conspicuous mainly by their absence."

tant culture of the United States by casting into doubt a white, Christian, heterosexual, "homogenous" take on culture and history at the expense of voices at one point not allowed or unable to speak for themselves, particularly those of African Americans, women, homosexuals, and the disenfranchised.

Among the outspoken, influential, and articulate critics of the Left and of American public culture that joined the debate was 1986 Supreme Court nominee Robert Bork, whose *Slouching towards Gomorrah* (1996) held that "liberal intellectuals" were responsible for the spreading of disdain, contempt, and disparagement of American values. To express his own aggravation with modern liberalism, Bork quoted Austrian-born Nobel economist Friedrich von Hayek: "The mood of [the West's] intellectual leaders has long been characterized by disillusionment with its principles, disparagement of its achievements, and exclusive concern with the creation of 'better worlds.'"[20] Furthermore, Bork continued that

in the 1980s, it seemed, at last, that the Sixties were over. They were not. It was a malignant decade that, after a fifteen-year remission, returned in the 1980s to metastasize more devastatingly throughout our culture than it had in the Sixties. . . . The Sixties radicals are still with us, but now they do not paralyze the universities; they run the universities.[21]

Bork's comments resonated into the following decade for many, gathering fellow critics concerned with the declining situation of American social life. But the early 1990s were blatantly characterized by a general distaste for politics and public life, which may explain, in part, the release of a spate of books dedicated to reconfiguring politics and civility by some, and recourse to cynical disengagement by others. Politics was particularly partisan and particularly nasty.

Recall that Congress was gridlocked over the Clinton administration's plan for healthcare reform; militias were making news for their radically antigovernment standoffs; the FBI blew up the Waco compound; Newt Gingrich Republicans launched a "Contract with America"; and Ross Perot became a serious political threat. There was general discord in Washington, D.C., and Americans heard the partisan clamor from Maine to New Mexico. Many Americans saw Washington as a giant playpen filled with bickering children. Disgusted, they turned further away from public life.

Thus in a countermove to the statistical studies of civic health and the intellectual sparring about civil society, a sub-battle of the Culture Wars, the mid-1990s saw a further surge of foundations and institutes dedicated to the particular task of restoring civility to public life and discourse in practical, policy-oriented terms. The Institute for Civil Society, based in Newton, Massachusetts, for example, was started with an anonymous $35 million grant to promote civility, hiring retired congresswoman Pat Schroeder as its spokesperson. The Forum on Civility was founded in the mid-1990s by former secretary of education, head of the National Endowment for the Humanities, and drug czar under the first Bush administration, William J. Bennett (children's book author/high roller). Recruiting Georgia senator Sam Nunn, the forum was launched as a response to "growing incivility in American public life" in the mid-1990s. Lamar Alexander, a former Republican presidential candidate, joined the Commission on Philanthropy and Civic Renewal as its chair in 1997, which is now funded by the conservative Harry and Lynde Bradley Foundation at the Hudson Institute of Milwaukee, Wisconsin.

Dozens of lengthy books on the topic of civic trust and civility, some mentioned above—about its makeup, its health, and its fostering—appeared every few months throughout the 1990s. Among some of the exhortations about the decline of American society and culture in this way were, in no specific order, Gertrude Himmelfarb's *One Nation, Two Cultures* (1999) and *The De-Moralization of America* (1995); Richard Stivers's *The Culture of Cynicism: American Morality in Decline* (1994); Michael Lerner's *Politics of Meaning* (1996); Stephen L. Carter's *Civility* (1998) and *The Culture of Disbelief* (1994); Robert H. Bork's *Slouching towards Gomorrah* (1996); Robert Putnam's *Bowling Alone*

(2000); William Bennett's *The Death of Outrage* (1998) and *The De-Valuing of America* (1992); Jeffrey C. Goldfarb's *The Cynical Society* (1991); Francis Fukuyama's *Trust* (1995); Amitai Etzioni's *The Spirit of Community* (1994); Robert D. Kaplan's *The Coming Anarchy* (2000); Morris Berman's *The Twilight of American Culture* (2000); Robert Bellah and his colleagues' *The Good Society* (1992); and numerous works by *Washington Post* columnist E. J. Dionne, including the edited collection *Community Works* (1998); among many other books and articles in such journals as the liberal *American Prospect* and communitarian *Responsive Community*—all of which to varying degrees dealt with the idea of America's ailing social health, the decline of culture, and the "devaluing" of America.

For some conservative critics, American decline begins with the Founders themselves; the sixties were merely the final culmination of our earliest principles.

For some of these, particularly for conservative social critics, that narrative of American decline begins in the eighteenth century with the Founders themselves; the sixties were merely the final culmination of all that was radically askew in the philosophical background of American founding principles. This thesis has helped to form a standard canon of response upon which many discontented with modern American culture and society still rely. The general story, made explicit and widely digestible by Allan Bloom's *Closing of the American Mind* (1987), himself influenced by the University of Chicago political philosopher Leo Strauss, goes something like this: the founding principles of American society as delineated in the Constitution by the Founders concentrate on the philosophical concepts of liberty and equality. Though sounding high-minded and worthwhile, these two concepts of modern philosophy—particularly influential in the thought of Thomas Hobbes, John Locke, and J. S. Mill—contain a decadent logic that has worked itself out for the last two hundred years, culminating in the apotheosis of individualism and the death of moral authority in the 1960s.

This abstract logic of liberty and equality addressed by Bloom and Bork—ensuring freedom from official interference in private life and demanding that individuals are treated identically before the law and government, regardless of birth or social standing—had the twin effects of releasing individual minds from the sense of duty, and of demanding the subservience of nature and a transcendent God to the will of man. Modern liberalism, while expanding the conditions of liberty for all people, not just the elect, has stripped social relations of the natural boundaries of ability and rank. The combined result of these logics resulted in a world of individuals who held themselves in incredibly high regard, had no conception of their appropriate relations to their fellow citizens, little or no respect for religious or familial authority, few or no limits set to their own personal gratification, and a refusal to submit their own wills and desires to the considerations of the larger community and to God. In order for society to be healed from the wounds of radical individualism and egalitarianism, we have to return to a time to before their influence was so pervasive.*

Gertrude Himmelfarb's *One Nation, Two Cultures* (1999) and *The De-Moralization of America* (1995) continued a variety of this line of thought with a special affinity for Victorian values. She argued that America was well into a state of moral decay, a state caused by the rel-

---

*A recent film takes this nostalgic yearning to concrete (and frightening) literalization. M. Night Shyalamalan's *The Village* (2004) appears to be set in late nineteenth-century eastern Pennsylvania. The entire film plays out with the viewer under the impression that it is a historical thriller. The surprise element, for which the director is known, is that the group living in the small community is actually the result of a self-imposed compact, agreed upon and entered into by cosmopolitans who became fed up with modern society and decided to hem themselves off from the modern world in the late 1970s. Founded, of course, by a *professor* of American history at the University of Pennsylvania, the group of ten moved to the eastern Pennsylvanian countryside and created, with the inheritance of the professor's wealthy father, a security-fence protected "wildlife preserve" where the community does its living and dying, as if it were one hundred years ago.

ativism and tradition-smashing counterculture of the 1960s and a decline of the Victorian ethos. Whereas the 1950s represented the result of an unbroken tradition of respect for political and religious authority, family values, and a deep belief in the objective standards of truth and beauty, the 1960s were the breeding grounds for a flight from personal responsibility, celebration of individualism, rejection of notions of objectivity, unrestrained self-gratification, and disrespect for authority. And as this counterculture moved to the center—seen in popular programming, music, and Hollywood—its lessons of moral laxity lowered entertainment and citizenship standards, creating a generation of Americans who will continue the tradition of disengagement from citizenship's responsibilities.

In the chorus of conservative critics, it was clear that we, particularly the younger we, have since apotheosized individualism and relativized values such that the primary goal of life is our own self-fulfillment. Society thus now finds itself in recent years trying to reclaim those values against the continued propagation of liberty and equality gone awry. Radical individuality and radical egalitarianism are to blame for the current decline in American culture. The result is citizen cynicism and the ironizing of life; there's no r-e-s-p-e-c-t.* Such a view was shared by critics such as Robert Kaplan in *The Coming Anarchy* (2000) and Robert Bellah's *The Good Society* (1992), both of which contended that not only had the 1960s caused some problems, but that the rugged and greedy individualism spawned by the Reagan years made things even worse, made citizens cynical toward moral and political authority. Wealth enabled and encouraged citizens further in the direction of hedonistic individualism.

Oppositely, in polemics such as *The Cynical Society* (1991) by Jeffrey C. Goldfarb and E. J. Dionne's *Why Americans Hate Politics* (1991), *both* voters *and* politicians are involved in this cynical logic. Politicians say things that they don't believe, that they need to say to get elected. Voters know politicians engage in such maneuvering and immediately

---

*I'm sorry. That was too easy.

look askance upon political speeches and promises. Cynicism—an entrenched disbelief, even "legitimization *through* disbelief"—is the dominant operating logic of the social body as a whole. While imagining that it is changing or uncovering the operative logic of a situation or power, disbelief further entrenches that logic.

From education and politics to literature and television, a knee-jerk disbelief, Goldfarb wrote, "defines our present-day situation. . . . Cynicism is shared by the haves and have-nots."[22] Such a view was echoed by Rabbi Michael Lerner, editor and publisher of *Tikkun* magazine, who wrote *The Politics of Meaning: Restoring Hope and Possibility in an Age of Cynicism* in 1996 as "an attempt to shift the dominant discourse of our society from an ethos of selfishness and cynicism to an ethos of caring and idealism."[23] Lerner saw contemporary America in the midst of a deep spiritual crisis, in search of meaning in a culture of cynical self-interest:

> Cynicism about ideals and other people's motives is one of the major correlates of this worldview. According to the dominant thinking of our age, those who pursue higher ideals beyond self-interest, who let ethical vision determine their life choices, must either be dissembling or deeply disturbed. In either case, the rest of us should keep our distance, because such people are either consciously trying to manipulate us or unconsciously seeking power and likely to hurt us in the process. This cynicism permeates daily life, undermining people's ability to trust others or to pursue ethical or spiritual vision.[24]

The Politics of Meaning purported that American society is an alienated society because it has become obsessed with the wrong goals, goals that do harm to the very conception of the good society. Though everyone knew that this was true, citizens did not know how to go about changing the ethos of the times in which they lived. People felt powerless to change things, and their own private lives were suffering because of it.

   Like Goldfarb and Dionne, William Chaloupka, author of *Everybody Knows: Cynicism in America* (1999), saw both politicians and the voting public as involved in a cynical logic, such that "confronted with cynical institutions, cynical media commentary, and intractable public predicaments, Americans are an angry lot. . . . [That] Americans are awash in cynicism . . . seems so obvious that it borders on the banal."[25] Taking cues from Sloterdijk's analysis of the cynic, Chaloupka navigated the meandering channels of cynicism as a *justified* disbelief in the political atmosphere of the present, and a well-honed mechanism of manipulation among political leaders. Speaking to and analyzing the cynical logic in some key exchanges by public figures such as George Will, George Bush, Newt Gingrich, Bill Clinton, William Bennett, Dan Quayle, and Dick Morris, Chaloupka not only uncovered the complex operating principles behind some of these exchanges, but showed how in attempting to "get beyond" cynicism, much commentary unwittingly and more deeply entrenched it. And when both sides were entrenched in this mode of enacting their agency in the democratic situation—a mode enhanced by a myriad of possibilities provided by modern mass media—then pundits frequently offered the "values remedy." This values remedy encapsulates the salves repeatedly applied: a return to civic and religious belief, respect for political and moral authority, and reinforcing objective standards of morality, beauty, and truth.

   The same salve was coming to be applied by a new generation unimpressed with cynical posturing. Issues of how private ironizing of public goals was affecting the broader conception of the "commons" were brought squarely to the fore in a small red book by twenty-four-year-old Jedediah Purdy in 1999. *For Common Things: Irony, Trust, and Commitment in America Today* came at the tail end of this debate and worry over civic engagement in the 1990s, and it raised the issue of how ironic disengagement was presently affecting civic trust, particularly among a young, educated, media-savvy generation. Purdy's volume sounded this concern in a new pitch by addressing an "ironic culture" pervading this younger generation as well as their elected officials, the media, and higher education. Irony was not something measurable or ubiquitous, though; it "does not reign everywhere . . . [but] the more time one has spent in school, and the more expensive the school, the greater the propensity for irony."[26]

Purdy saw the ironic personality as superficially adept at all kinds of social situations, comically filled with quotations from past movies, cartoons, and rap music. The ironic person is seen as the general social character described in some of the aforementioned critiques who does not believe in the adequacy of his own words, who has a constant, nagging feeling of inauthenticity and derivative behavior. "The ironist," Purdy writes, "is at ease in banter, versed in allusion, and almost debilitatingly self-aware."[27] Alert, socially mobile, aloof, and, ultimately, secretly melancholic about his inability to connect with others, the ironist holds up that "believing in nothing" is a measure of pride, and he thus refuses to commit to anything beyond the viewpoint of irony; in doing so, he does harm to civic trust. Since he maintains that he cannot be tricked by anyone or anything, he has become indifferent to public life. Irony has increasingly trumped civic trust because the ironist is ultimately afraid of being let down. The ironist is secretly scared and privately sad.

Faults and all, the book clearly touched a nerve: it sold out of its initial print-run of thirty-five thousand copies within six weeks and went immediately into a second printing. And in the weeks following publication it was reviewed voluminously. Purdy had indeed trespassed on some kind of sacred ground. Joshua Glenn, editor and publisher of the now-defunct *Hermenaut*, asked, "Why, then, are professional ironists so consumed with Purdy these days? One reason is because he said what so many of us already know: that we can't cleave to demanding values." And Gregory Wolfe, editor and publisher of *Image: A Journal of Arts and Religion*, wrote that "irony . . . is the hot topic of the moment. The trigger . . . is the recent publication of a book by a graduate student at Yale University. . . . The argument is that America is suffering from a pervasive attitude of irony."[28] There are a hundred other similar responses.

This mass of attention perhaps came from the fact that Purdy had reframed the debate involving irony, trust, and cynicism, casting them into living, breathing phenomena. *For Common Things* produced "a controversial event in American letters" that brought the abstract conversation about "social capital" out of the ether and put it into terms that many young, thoughtful people could see in their own lives.[29] The resulting openness of the discussion saw the topic of irony then addressed in media outlets ranging from *Time* magazine to National Public Radio, in publications from the *New York Review of Books*, *Social Policy*, the *American Prospect*, and the *New Yorker*, to the

> *In criticizing irony, Purdy had trespassed on some kind of sacred ground.*

Harvard Lampoon and *Crimson*, the *Yale Herald*, the *Charles Street Standard*, the libertarian *Reason*, and the all-purpose websites of *Salon*, *Slate*, and CNN, among others. Chatrooms "hummed" with discussion of the book, according to Benjamin DeMott, who described Purdy as a

> fierce scolder of elites, their cheerleaders, and their jesters, [who] chides Harvard students for moral indifference, Tom Peters for claiming "life is a hustle," Jerry Seinfeld for being "irony incarnate," and at times sounding like a mid-career Archibald Macleish pounding "the irresponsibles."[30]

Much of the criticism, however, was not so nice; often it was itself ironic and unfair—making ad hominem remarks and giving short shrift of the author's claims in exchange for clever one-upmanship, some even admitting as much, such as when *Time*'s Joel Stein ballyhooed that he only read the book plus a few sentences of Kierkegaard because he "wanted to seem smart" to his colleagues and maybe get a promotion. Though this attempted to be funny because it strutted what should have otherwise been an embarrassment, because it was true and written from the halls of the nation's most popular newsweekly, it was simply lame. Further, it fully confirmed Purdy's point that irony—even done badly—was king.

That is to say, in trying to address the issue of being sincere in an ironic culture, Purdy was often spoken of with irony and cynicism; again, further and oddly validating what Purdy had claimed to descry; he just could not win: "Why do the second- and third-rate musings of a twenty-four year old command our attention?" asked *Harper's* then associate editor Roger D. Hodge, for whom Purdy's writing was merely "unctuous sentimentality."[31] And in the now-defunct *Lingua Franca*, Caleb Crain accused Purdy of "sly disingenuous manipulative pseudo-sincerity."[32] Further, at the *New York Observer*, Adam Begley claimed to be "Against Irony, Really (Truly): Spongy Screed Wrings False,"[33] and the *New York Times'* ironically detailed "Why Seinfeld ('Irony Incarnate') Is So Menacing," by Christopher Lehmann-Haupt.[34] For Jesse Walker of *Reason*, Purdy was scarcely a real being, but rather a marketing ploy, whose book was "so richly bad . . . [that one] simply can't take it at face value. . . . Part of me suspects that Purdy doesn't actually exist."[35] Luckily some reviewers jabbed back with an appropriate tool: satire. *McSweeney's* published "Jedediah In Love" by Todd Pruzan.* A spoof on Purdy's perceived sanctimonious unfunniness, Pruzan's sketch draws a scene in the back of a stretch

---

*Todd Pruzan, "Jedediah In Love." *McSweeney's*, October 12, 1999, http://www.mcsweeneys.net/1999/10/12jedediah.html. Not long after the publication of this article in *McSweeney's*, I spoke with Jedediah Purdy (who will not remember) in Boston at a relaunch party for the *American Prospect*. He said Pruzan's yarn was tough medicine to swallow, and that, of all the criticism, he was hurt most by this one. Shortly thereafter I was introduced to Todd Pruzan (who will remember) at the Kingpin in New York City. He felt bad after he heard that Purdy was hurt by his article, and said he agrees mostly with what Purdy talked about in *For Common Things*. Pruzan's article about Purdy is, without doubt, very funny. Yet the article performs the act of satirizing Purdy's personality rather than engaging, like some of the other critiques, the ideas presented in the book. This is perhaps why it's the most fun to read, as well as the most effectual way to comment on the topic of irony in culture—through doing it well.

limo where he and Purdy are in a hot tub with beautiful Las Vegas hookers. As the two Las Vegas ramblers pop champagne and laugh uproariously, Purdy says, "You want to know what I think of the common things? What I really think? I looooove the common things. . . . And I really mean it." Nice.

As mentioned earlier, Purdy's interpretive turn was certainly not new; the critique of irony in culture has had a long and complicated history in philosophical thought. Irony in the Purdy debate and beyond, though, seems to have taken on a hypermagnetic character for commentary about civic trust, and the small treatise became the "whipping boy" of other political issues that were enervating Generation X pundits. It's as if the book was swarmed by the negative complaints about American society and culture that were evidenced in earlier complaints about cultural decline in the 1990s; and following the publication of Purdy's book these complaints were hurled at the scapegoat of irony. Such a conflation is undoubtedly seen in Rosenblatt's, Carter's, and Kloer's attack on the attitude immediately after 9/11.

This is partially so because there was a general consensus in much social criticism from both conservative and liberal commentators that the 1960s unleashed a self-absorbed hedonism that refocused the outward civic direction of the earlier part of the century during the 1950s to a more intense focus on the self. The decades following the 1960s, the general argument goes, were increasingly narcissistic and self-obsessed, materialistic, and continuing along the path of devolution, a loss of values, and an undermining of moral authority. The counterculture of the 1960s moved into the center of commercialism and became a widespread attitude—now the dominant force in American commercial culture. Disconnect from public life and hyperindividualism also come from the hedonism and greed fostered by the culture of the 1980s ("Greed is good," spoke *Wall Street's* Gordon Gekko).

In both cases a lack of commitment to the greater good signaled a remove from or apathy toward politics, and the public sphere became a place increasingly filled with consumerism and entertainment rather than social or political concerns. All of these kinds of critiques see social disconnect stemming from an overinflated belief in individualism and a lack of respect for moral authority and the broader community—a situation ultimately resultant from the very founding philosophies of the American Constitution in general: liberty and equality. These eventually turn into self-gratification without concern for others and a debunking of hierarchy in exchange for sole belief in the self. Combined, the two concepts define and delimit modernity. And as modernity and the ironic attitude are deeply intertwined historically and philosophically, one might see the ironic attitude as the appropriate magnet for the complaints about modernity and postmodernity themselves.

That is, the ironist is someone who stresses these characteristics, is somehow the evidentiary being that willfully corrodes society with his "ambuscading ways." He has a sense of superiority and a sort of hermetic self-regard. He is the narcissist, the inwardly directed, the morally uncommitted individual. Michael Lerner's *Politics of Meaning* tied "cynicism" and "selfishness" together as if they were the same social attitude, one ethos, one kind of personality. Dan Quayle equally observed that irony is that ill wind which encourages *selfish cynicism*. As a variety of selfishness, irony became what the theologian Reinhold Niebuhr called it decades ago: a moral "evil" that "is always the assertion of some self-interest without regard to the whole."[36] The ironist masks hostility and appears always restrained, self-withholding; he is unflappable, unmoved—and ultimately uncommitted.

To bring the discussion back to the present, the interesting and lively thing about recounting the various condemnations and assessments of the above books—and why I give only a brief overview of them here—is that many of them have become quickly predictable, producing boredom and thus oddly confirming a view of the citizencynic's prepared defense. Many of these polemics play into prefabricated caricatures that make it tempting to swiftly deduce palliatives from certain complaints: not enough religion? Get citizens to go to church. Too selfish? Create a common enemy to have citizens see beyond themselves. Every social diagnosis of cynicism—every successive jeremiad—renews the call to believe. Moralists announce that we must refurbish belief and community that have fallen out of favor. How authority should be presented, how the media and institutions should be reformed, are successive recommendations that always join these lamentations. The "values remedy" is the antidote. "If cynicism is the problem," Chaloupka writes, "the answer must be belief—in leadership, education, obedience, and the responsible application of moral criticism."[37]

What this passage suggests rings completely familiar. One knows what to expect as soon as the diagnosis of cynical society is put forward. So the basic complaints that run through many of these thoughtful and considered diagnoses can be summed up thusly: social conservatives and communitarian liberals are understandably saddened by the lack of respect and regard that human beings have for one another in the contemporary culture of the United States. Cynicism and ironic remove result from a lack of respect and regard for hierarchy, and their effects are seriously corroding public life and unified commitment to social well-being. Some see the contemporary culture as being radically off track, and some just slightly.

There is nostalgia involved in much of this criticism of contemporary culture, such that, as the Canadian philosopher Charles Taylor has noted, "root-and-branch critics of modernity hanker after old public orders, and they assimilate personally resonating visions to mere subjectivism. Some stern moralists, too, want to contain this murky area of the personal, and tend as well to block all of its manifestations."[38] Unable to compromise or investigate how "authenticity" has played a role as a moral value, many critics missed the chance to engage a formidable philosophical idea: that a desire for a sense of authenticity had trumped notions of ethical responsibility, instead relegating all ethical change under the rubric of relativism. This sits in direct opposition to some of the deepest assumptions that inhere in the modern, unspoken social contract.

CHAPTER FIVE

Trust, Civil Society,
and the Social Contract

Very concrete and ascendant social problems . . . are
behind much of the contemporary feelings of anxiety,
despair, and dread.
> —CHRISTOPHER BEEM, *The Necessity of Politics* (1999)

Bombs are flying. People are dying. Children are crying.
Politicians are lying, too. Cancer is killing; Texaco's
spilling. The whole world's gone to hell, but how are you?
> —I'm suuuuuuuuuper! Thanks for asking!! All things
considered I couldn't be better, I must say!
> —BIG GAY AL, *South Park: Bigger, Longer, and Uncut* (1999)

The discussion about civic trust brings other concerns with it. It
assumes certain values that irony was conceived of as eradicating:
trust, sincerity, authenticity, and seriousness. While irony does indeed
seem to trump these values, as an attitude it hides what it means under
the guise of its opposite. Because of this, initial hints to the tension
between the ironist and the serious pundit are revealed when consid-
ering the role of the ironic attitude's assumed polarity—civic trust.

As a moral attitude we have toward the strangers that surround us
in daily life, trust is the most essential component of modern social
cohesion and has been written about voluminously over the past sev-

eral decades. Such a concentration bespeaks trust's troubled trysts in contemporary social life and its preeminence in the concerns of political scientists, sociologists, and politicians—who need to accumulate trust to win. The concentration of this concern has been evident in the United States and Britain.* For them, maintaining civic trust has become problematic.

Premodern societies in the West were based on given, inherited social roles stemming from feudal or familial ties, which while often certain, were confining. Members of modern society saw themselves thrown into a web of strangers bound by abstractions, such as capital or legal relationships. Modernity, for the most part, meant the onset of an urban existence among strangers. The *self-regarding* feature of individuals makes them, then, in some way, unknowable.[1] Trust mediates this estranged situation and forges the sacred bond among society's members, allowing modern democracies to work. Necessary in this situation—what Emile Durkheim famously called "precontractual solidarity"—is a trust that emerges at a near-theological level; it is categorized in the realm of the sacred. It requires the proverbial leap of faith. One must first believe in trust before outwardly acting in a way that evidences it. Trust is something you *give*. The more outwardly enforced, the less internally believed. As Friedrich Nietzsche

---

*Conversations about civic trust in Germany—due to the state's lagging performance in ability to provide social services, barely sinking unemployment rate, and widening economic disparity—are beginning to appear. A lecture in October 2006, "Was hält unsere Gesellschaft zusammen?" (What holds our society together?) by historian Paul Nolte, edged closer to questions about social trust and civil society that have been occurring in the United States for the past thirty years. In Germany, at least, this erosion is resulting in a class of people dubbed the *prekariat*, a sociological term used by politicians that is the equivalent of our "poverty line," or "poor," not to be spoken about in a country priding itself on providing, as the outrage by some other parliamentary contingents and media were quick to display. The damaging effects of globalization on social structure and services take time—as well as an eventual compromise of European measures of good statecraft and civic stewardship. *Schade.*

observed, "If someone assiduously seeks to force intimacy with another person, he usually is not sure whether he possesses that person's trust. If someone is sure of being trusted, he places little value on intimacy."[2]

Civic trust is an intimate matter in the commentaries cited, because without it there is no society; there is but a Hobbesian vision of all clammering for survival, individual against individual, unmediated by the mutually agreed-upon laws—which *must* be taken seriously because they have consequences—that govern individual and social behavior. It is, to be sure, the image of society often painted by a government cynical of its own power. Many of the pundits mentioned, to their credit, provide a critique that is as anti-Machiavellian as it is anti-cynical. Both the Machiavellian manipulators and the "Seinfeldian" ironists make for bad company. Recall that Jerry, Elaine, George, and Kramer were all put in jail in the last episode.* Thus, to not be serious about one's responsibility for sustaining civic trust by being sincere in one's dealings or recognizing the full and equal humanity of strangers, is to contribute to the dissolution of social cohesion—condemnable.

Trusting behavior should flow outward from the self to larger systems created by institutional and organizational confidence. As citizens we aspire in various associations, groups, civic clubs, corporations, and charities to an ethical relationship, a civility, we hope will hold society-wide, not just in our private relationships. We abstract trust relations from local to national and beyond. To trust is therefore also to risk disappointment and the failure of others to fulfill their responsibility of being trusted. It is to have faith in the ethical reciprocity of strangers, even while knowing the risks.

The ironic attitude's *apparent and selective* relation to trust—essentially its opposite, its skepticism toward social roles and relationships, its not always taking seriously the words of others or itself, its view of contingency—reveals an entrenched meta-disbelief in modern society's necessary trust among its members, casts doubt upon the intelli-

---

*I don't even know where to begin in taking this apart.

gence of trusting. The risk is too much, because it's so often been corroborated. Ironic detachment appears to point out the naïveté of holding a stance of belief in others and antagonizes civic belief. In its stead, it values a constant, unyielding skepticism. Knowingness assumes pregotten knowledge. The ironist is thus often intimated as a sort of secularized agnostic: he does not fully believe in the public's benevolent bond among its members. He does not live up to his end of the unspoken bargain of the social contract: trusting strangers is required for the modern democratic situation or community to work; one must suspend disbelief.

The exchange over civic trust that occurred in the 1990s took place within the larger context of the health of American civil society; trust should take forms of behavior that ideally radiate through the national family. A *civil society* is thus composed of private citizens who actively participate in social affairs and who expect mutual and implicit *recognition* of each other as citizens. As far back as Aristotle, civil society has been understood as the opposite of "barbarism"; that is, it is the acknowledgment of the rule of law over the rule of force, the recognition of others' free agency and free ability of self-determination, of self-possessed individuality. It therefore implied certain *types of behavior* circumscribed within its realm.

Between 1750 and 1850, the time of romanticism's influence over cultural consciousness, however, modernity's march begins to corrode an inherited concept of civil society, so much that the virtues of the old social order—a sense of one's social place, of being bound to the past, the land, community, a sense of stability over time—were slowly dying. Society morphs to become, in comparison, more rudderless, more individualistic, an arena of self-interest and quest for material possessions.[3] This image of social collapse was wrought by modernity's new organizational structures, which many social commentators today point to as the beginnings of social and cultural "decline." An attendant nostalgia is a near-constant traveling companion to analyses of social breakdown, as we've seen, usually evidenced and tied together in a host of related social problems, such as crime rates, illegitimate births, and ethnic or generational tensions. Indeed, beliefs about fraying social fabric are linked to, in the opening quotation, a "verifiable increase in a variety of social pathologies. Very concrete and ascendant social problems . . . are behind much of the contemporary feelings of anxiety, despair, and dread."[4]

Recommendations for adjusting behaviors within the social body in order to repair the social fabric—in part, jeremiads, moral outrage, protest—are conceived of as part of the solution to general unease. From Aristotle through Erasmus through Hegel, the idea of civil society has always contained within it prescriptions for individual civil conduct, particularly when the present seems to be going awry. And so it is within the current civil society debate that *civility* becomes an important catchall word and persistent concern. It comes with certain expectations and normative standards that are assumed to increase or maintain civic trust and respect. Civil society has the function of instilling in the citizenry a sense of duty and responsibility.

An attendant nostalgia is a near-constant traveling companion to analyses of social breakdown.

The year 1998 saw the publication of Stephen Carter's *Civility*, a centrist required-text, that claimed the culture of market capitalism was not fostering sufficient instruction for human happiness; America had suffered a crisis in civility because of it. Referring to things such as courtesy, public control of the emotions, respectability, and regard for others, Carter conceives civility—as did Erasmus, whom Carter invokes in his introduction as an early proponent of the notion that civility has a *moral* component—as willingness on the part of individuals to act in accordance with social rules even when they would prefer not to do so.* To be civil is to curtail one's personal freedoms on behalf of the greater good, for

*In 1530 Desiderius Erasmus published his book on proper table manners and behavior in polite society, *De civilitate morum puerilium (On Civility in Children)*. It quickly became a dog-eared reference for the emerging bourgeoisie.

we live in society as in a household, and . . . within a household, if we are to be moral people, our relationships with other people . . . are governed by standards of behavior that limit our freedom. Our duty to follow those standards does not depend on whether or not we happen to agree with or even like each other.[5]

Throughout his influential book—known to be a favorite of President Bill Clinton's—Carter makes broad claims about "growing incivility" and "the disintegration of social life" in America. Though he is careful not to hark back to a golden age (he is conscious of this tendency in so many other books of virtue-lament), Carter does write that the "current level of incivility is morally intolerable and getting worse." Ulti-

---

The volume was also meant as an instruction manual for raising young boys born into this social class (the book was written specifically for noble boys and was dedicated to a prince's son). *On Civility in Children* concerns itself generally with what was coming to be conceived of as proper behavior in society, but also with "outward bodily propriety." As the resourceful German sociologist Norbert Elias has written of the treatise, "It contained simple thoughts delivered with great seriousness, yet at the same time with much mockery and irony, in clear, polished language and with enviable precision. It can be said that none of its successors ever equaled this treatise in force, clarity, and personal character." This passage is from Elias's seminal study, originally published in 1939, *The Civilizing Process: The History of Manners and State Formation and Civilization*, trans. Edmund Jephcott (Oxford: Blackwell Press, 1994), 44. This remarkable work provides not only an engrossing account of the development of bourgeois manners from the thirteenth until the early nineteenth century, but is also, because of Elias's extensive use of direct source material, extremely entertaining. For example, Erasmus notes in his treatise that a boy "should retain wind by compressing the belly. Yet it is not pleasing, while appearing to be urbane, to contract an illness" (Elias, 106). Thus, "Let a cough hide the explosive sound." And "Turn away while spitting, lest your saliva fall on someone" (126). Lastly, for now, "It is very impolite to keep poking your finger into your nostrils, and still more insupportable to put what you have pulled from your nose into your mouth" (120). The numerous examples from German, Dutch, French, and English instructional guides provide many, many more laughs.

mately, he sees the problem as one of declining trust and increasing cynicism, the latter "the enemy of civility [that] suggests a deep distrust of the motives of our fellow passengers, a distrust that ruins any project that rests, as civility does, on trusting others even when there is a risk."[6] In order for civility to return, the book argues, there must be an increase in the amount of trust and understanding that Americans display toward those with whom they disagree.

To do that, the situation of trust necessary in civil behavior is, fundamentally, the recognition of mutual agency. "Civiltarians," for lack of a better term, believe that citizens need to fully acknowledge the *selfhood* of others and the ethical relationships that come with it. Civil behavior thus makes possible this sort of relationship because it recognizes the free will of the other—and simultaneously the possibility of disagreement. A certain internalized distance thus recognizes others' self-regarding aspect—the gap that exists between individuals necessary for the fundamental recognition of *privacy*. The recognition of this social space and the other's agency should motivate certain behaviors: courtesy, generosity, deference, consideration, and sincerity. They are enacted only when there is significant trust within the social body such that enacting the behaviors goes along with being able to trust the social actors with whom one always lives.

Incivility, on the other hand, evidences a lack of generalized trust; it is perceived most often as a disregard for one's neighbors or fellow citizens, rude or disruptive behavior, discourtesy, and indifference to generally accepted norms of public interaction. Such incivility takes as its starting point a suspicion or disregard of others and a withholding of trust. Incivility does not recognize the full humanity and self-possession of others, or, moreover, the real state of interdependence. These kind of withholdings are indicative of social breakdown.

What the normative citizen certainly does *not* exhibit or foster are characteristics such as unrelenting sarcasm or permanent ironic detachment to the degree that he loses the trust that is the default expectation put upon him as a citizen. As political philosopher Robert B. Pippin aptly notes: "A society of suspicious or sarcastic or cynical or judgmental or self-involved persons—let us say a world full of *Seinfeld* characters . . . corrodes and undermines . . . the modern *civitas*, [which involves] some sort of appreciation of the dependence of life on others."[7] With this, the good citizen, because he is enmeshed in a network of trust relationships, needs to be serious and honest about the things that are required of him. His sense of moral commitment to the community and to the nation is not to be taken lightly. He needs not only to *perform* his role in the social realm, but to *believe* that it is good and worthwhile. He cannot take himself too seriously or value himself to the extent that he shuts out others around him or neglects his community. The public role in the traditional model of citizenship needs to be "readable" or "transparent," for hiding meaning or intention exploits someone else's good-faith efforts at understanding.

This sort of picture of the social actor's role in society may be characterized as the traditional-moral conception of the individual's duty toward society. "From a traditional religious perspective," the Hoover Institute's Stanley Kurtz explains, "humans strive to create a community based on shared moral standards. Conscious of his own weakness . . . the individual places himself under the authority of its moral norms. He knows that both he and others will at times fail to meet those norms. Yet a refusal to articulate and impose moral requirements on himself and others would be a betrayal of the community itself. It would, so to speak, be *unbrotherly*."[8]

To summarize the rest of Kurtz's point: the aesthete, the ironically disengaged, is, unlike the first model, foremost an individual. He substitutes personal expression for moral judgment. To him the moralist's judgments are oppressive attempts to stifle the inner self. Music, sex, and drugs are part of the self's expansion and expression. For the traditional moral man, this aesthete's refusal to make judgments is the equivalent of withdrawal from the community. The traditional moral man interprets the pleasures of the aesthete as a form of idolatry: an attempt to turn all that is selfish in man "into a substitute for God." That is to say, the community exists for the ultimate salvation of the individual wanderer, and thus each must submit to the will of the whole. The community is an older, more fundamental entity than the *aesthetic individual* (whom Kierkegaard, again, equated with the ironist); he is the individual that has replaced God or community with his own pleasure and entertainment.

This all rings a familiar bell; we know it to be true. Being a selfish jerk who does not care about anyone but himself is not good. The interesting question here is: where did this notion of the good citizen come from and why has it garnered such attention in America? This will help us to better understand the misplaced outrage unleashed upon irony.

Social Contract

Civic trust, conveyed in earlier terms, is essentially a spiritual (that is, invisible) union—conceived in America's Puritan past as the transfer of God's bond with the individual to a bond among individuals within a community; this gives social trust its religious tenor. In this older terminology (indeed resonant if not explicit in today's debates), the ironist-aesthete displays no *faith*. He is, by extension, not among the saved. He is without grace. He is cast out. These are old and religious terms, of course, but in a day and age in the United States when overt religious language and belief is playing an increased role in political life, the very implications mean trouble for the ironist, who is himself just as much, if not more, a diehard moralist.

Ideas about social contract originate in Stoicism, which saw people as solitary wanderers, and from a medieval theory of rights, which extended civic privileges through "divine" permission. In the modern age, the social contract relies on a rationalist conception of "disengaged reason" (Descartes) and Locke's idea of a "punctual self," both of which understand people as reasoning, atomic, and self-possessed entities. These isolated selves are held together by a series of agreements.

Theorists in the seventeenth century, such as Grotius and Pufendorf, helped to further this view.[9] This is not so interesting, as it is incredibly clear and normal for us.

The social contract in English political philosophy, the intellectual harbinger to modern democratic governance, reflects an idea of personal salvation through the healthy state of social cohesion, as something devoid of serious conflict within the social body. The Puritan roots of this dichotomy between inward salvation and outward care for one's fellows were "formally bound . . . into a 'Civil Body Politic' . . . most convenient for the general good," writes historian John Demos.

> [But] there were also in the first group a number of "strangers"—people not primarily committed to religious aims and values. . . . In subsequent years there came others to be known as "particulars.". . . Some individual "strangers" and "particulars" became trusted and valued citizens, but others continued to seem different and more or less suspect.[10]

The idea that one should only be concerned with one's own salvation gave way slowly to a conception of salvation that occurs only by immersion within a community of like-believers.

That is to say, to have one's identity bound to those within the association of the contract also created those who do not abide by the contract. To be outside of this association, to opt out of participation, resulted in being ostracized. And not to be committed to "religious aims and values" was to be a "stranger," to be untrustworthy. Without a fundamental connection to others, the individual self is lost. The idea that one should only be concerned with one's own salvation gave way slowly to a conception of salvation that occurs only by immersion within a community of like-believers, where one's upright behavior could be displayed and confirmed.

What is important to remember here is that ideas of the social contract in Puritan communities were propelled by the inescapable energy of the Reformation's stress on *individual commitment,* something enabling and fomenting commitment with the *full will.* The social contract is thus an individual covenant first with God and later between people; the modern social contract begins as a religious concept. The ultimate purpose of such a bond was to glue together a Christian community, agree on the source of secular power, and to enable the further possibility of individual salvation via an association of the saved. This association, as something gravely and existentially serious, trumped familial and traditional relationships. Society had to be entered into with the adult's full will, with individual consent.

This sort of consent was only achievable once there was a conception of the individual as a self-possessed being able to direct his own will *toward* the social good with total commitment. This led to an idea of a community of like souls after whom one should look. Without doubt earlier Puritan reformers valued greatly the idea of this covenant, and crucially for them it garnered the character of the sacred: given a godly community fully committed to salvation and their own private relationships to God, one's moral duty was to be extended to caring, as well, for one's neighbor. Not to attempt to join with the whole was to enable the growth in the community of "rebels against the commone good, all [of them] private respects of mens selves."[11] Individuals not fully honoring the covenant created social problems and mistrust. The first duty is acceptance of God's will; the second is guarding the covenant against all transgression. For Calvinist, particularly Puritan, societies, this directive was of particular concern.

The relationship between individuals, therefore, at the very founding of America's quasi-mythic beginning was such that "the covenant, the agreement between God and his people," philosopher Charles Taylor writes, "begins to develop into an understanding of society as based on a covenant between its members. In a godly community founded on personal commitment, the two [are] facets of one and the same covenant."[12] That is, the bond between Puritans was a transfer of the covenant between God and each member. This bond extended the circle of ethical responsibility by radiating outwardly, and with the force of moral obligation, into realms yet unconquered. The consequences of this social contract theory for setting up God's commonwealth, particularly in New England, "were momentous." And while for Calvinists salvation can never be *earned*, engagement with others, writes Andrew Delbanco, "who are alike in behavior and piety is a *sign* that it may be granted."[13] In more worldly terms: you don't get good by hanging out with the bad.

But the originally religious covenant of the Calvinist founders becomes increasingly secularized in America over the course of the eighteenth century. Salvation becomes trust—the same trust we're talking about today and a trust lying deep in the expectations of social responsibility. Specifically, in the decades leading up to the Revolution, there was an increasing conflation of personal salvation with a burgeoning social feeling found primarily in sermons of the time. Concurrent with this slow growth, revolutionary sentiment in the colonies is stirred to new heights; the *political* fate of all is bound to *personal* salvation, however much revivalism attempted to reassert the primacy of personal piety.

This is not at all to downplay the enormous reception of revivalist speakers such as George Whitefield, Gilbert Tennett, Samuel Davies, or Samuel Finley. But "the struggling Christian has but one comfort in this moment of extremities," offers historian Robert A. Ferguson. "An immediate choice between heaven and hell is suddenly *communal* in its stress upon the *present* moment. . . . Revivalism provides the assurance that no decision need ever be made alone. Its thrust toward immediate conversion . . . is one more sign of the desirable possibilities in union and, beyond, of a far more glorious opportunity for all."[14] Christian salvation had slowly become a national concern; social trust becomes more palpable; and the revolutionary cause becomes supported and justified by the very God that slightly over a century prior was concerned foremost with individual redemption. The influence of Enlightenment rationality, political thought, and, importantly, a sense of shared destiny set against publicized British affronts, had taken slow root in the minds of intellectuals in the colonies, leavening Calvinist religiosity of prior generations with the tempered deism of the mid–eighteenth century. Coming from the rationalist critique of religion by figures like Tindal, Shaftesbury, Blount, and other English and French writers years prior, the deism developing in America was welcomed and enlarged among the educated in urban centers— Boston, New York, Philadelphia.

Simultaneous with the pickup of deism, revivalism as a cultural and political force was influential primarily in the colonies of Virginia, Rhode Island, Pennsylvania, New Jersey, Connecticut, and Massachusetts, and it was indeed a significant intellectual force on the national stage; yet these colonies were the most influential in determining the sense of unity. Because of revivalism's influence, moreover and slowly, the salvation of the individual was "nationalized" to the salvation of the whole of those wishing to detach from colonial authority. God's selection of a representative person was thus exteriorized to the selection of a people in a variety of sermons, religious tracts, and speeches. That is to say, revivalism paradoxically brought about only further erosion of old-school Calvinist tenets.

In 1762, for example, Pastor Abraham Williams of Boston tenably equated the "voice of the people" with the "voice of God"; Jonathan Mayhew a year later in *Observations on the Charter and Conduct of the Society for the Propagation of the Gospel* praised the American people as the heirs of the "divines of the common people in England"; Charles Chauncy delivered a sermon on Thanksgiving Day that was able to transform the will of the people into something *divinely* inspired: "It was under God's all-wise, overruling influence that a spirit was raised in all the colonies nobly to assert their freedom as men and English-born subjects."[15] This sentiment seemed to spread, regardless of religious affiliation: "Glory out of crisis, optimism from revolutionary change . . . deliverance through America, the value placed upon union, the miracle of sudden nationality," Ferguson writes. "Salvation, the original source of [this] rhetoric, thus enters into a sense of general well-being that all citizens share irrespective of their religious state of mind or preference."[16]

The original voices of religious liberty come to be infused in political speech by "insisting that faith and liberty are inextricably intertwined."[17] Political liberty in the sermons and speeches of many a Protestant preacher becomes possible only through that very liberty being contingent on the will of the people, a thing now divinely inspired. Though there were hot disagreements between "Old Lights" and "New Lights" during the sweep of revivalism, it is important to note that in the fury of theological exchange the debates shift from God's strictures to problems in individual and community life.

Elisha Williams, rector of Yale College in 1744, writes in *The Essential Rights and Liberties of Protestants* that "the Rights of Conscience and private Judgment in Matters of Religion [in biblical, legal, and philosophical traditions] are unalterably the same."[18] Protestantism's original antiauthoritarian impulse finds a home in this sort of rhetoric, one infused with a radical Protestantism that "favors the spoken word . . . the courage of revolutionary action depends upon the immediacy of speech."[19]

This small offering of examples highlights the transformation of an originally English Calvinist social thought regarding a person's proper relationship to society, his duties and responsibility toward social order, into something that was slowly *exteriorized* in America when its national identity was forming. The transfer of man's covenant with God becomes the bond between the individual and society. Salvation of the individual believer becomes contingent upon the salvation of the whole. The original divine bond among individuals within a community permits a shift to a *modern* conception of what binds the society of the saved together, from metaphysical to secular, which occurred slowly and messily during the Enlightenment and Revivalism.

This is all to point out that a new kind of social bond was made possible, in part, through a reconstruction of how salvation occurred, a redescription of metaphysical accounts of how beings were bound together, and would result in the *secularization* of the divine union, from God-to-man to man-to-man. Worth quoting at length is the historian of religion and economics Adam Seligman, who recounts this historical change in *The Problem of Trust* (1997):

> Ultimately, the introjection of grace within the individual believer . . . led to the loss of its transcendent locus. The *deus absconditus* of Calvinist religiosity increasingly lost all relevance to the world of man. As grace became secularized into such ideals as the romantic imagination and national virtue . . . faith could no longer be supported by the armature of a transcendent God. . . . What took its place was, in the broadest terms, *a search for trust*. In fact . . . the process of secularization and the replacement of godly by human attributes also implied the *replacement of faith by trust* (or rather, the search for faith with the search for trust).[20]

Trust as a social glue is the *replacement* for faith in a transcendent order that guaranteed the invisible, sacred bond between people. Modernity, as it did in all things, instituted a process of secularization in the social contract, the replacement of godly by human attributes; this implied the replacement of faith by civic trust.

Furthermore, this sort of connectedness, this inspired trust, be it conceived "nationally" or "socially," would result in the foundation of basic social order— indeed the motivation for "back to basics" behind any number of modern jeremiads. The Puritan brand of Reformation thought was

Trust as a social glue is the replacement for faith in a transcendent order that guaranteed the sacred bond between people.

mortified by social disorder, which was to be corrected with an outward activism dedicated to putting the world back in order by the elect.[21] Social order as a state of society results, then, from the original contract; God will help a society along if its house is in order. This is to be done first by inward commitment, and second by all who have similarly chosen their walk of life together, as evidenced in contract. The result is a social body of individuals, introjected with discipline, "who rule themselves in their own personal lives."[22]

Protestant Values in the Social Contract

Social trust, in this tradition, then, necessitates an inward disposition that transcends self-interest in favor of public well-being, in favor of committing oneself to social order. In doing so, citizenship within that social body, as should be clear, must be performed *sincerely*—it must be entered into with the force of self-motivated agency. To engage the civic body and to be trusted, one must be perceived as being sincere in one's engagement, not merely doing so because it is an obligation or to use the face of sincerity to get what one wants. As Lionel Trilling contended in 1971, when sincerity was already a suspect declension of character:

> Society requires of us that we present ourselves as being sincere, and the most efficacious way of satisfying this demand is to see to it that we really are sincere, that we actually are what we want our community to know we are. In short, we play the role of being ourselves, we sincerely act the part of the sincere person. . . . [But] if we speak [the word *sincerity* today], we are likely to do so with either discomfort or irony.[23]

The Watergate investigation haunts this statement—*Sincerity and Authenticity* being published in 1974—bringing the blanket of political cynicism and skepticism over the apparent sincerity of political statements. Nonetheless, the point is taken. Sincerity is being true to others; society requires it; we have to reveal to them our authenticity, our being transparent in word and deed. We have to "mean it."[24] Irony only makes sense if it appears sincere and if there are otherwise attempts at sincerity, directness, earnestness, and honest engagement set against it, that it apes and satirizes.

As a personal attribute, sincerity rose to coveted status, Trilling explains, during the English Renaissance, particularly with Shakespeare, who used the word with no pretense or metaphorical leanings. Sincerity had not always been a *moral* value. Originally *sincere* meant "uncorrupted," having entered the English language, according to the *Oxford English Dictionary*, by 1540. The term, derived from the Latin *sine cera* (without wax, as a patching agent) was used to describe things such as wine or glass, things that would possibly contain impurities but that did not, earning them the mantel. Something that was unadulterated, that existed in its pure sense was considered sincere. Even Samuel Johnson gave priority to the word as regards things, not people.

In the sixteenth century, however, parts of European society saw increased social mobility and the slow decline of clear social bounds and roles. Men and women alike, especially in England and France, left their inherited classes for the betterment of their social status. Such movement required that when one moved on and met others, one should display one's true intentions outwardly; only "villains" and non-Christians were "dissimulators," intentionally showing themselves falsely to others for personal gain. Such a person was morally reviled, for he attempted to rise above the station in which he found himself by guile, false avowal, and cunning. This mode would eventually be dissected for all of its modern implications, its telltale Romantic acuity, in Denis Diderot's *Rameau's Nephew* (1805).

A mock conversation between the author *(Moi)* and the obsequious nephew of the composer Jean-Philippe Rameau *(Lui)*, *Rameau's Nephew* sets two modes of moral behavior in opposition: the straightforward rational moralist and the deceptive young man who both openly discloses his desires and who performs socially to get what he wants. Reduced to shameless self-abasement for the purposes of self-promotion, Rameau is seen by Diderot as his own worst enemy in the moral errand of obtaining a purity of heart. He is his own opposite. Above all, these characteristics occur because Rameau is concerned with his place in society and how to better this standing, how to achieve fame as an artist.

In explaining the course that Rameau takes in order to do so, Diderot pitches the nephew as running his spiritual course *within* the realm of society. This process, as something detached from nature, Diderot sees as corrupting the individual soul. By trying to appease and raise himself beyond his standing, the nephew becomes alienated from his own interiority. Aping the gestures and rituals performed in polite society, he is hyper-self-conscious to all the cues and commands that social dictates impress upon him. As such, the dialogue as a whole, Trilling writes, "lays bare the principle of insincerity upon which society is based and demonstrates the loss of personal integrity and dignity that the impersonations of social existence entail."[25]

Additionally and importantly, Rameau, by reducing the behaviors of socialites to mere gestures, triumphs the truth of art in performing an opera at the end, and in doing so *transcends through art* the accreted traditional categories and dictates of morality. He assumes various roles (the appearance and performance of the self in the public sphere), and in doing so, elevates the individual spirit beyond particularity into the universal, here characterized as becoming more free. Diderot, like Rousseau, thus exemplifies the tension between pure interiority and social violation, the necessity of the free creation of identity to escape the confines of society.

Though a complete account of sincerity as a moral value would require far more space, even a lengthy digression would have to immediately lay claim to the fact that the value of sincerity has its direct roots in, and was an explicitly supreme value of, the Reformation. As British historian J. M. Roberts states, "The Protestant Reformation displaced so many traditional values by the one supreme value of sincerity."[26] Given the central emphasis that Luther placed on direct communion with God and the ultimate legitimacy for this communication as seated within the individual himself, to feign sincerity of salvation was ultimately to do harm to oneself. And doubly so: for one was not only sure of the secret knowledge that one was not saved, but also the knowledge that one had been untruthful—an injustice to the precepts of the faith. To feign this in society was to do an injustice to the attempts at social cohesion that were built on sincere interaction.

Acting against oneself, besides requiring insincerity, was consequently do harm to one's *authenticity*, a value implied in the discussion of civic trust, because such a state is conceived of as the fundamental quality of one's experience, of abiding by that experience with others. Authenticity stems directly from the moral mood of sincerity. But whereas sincerity implies the description of an activity of *expression* of the self (actions and words), authenticity, in the "jargon" of philosophy, implies a *characteristic* of a moral being. To clearly represent the state of one's interiority without dissembling or acting is to *be* an authentic person. Being a sincere and authentic person is required for the social contract and the binding together of civic life to function at all.

Authenticity as a moral value in *modernity*—indeed the primary value espoused by romanticism—is often trampled upon with words like *narcissism, hedonism,* and *relativism,* because authenticity implies the self's recognition and judgment of itself. This reflexivity and interiority camouflage the *moral* impetus behind the individual's reach for authenticity. Though problematic, this is simultaneously to hold the value of "being true to one's own values" higher than that of fashioning one's behavior to ideals that one did not choose. Adherence to such values would be "inauthentic," "selling out," or "rigid."

The moral ideal of authenticity, then, having stemmed from the Romantic insistence on sincerity and the overlay of action and inner feeling, has become, in its own right, the dominant modern moral value—that is, an ultimate aspiration because it helps people feel integrated and whole; it points toward the good life, the best way to live. To consciously aim toward an inauthentic existence (as remarked by Tolstoy, Dostoyevsky, Kierkegaard, Heidegger, Sartre, Camus, et al.) is to sacrifice the existential responsibility of living a life, however difficult it may be. Stemming from an insistence that morality is a voice within, authenticity urges a sincere attempt to adhere to that voice. An authentic being, then, is one who has to some degree shunned external directives and morality in exchange for his own direction; he "does his own thing" and can say, "I did it my way."* The valuation of authenticity sometimes counters commitment to community.

Jean-Paul Sartre Acting French

This inner urge, this flight toward inward authenticity, is absolutely, on both sides of the political aisle, "unrepudiable" by moderns.[27] There is therefore a deep conflict between traditional moral pictures, which hold objective standards for behavior regardless of how one "feels" about doing them, and this urge toward authenticity. Or, better stated, the inward urge toward authenticity touted by romanticism and modernity, when held as a higher value, can trump traditional notions of moral behavior and thus be characterized as "hedonistic" or "anticivic." Our predicament is to be stuck between these two senses of commitment.

If one conception of the self and human beings is that they are fundamentally survivalist atoms prone to manipulation and self-serving instrumentalism, being sincere is troubled, for now *appearing to be sin-*

---

*The value of authenticity in the face of politics was on display at outgoing German chancellor Gerhard Schroeder's farewell ceremony, when the army national band played, instead of the formal departing music, Frank Sinatra's "I Did It My Way." Interviewed later, Schroeder said that it most accurately described his political career.

cere becomes *useful* to getting what one wants. Yet to admit openly that one is manipulative and shameless in one's use of feigning sincerity is to be authentic—the supreme moral value, as Thomas Frank has written, of the modern American mind.[28] The values of sincerity and authenticity in our case have come unhinged. It is now possible to be authentic (with regard to ourselves) without being sincere (with regard to others) because one may be insincere to be self-interested, which is still authentic. And thereby it is also possible to be honest to oneself while being manipulative. The results are *The Apprentice* and *Survivor.** If such values hold sway in a social situation—or in influential prime-time television slots—it is clear that such a state presents a large problem for being trusted and trusting others. That is, for being serious.

There were two camps spelled out very clearly by the columnist Roger Rosenblatt in his diatribe against irony after 9/11, which set up the unreality of ironists against the belief in "what is real" of the true believers:

> In short, people may at last be ready to say what they whole-heartedly believe. The kindness of people toward others in distress is real. There is nothing to see through in that. Honor and fair play? Real. And the preciousness of ordinary living is real as well—all to be taken seriously, perhaps, in a new and chastened

---

*Insincerity as an increasingly chosen cultural option is also seen as something of a moral problem caused by Christianity itself. As Max Horkheimer wrote in *The Eclipse of Reason* (New York: Seabury Press, 1974), following the Nietzschean interpretation of Christianity's quelling of superior, dominating instincts: "By the very negation of the will to self-preservation on earth in favor of the preservation of the eternal soul, Christianity asserted the infinite value of each man, an idea that penetrated even non-Christian or anti-Christian systems of the Western world. True, the price was the repression of the vital instincts and, since such repression is never successful, an *insincerity* pervades our culture. Nevertheless, this very internalization enhances individuality" (137–38).

time. The greatness of the country: real. The anger: real. The
pain: too real.[29]

To be real and to be serious here fall in line. The phrase "there is nothing to see through in that," directly implicates the ironist as someone
who is going around "unmasking," things or "seeing through" motivations. What is serious is reality, and what is real is serious. "Are you
looking for something to take seriously?" Rosenblatt asks: "Begin with
evil." Being *serious* about one's duties as an individual in society, about
one's ethical commitments, about one's political citizenship and
humanity is the historical model not only of good citizenship, but also
in moral personhood. For being serious says that actions will follow
the things one has said. Seriousness implies commitment to future
actions, an agreement to bear or mete out consequences when those
commitments are broken.

Seriousness, like sincerity, implies an alignment between appearance and reality. Unseriousness, on the other hand, whether inten-
tional or not, is the incongruity of what is said and what is done.
Whereas seriousness implicates alignment of inner and outer, playful-
ness, sarcasm, jokes, inauthenticity, insincerity, falseness, whimsy,
caprice, deception, frivolity, and the like signify the lack of alignment.
We ought to know the difference. It's increasingly difficult. What is
the structure of irony if not a "lack of alignment" between avowal and
meaning, between expectation and delivery?*

---

*The year 1996 saw Alanis Morissette's now-iconic, talked-about-one-mil-
lion-times-as-not-really-ironic song "Ironic," which spells out several situations that actually are not. (It's impossible to pass up.) That is, as situational
dramas, the scenarios described do not in the least partake in situational
irony: *It's a black fly in your chardonnay:* not irony, just gross; *A traffic jam when
you're already late:* certainly unfortunate, as now you'll be even later; *A free ride,
when you've already paid:* not irony, but proof that you're an idiot; read the sign
above your head that says, "All Rides Free"; *It's a death row pardon two minutes
too late:* Likely from the guy in the traffic jam. Not irony, just more evidence
of God's cruel wrath for the guilty. Or maybe guilty. Anyway, an additional
comment explained very eloquently by VH1 commentator Mo Rocca: "Rain

As forms, then, sincerity and seriousness have much in common. Seriousness has staying power; it has life-altering power. Seriousness goes to the core of the human experience, as opposed to the superficiality of custom, tradition, mores, and protocol. When something is serious, these sorts of social behaviors are forgone in order to react in an existentially direct way to life and, more frequently, to death. And so the proximity to death, pain, or confinement is directly proportional to the degree of seriousness with which we take something. Seriousness orients itself toward the future with all the force of the past. As Nietzsche jovially thundered, "The past, the longest, deepest, and sternest past, breathes upon us and rises up in us whenever we become 'serious.'"[30]

Friedrich Nietzsche as Gay Biker

Also for Nietzsche, as an interesting counterweight to those not yet taking seriously the force of

on your wedding day is not ironic, it just sucks. Now, it would have been ironic if, say, you normally lived in rainy Washington state and went to the Arizona desert for your wedding to escape the rain, had checked the forecast, and it then rained in the Arizona desert and all of Washington state was sunny and warm. That would be ironic." Yes, it would: formally, situational irony exists when there is an incongruity between what is expected to happen and what actually happens due to forces beyond human comprehension or control. Morissette subsequently, in 2004, noted publicly that her song did not contain any examples that lived up to the definition of irony, which, in turn, is the true irony. Good save, Canada. (Actually so with "My Humps.")

satire in the current cultural environment, to take things seriously was nothing more than the intellectual inability to think well and laugh simultaneously. This is merely a prejudice, not an inherent problem in being human:

> *Taking Things Seriously.*—The intellect is with most people an awkward, obscure and creaking machine, which is difficult to set in motion: they call it "taking things seriously" when they work with this machine and want to think well—oh, how burdensome must be good thinking to them! That delightful animal, man, seems to lose his good humor whenever he thinks well; he becomes "serious"! And "where there is laughing and gaiety, thinking cannot be worth anything":—so speaks the prejudice of this serious animal against all "Joyful Wisdom."—Well, then! Let us show that it is prejudice!

Sometimes this seems true, and sometimes we would love to believe that it is readily possible. But real seriousness has a way of sticking around without laughter, has a way of canceling out jest very, very quickly. Rosenblatt's concern hits squarely in the chest and resonates gravely about the seriousness of evil and pain, our common susceptibility. Seriousness is always grounded in a worldview and set of values prior to the situation requiring the serious response.

So given the historical grounds for the legitimization of the social bond (trust as secularized faith), to offend social trust by dissimulating, wearing a mask, presenting the self as opposite or at variance with what it knows itself to be, is also, by proxy, to transgress a sense of the sacred that is inwardly committed to create outward order. Irony requires a community that understands what is happening and one that does not. It pits getting it against not getting it, implying an intellectual or aesthetic superiority (though never explicitly moral, for *speaking directly* of morality is prudish and controlling). This attitude is frequently "arrogant," "elitist," "bitter," and "smartass." Each of these descriptions—from *Time* columnists back to Aristotle—sets up ethical polarities of donning the ironic mask. It refuses to treat all others as equal; it implies arrogance toward those who are not in the understanding community; it denies full humanity to those who are not. This dynamic rubs against the moral values of normative citizenship—and puts into relief why the ironist is condemned for not honoring and *displaying* them. This infringes upon perhaps the most fundamental assumptions about what it means in the West to be a "good person," who is also, by extension, a "good citizen." Seriously.

CHAPTER SIX

The Descent of Inner Dependence

Give me beauty in the inward soul; and may the outward
and the inward be at one.
  —Socrates

Any moment you choose you can retire within yourself.
Nowhere can man find a quieter or more untroubled
retreat.
  —Marcus Aurelius, *Meditations* (AD 167)

Do not go outward; return within yourself. In the inward
man dwells truth.
  —Augustine, *De vera Religione* (AD 390)

The inner man and its liberty . . . needs neither laws nor
good work; nay, they are even hurtful to it.
  —Martin Luther, "On Christian Freedom" (1520)

Morality is character, character is that which is engraved
. . . for character is really *inwardness.*
  —Søren Kierkegaard, *The Present Age* (1846)

What's gonna set you free? Look inside and you'll see.
  —The Beastie Boys, "Gratitude" (1992)

There is a larger picture prior to the modernist model of how irony
functions within the subject; it's also a model essential to the role of

the self in the social contract. Romanticism requires a certain view of the self to operate. Civility operates upon the same logic of social distancing. Both require certain self-imposed regulations and desires for the self's public presentation. But for even this division to be possible, there first must be a valuation of private interiority; there must be an view of the self as something existentially special when contrasted with the world of objects and events. There is mind or spirit, internal to a being, and there is matter, external to the being and in the world. This view is incredibly commonsense for us, for it forms the very philosophical foundation of modern personhood. We no longer have to think about it.

Both Romantic irony and civility require certain self-imposed regulations for the self's public presentation.

But we may have to in order to address the source of our current cultural jam. How did this picture come to be? What would the self have to look like in order to conceive of it as a place to turn to for guidance and standards by which to judge the world? What are the philosophical narratives that went into establishing this distance from the world such that one could actually judge it? What sorts of specific religious directives encouraged this movement—and more importantly, why? Prior to psychoanalytic theory or discussions of how *cool* defends the ego from attack, how did this picture of the self as something that needs to (or could) be defended originate?

These are hyperbolically enormous questions that I cannot fully cover responsibly here. Still, they remain interesting questions, and it is important to recount, however briefly, the story of this valuation and turn toward "inwardness" in the Western religious and philosophical tradition, as such directional change plays a vital role in the creation of irony as a worldview. This story comprises a major narrative in Western philosophy, and thus, in the modern liberal conception of individual subjectivity.

But in order that I do not myself overstate, generalize, and simplify,

I will first say it in another's words. This way you can blame him. The political philosopher Charles W. Anderson has keenly observed of this tradition and narrative of inwardness:

> [That] the individual has the power to transcend, and thus to assess, culture is a view that is fundamental to the liberalism of Kant and Hegel, Mill and Dewey, as well as to the individualism of Plato and Aristotle, the Roman Stoics, and all of Christianity. This idea of individuality runs deep through our philosophical heritage. It is, I believe, fundamental to our liberal public philosophy.[1]

That is to say, the notion of private interiority as carved out by philosophical ideas of personhood, and as being the fundamental "location" and "guarantee" of individuality, would eventually create the foundation for the entire notion of outwardly extending privacy—including property, space, and constructs of the legal rights of persons. It is the foundation of individual autonomy, of the person as a self-possessed entity, implying a certain detachment and disinterestedness, the basis of liberalism in the West—indeed a continuing set of values that guides the behaviors of nations and laws in the present age.

Augustine

Augustine had much to do with our modern notions and images of the self as a private place inside of us, something sacred to be protected. Augustine's view of the world was, in part, much like those of his contemporaries. He inherited the Platonic conception of a reflective world—passed on by Plotinus and the Pseudo-Dionysus, among others—which saw the objects and events in the world as symbols, as reflections of God's thoughts: the world behind the world.* Since God,

---

*The idea of a real world behind our world is the Platonic basis of most films starring Keanu Reeves: *The Matrix*, *The Matrix 2*, and *Constantine*. Sadly, not *Bill and Ted's Excellent Adventure*.

the creator of that world, is all good, everything that exists must also be good, and the universe exists for a purpose known ultimately only to God. The universe of objects and events is ordered—nature—according to the mind of its creator. The world of forms, hidden behind the perceptible world, is the ultimate reality. And, finally, for the good of humans, whether they understand or empathize with the world they see around them, they should see and *love* the order that God has created in the world. It is there for their discernment and wonder.

It is in this notion of love, as observed by philosopher Charles Taylor, that Augustine breaks with Plato. Augustine refers to the Platonic differences between spirit and matter, higher and lower, eternal and temporal as the difference between *inner* and *outer*. There is the inner and the outer man; the outer is the body, the inner is the soul. As Augustine writes in the opening quotation: "Do not go outward; return within yourself. In the inward man dwells truth." In this sentiment lives the Stoic tradition of Seneca, Marcus Aurelius, and Cicero, all of whom praised turning inward to the "inner citadel" for the true source of strength, virtue, courage, and wisdom; Augustine's early studies of Cicero (recall his fondness for being called an ironic sort) informed and influenced his views of inner sacredness.[2] The outside world may have man in bonds, he may be subject to peril, coercion, and death; the world may tempt him with riches, bodily pleasures, and opportunities for avarice and umbrage, but with a view of himself as containing total and infinite inward freedom, the possibility of release from the external world to the ultimate rock of the divine inside, he is saved; nothing can harm him; he has joined the eternal and unshakable foundation of the universal mind. Go inward, this tradition exhorts; set sail for the safe harbor of the soul.

Thus for Augustine, as for his Stoic predecessors, the inward turn is the way to God. And as God is equated with Truth, turning inward was the way to find Truth in the world. The principal way to God, in Augustine, then, is not simply in the created order of the world, but in ourselves; it is the very support of our being. Beauty existed as a harmonious relationship between the inner and the outer.* Further, man was joined to God in an invisible chain of being; the likeness of his innermost part to that of God was what bound him inexorably to the highest power. Man thus directed consciousness toward this inward connection. This shift in direction stresses and fosters the language of inwardness, and encourages the subject to take up a reflexive stance. "Augustine's turn to the self," Taylor writes,

> was a turn to radical reflexivity, and that is what made the language of inwardness irresistible. The inner light is the one which shines in our presence to ourselves; it is the one inseparable from our being creatures with a first-person standpoint. What differentiates it from the outer light [of Plato] is just what makes the inward light so compelling, that it illuminates that space where I am present to myself.[3]

Augustine thus introduced the inwardness of radical reflexivity and bequeathed it to incipient Christian ideas of internal divinity, particularly as set against secular authority and its varieties of emotional and psychological captivity. That "place" of inner light would eventually come to be known as "conscience" or "soul." It is the ultimate guide to moral behavior; it is that sense which guides our outward actions as if

---

*The notion of alignment, of a proper relationship between the divine and the earthly beholder, is particularly explicated in medieval aesthetics, and more specifically in the theoretical explanations of the aesthetic *experience* found in Plotinus, Augustine, Boethius, Erigena, and Aquinas. For a fascinating and thorough history of medieval aesthetics and their relationship to morality and the birth of scientific understanding, see Wladyslaw Tartarkiewicz, *History of Aesthetics*, trans. C. Barrett 3 vols. (The Hague: Mouton, 1970–74); Edgar De Bruyne, *The Esthetics of the Middle Ages*, trans. Eileen B. Hennessy (New York: Frederic Ungar, 1969); Johannes Huzinga, *The Waning of the Middle Ages*, trans. F. Hopman (London: Harmondsworth, 1965); and Umberto Eco, *Art and Beauty in the Middle Ages*, trans. Hugh Bredin (New Haven: Yale University Press, 1986).

given direction by an inward captain. This story—religiously inter-preted—tells us that it is by the spark of the divine inside that we find our way in the world.

Reformation

This notion of the inward self, the "inner man," is motivated by a desire to observe more closely the nuances of, in Christian terminology, the movement of the soul.* And it is, jumping forward now, the Protestant Reformation's main revolutionary inward turn—inherited, in part, from Augustine and the Stoics—that enables a view of the self, a story about the self, necessary for democratizing the belief in sacred individ-ual interiority shared by all (the motivation behind conversion and evangelical missionaries). Consciousness for the believer is directed inward to find God instead of outwardly toward the world of objects, toward ritual, toward the symbolic order of God's creation. For the Reformed Christian, spirituality becomes inwardly free. "Worldly authority cannot force us to believe," Luther wrote, "it can only out-wardly prevent people from being led astray by false teachings."

A sense of inward value, of self-possessed certainty, of skepticism toward secular authority and the moral and spiritual dictates of

---

*The Eastern Orthodox St. Gregory of Palamas, part of the inward-turning among Orthodox monks in the late thirteenth and early fourteenth centuries, promoted the use of mental prayer (or "prayer of the heart"). Because it required solitude and quiet, this kind of prayer was known as "Hesychasm" (from the Greek *hesychia*, meaning calm, silence). Gregory's followers were mocked as "men with their souls in their navel" (Greek: *omphalopsychoi*), because in meditation they focused their eyes on a spot below the chest, sup-posedly in order to heighten the mystical experience. The debate over this way of inner contemplation dominated subsequent Orthodox theology, much in the way that the debate over faith versus works dominated Western reli-gion. More importantly, the practice of Hesychasm is the origin of the term *navel-gazing*.

Catholicism, of a sense of unique identity and *individual* relationship to God—all of these elements, created by the Lutheran Reformation's view of man's place in the world and his relation to God, are components of the burgeoning of individual subjectivity of the sixteenth century.

Yet already present in autobiography of the late Middle Ages was the shift toward further concentration upon private life.[4] French historian Georges Duby notes that the turn toward increasing self-consciousness is already present—evidenced in sculpture, writings, and paintings—in the twelfth and thirteenth centuries. Ideas of salvation, prior to the Reformation, had begun to turn insofar as

> salvation was not acquired simply by passive, sheeplike participation in religious rites but was "earned" by an effort of self-transformation. Because sin was now held to reside not in the act but in the intention, in the most intimate recesses of the soul, the new view was an invitation to introspection, to exploration of the conscience. The apparatus of moral governance was shifted inward, to a private space that no longer had anything to do with the community.[5]

But the Reformation, incipient in the late fifteenth and flowering in the early sixteenth century, took to new heights of exaltation and persistence the idea that absolute individual commitment to God, that is, salvation by faith alone *(sola fides)*—the total inward turn—was a key to salvation and grace *(sola gratia)*, along with a personal reading of the Bible *(sola scriptura)* and the acceptance of Christ *(sola Christus)*. Whereas Catholicism continued to hold that this commitment was reserved for the elite "counsels of perfection" (see: pope and friends), Reformers demanded that *each and every* Christian must *commit* himself or herself wholeheartedly, for "personal commitment must be total or it was worthless."[6] Protestantism's crucial and history-altering claim that true salvation was located only in the interior self and to be given by God alone—in a justification by faith alone—created at once a sort of distancing within the self and from the social that allowed and encouraged subjects to cultivate interiority.

It is oft said that Luther, in one swipe, thus dignified all kinds of work, from everyday chores to the running of a principality. So long as it was done with commitment and faith toward God and others, work was justified. "No way of life is truly good," wrote Augustine, who influenced Luther more than any other theologian, "no matter how much it is line with nature, unless it is endorsed with the whole will"; the inability to will fully was Augustine's conception of sin.[7] It was this idea of commitment and complete willfulness, the guidance of conscience, and the valuation of inwardness that will serve as the tinder in the fiery Reformation thought of Luther, John Calvin, Philipp Melanchthon, Huldrych Zwingli, and John Knox.

The Christian conscience, as something separated from all outward considerations, becomes, with Luther, fundamentally free.

Luther's stress on the split between inner freedom and the secular world (including the civic world) separated, for a time, individual conscience from civic life; it also freed economic activity from ethical and religious constraints. Thus the causes of the Reformation were not only religious and social, but also, like all things that move the world, political and economic.[8] The Reformation's stress on individual faith and conscience also fostered economic and religious individualism; the Christian conscience, now described as something separated from all outward considerations and abeyance to even church authority, becomes fundamentally free. It was now the seat of free moral agency, the foundation of our very ideas of what a *person* is. As Marcell Mauss wrote:

It is the Christians who have made a metaphysical entity of the "moral person," after they became aware of its religious power. Our own notion of the human person is still basically a Christian one. . . . From a simple masquerade to the mask, from a "role" to a "person," to a name, to an individual; from the latter to being a being possessing metaphysical and moral value; from a moral consciousness to a sacred being: from the latter to a fundamental form of thought and action—the course is accomplished.[9]

And therefore, by imbuing the individual with moral power for self-regulation and self-possession, Reformation theology spiritually justified individual worldly activity.* A plethora of autobiography, journals, and first-person narratives would follow. It is at this time, as many scholars of the late Middle Ages and Reformation have contended, that "men became individuals." Previously individuals did not have so much an awareness of "internal space," a private interiority that was "one's own." The resulting conception, then, is one where there now exists an external domain of objects and an internal realm of divinity to which individuals and communities would respond in numerous ways.✝

Thus the Reformation's major considerations—inwardness, sincerity, recognition of particularity, and commitment—comprise our con-

---

*For the full and contested thesis, see, naturally, Max Weber, *The Protestant Ethic and the Spirit of Capitalism*, trans. Talcott Parsons (New York: Routledge, 2001). The London School of Economics' Anthony Giddens devotes several pages in his introduction to the book that spell out the arguments against Weber's analysis, though he notes that many of the earlier critiques of Weber's analysis are themselves flawed. Giddens cedes that Weber was mistaken on the following accounts: the distinctiveness of the notion of a calling (*Beruf*) in Lutheranism; the supposed lack of an affinity between Catholicism and regularized entrepreneurial activity; and the degree to which Calvinist ethics actually served to dignify the accumulation of wealth in the manner Weber suggested.

✝For Charles Taylor, the idea of magic and witchcraft is tied up with the idea that God is in the world and not "in" humans. For the concept of witchcraft or possession to work, there must be a credible worldview in place that holds that an outward power is capable of going inside of an individual to possess her individuality. He describes the persecution of witchcraft in sixteenth-century Protestant societies and in Puritan New England in the mid–seventeenth century as essentially the contest between the encroaching worldview

ception of the self as something "anchored in our being." Considered in opposition to a worldview that held valuation and ideas as things "in the world," or, in Platonic thought, in the transcendent realm of the Forms, the resulting existential feeling of subjects as having thought and feeling (that is, ideas and valuations), in their own *private* "psychology" (though that word is entirely inaccurate for the time), was one both of inward freedom and of simultaneous disengagement from the social world. This revived notion of spiritual freedom created in individuals an image that there was a core to their being existing in an internal *space*.

For Luther, surrounding this space of the soul—where faith is the innermost core of the person—was a set of moral laws through which one acted. Faith in this sense was inexpressible directly, was an inner cosmos, an inward qualification of the spirit. And around the core of this faith are moral rules *through which* it is expressed. The true Christian would enact his faith through the *spontaneous expression of virtue* through this scrim of moral precepts. Signs of grace were determined

---

that valued the individual's self-possession and a worldview that remained true to the belief in the omnipotence of an outside, universal force. The latter view was, essentially, he argues, tantamount to a residual Catholicism. Taylor writes, "Perhaps the obsessional concern with witches, and the spectacular rise of belief in and sense of threat from them, can be partly understood as a crisis arising in the transition between identities" (*Sources of the Self: The Making of Modern Identity* [Cambridge: Harvard University Press, 1989], 192). Working against this worldview was incipient Protestant valuation of self-possession. Taylor, again: "One of the most powerful forces working against magic, and for the disenchanted view of the world, was the Protestant Reformation, which was profoundly suspicious of such meddling with occult forces. Magical practices couldn't be allowed as a proper use of divine power, because that would be to assume human control over this, which was against the very principle of the Reformation" (191). For an extended work on witchcraft from a similar perspective of conflicting identities and understandings, as well as the medical approaches to "curing" (very painfully) the mental illnesses perceived to have arisen from sin, see University of Virginia historian H. C. Erik Midelfort's *A History of Madness in Sixteenth-Century Germany* (Stanford: Stanford University Press, 1999), as well as his *Witch Hunting in Southwestern Germany, 1562–1684* (Stanford: Stanford University Press, 1972).

by the spontaneity of moral conduct as well as by the recognition of one's honest evaluation of the presence of faith.

From the viewpoint of this new sense of self-possession, of self-consciousness of interiority, there is a kind of "freeing" of the subject from the external world, a new kind of self-awareness, as well as an imagined "closer" relationship of individuals to the divine. The innermost part of one's being was, thus, through faith, connected to the divine in an immediate and experiential way. As Luther wrote, "No one can understand God or God's word, unless he has it directly from the Holy Spirit, and no one has it unless he experiences and is conscious of it."[10] No one can judge your inward life but yourself and God; you and God are the only witnesses to your most intimate commitments and thoughts.

Thus Protestantism eliminated intermediaries between man and God, heightened a sense of human independence, and focused attention upon the individual religious consciousness. The Scottish sociologist of religion Harvie Ferguson

Martin Luther with *People*

writes that at this time in Western religious history, "all the medieval theological categories had been abolished to be replaced by a single remaining qualitative distinction . . . between the 'inner man' [and] all forms of external coercion."[11] The difference between the Catholic and Protestant believer at this time was such that the Protestant must not only understand and accept God's salvation, but believe that it applies to him. He must not only believe it, he must believe *in* it. *Faith itself* is the sign of salvation. The Protestant, as long as his faith is secure, "enjoys a peculiar sense of certainty and finality," writes historian Ralph Perry, "His strength lies in this, as does his tendency to cock-sureness and self-righteousness."[12] Or, as the Beastie Boys would have it, "What's gonna set you free? Look inside and you'll see." We're all, to some degree, Protestants now.

Calvinism and the Self

The Counter-Reformation as a social and political force was a fierce enemy that John Calvin saw must be opposed with great vigor and total discipline if the tenets and achievements of the Reformation were to remain influential as a spiritual revolution. Encroachment from the world and corruption by the flesh could lead to a dissolution of identity through the compromise of the Protestant religious ideals inherent in one's person. In an attempt to rescue Lutheran reforms from the dangers of complete social withdrawal and against the Counter-Reformation, the sixteenth-century ethics of Calvin—ruling over the virtual theocracy of Geneva—indeed continued the Augustinian notion of sin as the inability to fully commit oneself to moral precepts, one's salvation, to God.*

Calvinism (as distinct from the faith and order that Calvin himself set up in Geneva) attempts, then, in part, to rescue the central tenets of Protestantism from what it saw as its inherent tendency toward social dissolution made possible by a radical inwardness, which had the effect of shearing off the individual, of leading to self-absorption—just as much a sin. Individualism and direct communication with God could lead to withdrawal from the congregation; it also threatened, of course, social and political hierarchy. Rather rigorous means and

---

*The same could be said for John Knox's disciples in Scotland; and many of Oliver Cromwell's supporters in England had hoped for the same. See Walter A. McDougall, *Freedom Just Around the Corner: A New American History, 1585–1828* (New York: HarperCollins, 2004), 55.

structuring of society were upheld in Calvinist communities, such as mandatory church attendance, tithing, strict rules of personal and communal behavior, corporal punishment, public inquisitions, and death and banishment to heretics.*

The daily temptations of the earthly world that lead to sin were to be defended against ultimately with the *conscience*, that inward guide directing one from concerns of this world and toward the work of God. It was a duty to protect one's neighbor from these temptations; if one was to protect the sanctity of God in preparation for his rewards, it would be at all costs. If the individual could not avoid wrongdoing and sin, Calvin believed, other Christians had the moral obligation to be their "brother's keeper." He used the pulpit to warn potential sinners.[13]

Calvin's thinking was theologically systematic, yet he paradoxically proclaimed that inward direction toward the way of God must be so total that we should cultivate a deep hatred of the world. "If we would truly glorify God," historian Thomas Greer describes in his explana-

---

*Some of the examples of punishable prohibitions in the early days of the Massachusetts Bay colony, in 1655 in Essex County, were "eavesdropping, meddling, neglecting work, taking tobacco, scolding, naughty speeches, profane dancing, kissing, making love without consent of friends, uncharitableness to a poor man in distress, bad grinding at mill, carelessness about fire, wearing great boots, wearing broad bone lace and ribbons." Between 1656 and 1662: "Abusing your mother-in-law, wicked speeches against a son-in-law, confessing himself a Quaker, cruelty to animals, drinking tobacco, i.e. smoking, kicking another in the street, leaving children alone in the house, opprobrious speeches, pulling hair, pushing his wife, riding between two fellows at night (if a woman), selling dear, and sleeping in meeting." And up to 1670: "Breaking the Ninth commandment, having a dangerous well, digging up the grave of Sagamore of Agawam, going naked into the meetinghouse, playing cards, rebellious speeches to parents, reporting a scandalous lie, reproaching the minister, selling strong water by small measure, and dissenting from the rest of the jury." These and other hilarious examples can be found in George Francis Dow, *Everyday Life in the Massachusetts Bay Colony* (New York: Dover, 1988), particularly the chapter "Crimes and Punishments," 199–226. For its simultaneous bizarreness and reality, well worth a read.

tion of Calivinist zeal, "we must first rid ourselves of distractions of the flesh; we must achieve, in short, a contempt for the world."* Prayer is one way for a person to withdraw from the tumult of life; it is a waiting for the Lord to appear inwardly; it is shunning the world, protecting the self. For Calvin, prayer can be said to be carried into one's wakeful life, such that we "ought to cultivate an indifference to the world of the senses."[14]

The rejection and revulsion of the external world in original Calvinism went to the extreme of denouncing friendships and social proximity, particularly from those doubting or not cognizant of the way to salvation. This sort of early revulsion in Calvin—though radically altered throughout Calvinism's development in England, Holland, Germany, and America—was inspired, in part, by Old Testament directives, such as that found in, appropriately, Jeremiah 8:4–6:

> Beware of your friends; do not trust your brothers. For every
> brother is a deceiver, and every friend a slanderer. Friend
> deceives friend, and no one speaks the truth. They have
> taught their tongues to lie; they weary themselves with sin-
> ning. You live in the midst of deception; in their deceit they
> refuse to acknowledge me, declares the Lord.

The true Christian, in this Calvinist sense, should always be suspicious of friendships and dwell only inwardly; he should remain primarily conscious not of the personality of the individual, but of his obedience

---

*Dow, *Everyday Life*, 313. In using the word "zeal," it is important to note the clarifications that Puritans themselves made in handling it, lest we continue the *Crucible*-like caricature of the Puritan mind; the clarification is made especially clear by Perry Miller: "Mere zeal alone, however sincere, was not sufficient. The ideal was guidance of the heart by the mind, and while God requires zeal of his people that they may be 'active and forward in the pursuit of the things which they engaged,' yet in order that zeal may be truly serviceable, 'it had to be well regulated with a right and clear understanding of what they do.'" *The New England Mind: The Seventeenth Century* (Cambridge: Harvard University Press, 1939), 68.

to the law of God. One's chief concern, above all else, should be the state of one's salvation.* This placing of all human relationships as subordinate to that with God had the effect of a profound introjection of consciousness, alienating man at his core, save his being with God. The English Puritan Thomas Adams maintained this aversion to the world in *A Commentary Or, Exposition Upon The Divine Second Epistle General Written By St. Peter* (1633), when he recommends that, every morning before going among others, the person imagine going into "a wild forest full of dangers, and to pray God for the cloak of foresight and righteousness."[15] Inward, Christian soldiers.

The self-reflexive disposition, the internal concentration, the hyper-self-awareness, all had the ultimate goal of determining the subtle inward signs of whether or not one was saved, whether one had been a recipient of grace, whether the Devil was working his ways upon the watery soul. But—and this is the glaring existential snare of Calvinism: nothing could be done about it. This was so because clearly in the Calvinist theology—set as it was against the Catholic doctrine of works—one could not make efforts toward grace; one's fate had been predetermined since eternity by God alone. Any effort in the direction of "lifting oneself up" was to exhibit a will that believed itself free, which it was not when it came to regeneration. That is to say, in the Calvinistic conception of the state of man, human agency was simultaneously both given—in that it saw beings as privately autonomous—and taken away—in one's inexorable fallen-ness. Because one could not help oneself, and no one could *ultimately* help

---

*As Miller, again, has pointed out on several occasions, this salvation-obsessed caricature of the Calvinist Puritan mind should not disallow recognition of their highly logical thought and philosophical reflection, though "they did indeed subordinate all concerns to salvation, and they did force their social and philosophical thinking into conformity with religious conclusions, but they were incapable of confining themselves solely to dogma or giving over the arts and sciences into the keeping of the unregenerate. They were first and foremost heirs of Augustine, but also they were among the heirs of Thomas Aquinas and the pupils of Erasmus." *The New England Mind,* 66.

another, the individual was utterly powerless to act toward his own salvation; to act was to exercise willfulness, further proof that one was not of the elect.

Only detailed conversion experiences led to a changed and saved life. "Conversion was seen as a humbling of the heart," writes the Americanist Perry Miller, "but it was also construed as enlightening the mind, and humiliation unaccompanied by a considerable degree of information was worthless."[16] Knowledge without grace was possible but flawed; grace without knowledge, perfect proof of salvation. No one was spared; "even the meanest believer must give the grounds for his belief."[17] True knowledge of God only comes by this conversion experience. By himself alone, for the Calvinist, man is fallen, corrupted, depraved, infinitely miserable, forever unhappy, wicked, and utterly imperfect. He is blinded by self-love and greed. God's grace is required for salvation.

For the understanding of the place of the individual consciousness in the world under Calvinism, it is important to understand, briefly, the denomination's five founding tenets, or Five Points, commonly remembered with the mnemonic TULIP: *Total Depravity, Unconditional Election, Limited Atonement, Irresistible Grace, and Perseverance of the Saints.* These precepts were part of the Puritan religious mind.*

---

*This clearly leaves out consideration of Captain John Smith's 1607 founding of the Jamestown colony, thirteen years prior to the Plymouth landing. I am aware of the discrepancy and here lean on the general character of the religiously inspired search for freedom as relevant to "intellectual origins," rather than the earlier excursion to Virginia, undertaken for business and profit under the auspices of the London Company. Whereas the Massachusetts colony worked quickly to establish a viable community and centers of worship, and also included women and children in the task, "The promoters in London," the historian Alan Brinkley writes of the Jamestown effort, "diverted the colonists' energies into futile searches for gold and only slightly more successful efforts to pile up lumber, tar, pitch, and iron for export. These energies would have been better spent on growing food. The promoters also sent virtually no women to Jamestown. Hence, settlers could not establish real households and had no permanent stake in the community." *The Unfinished Nation*, 4th ed. (Boston: McGraw-Hill, 2004), 28.

Total depravity (or total inability) is the original state of man after the Fall; sin has extended to every part of his personality—his thinking, his emotions, his will. And because even his will is depraved, he is unable to help himself. Without the power of the Holy Spirit, the "natural" man is deaf to the message of the gospel. Unconditional election is the doctrine of Calvinism that holds God has already chosen the elect. This selection is not based upon any merit shown by the subject or upon who "accepts" the offer of the gospel. God has simply designated some for glory and others for eternal damnation. This was done before the foundation of the world. This doctrine does not rule out, oddly, man's responsibility to believe in the redeeming work of Christ. The elect are saved to do good works in the world. And although these works will never bridge the gulf between man and God, they are a *result* of God's saving grace.

Possessing the fruit of good works—a convenient and oft-utilized, if not oft-spoken, justification for material accumulation—is an indication that God has sown seeds of grace properly. Man's *choosing* to do these good works in order to be saved is further evidence that he is not, for one has exercised an already ineffectual and marred will. Limited atonement is a doctrine offered in answer to the question, "For whose sins did Christ atone?" The Calvinist answer, in coherence with the above, is that Christ died, indeed, for many people, but not for all of them. Specifically, Christ died for the "invisible Church"—the sum total of all true Christians. Irresistible grace is thus the inward response by the elect to the call of the Holy Spirit. One cannot refuse grace or the call of Christ. Here again, one's will is totally ineffectual; one is simply an agent of the Lord. (Condemning Calvin's teachings, Erasmus believed that this reduced man to the figure of a puppet. Specifically, I think it was Alf.) Lastly, perseverance of the saints is a doctrine that states that the saints (those whom God has saved) will remain in God's hand until they are glorified (dead) and brought to abide with him. Calvinists believed that Christ assured the elect that he would not lose them along the way, and that they will be glorified on the Day of Judgment. The Calvinist thus invests himself wholly in the promise of God, trusts that Christ will fulfill the will of God in saving all of the elect according to the preordained plan laid out before time.

The sum total of these tenets as a body of belief, if one was not somehow assured of already being a saint, had the effect of creating a feeling of deep spiritual loneliness, helplessness, and absolute lack of control over one's fate—a lone, perhaps hopeful, consciousness in a sea of temptation and depravity with not a spot of chance that one could do anything about it. Strict Calvinism was a rough doctrine, and it did violence to a sense of benevolent human nature. This internal discerning and attempts at outward evidencing, of course, required quite a bit of conscientiousness about one's behaviors; often, too, because Calvin's God (not surprisingly like Calvin himself) was a righteous and severe judge, as would be his followers.*

John Calvin with Stars and Bars

---

*The famed story of Calvinist retribution is here worth recounting: when the Spanish theologian Michael Servetus challenged the doctrine of the Trinity in 1553, and Calvin, in Geneva, caught word, he warned the Spanish theologian to stay away. When Servetus did not heed and visited Geneva, Calvin had him arrested. Charged with heresy and swiftly "convicted," Servetus was burned at the stake, whereby Calvin cited Deuteronomy 13, saying "God makes plain that the false prophet is to be stoned without mercy. We are to crush beneath our heel all affectations of nature when His honor is involved. The father should not spare his child, nor the brother his brother, nor the husband his own wife, or the friend who is dearer to him than life." Quoted in Thomas H. Greer, *A Brief History of Western Man* (New York: Harcourt, Brace, and World, 1968), 314.

Self-knowledge begins in knowledge of the corruption and blasphemy of one's own soul. One was confronted with the alternatives of salvation or eternal, hellish damnation, which, because one was powerless to prevent it, filled believers with a stable of anxieties. So this desperate spiritual situation provides an irresistible motivation to reach beyond the boundaries of the self and into the world through action and deed; and this made for a fundamental anxiety, contradiction, spiritual confusion, and deep tension in the Calvinist mind.

If you were a saint, however: much easier. The logic of the tenets did, though, "place a great onus on those who were convinced of their salvation," writes historian Walter McDougall in his opus on early Americans, *Freedom Just Around the Corner* (2004). Such figures had to "demonstrate sanctification each waking hour and indeed in their dreams," which placed even greater spiritual stress "on those who had not had a wrenching conversion. They asked what they could do to escape eternal damnation, and had to answer nothing at all."[18]

The idea of the elect had practical, evidentiary confirmation in the notion of *piety*. Those who displayed piety were part of the "visible church," and they were rewarded in material fruits ("seek ye first the kingdom of God and all this shall be added unto you"). Piety became the movement outward from saved self into the world, and was evidenced in an obligation to help others, to reach into the sphere of civic life, to uphold the social covenant, even though one knows that doing so may be for naught. The covenant was the agreement between God and man under which people agreed to abide by Christian principles and obey the "Heavenly King in return for His blessings in a Promised Land."[19] And this covenant with God is a collective one: if the good Calvinist is to live up to it, he must remain concerned with the general welfare of the community, how other people in the community are living up to the covenant. What one person does affects what others do. This logic says: You will be punished for what I am doing, and I for what you do.

In the exacting Calvinism of the early generation of American Puritans, confirmation of having received grace came solely by the already-elect agreeing that one's behavior was that of someone who was saved. The connection between conscience and piety was that the latter was outwardly visible, while conscience remained interior, implanted by God. What was invisible to others was most visible to the believer's inward perception. Piety is how one "displayed" a God-inspired conscience, so to speak, that played out in public. And it substantiated itself not by withdrawal into its own sphere, but by excelling in every region of secular life. The man of God should not only be a braver warrior, an enlightened ruler, or a skillful artisan, but also a successful tradesman; all of this would corroborate divine appointment.[20] (Indeed those comprising the elect were the only ones with, conveniently, full voting rights in the community and full membership in a Puritan congregation.)

Piety, in other words, is a sort of objectified salvation. It was evidenced in material and social rewards. A man should therefore behave *as though* he were one of the elect, as if he were already a perfect Christian ("nothing succeeds like the illusion of success," famously wrote Christopher Lasch). And Reformed Christianity, particularly in the dictates of Martin Luther, fundamentally demanded as much of *all* Christians; they must behave as such because they have the *ability* to have faith. Yet still, so impossibly collapsed was the state of mankind under the Calvinist conception, and so deterministic was the fate of man, so impossible was any inclination of his will, that John Milton famously penned, "Though I may be sent to Hell for it, such a God will never command my respect."[21]

The relevance of mentioning these Calvinist imperatives is to address how the believer reflected upon his own private interiority, his newfound home that the Reformation had forged. Early American and British writings on the troubles of this interiority, in the form of spiritual autobiographies, reveal a bizarre fascination with the self so that it may be obliterated. First-generation Puritan journals and autobiographies see the self snap back at itself with a dark vehemence for its own destruction—a fostering of a radical subjectivity that in turn violently rejects the recognition of its own radical subjectivity. Yet it was inward recognition of this inward place—presently perhaps best understood as ego—that blocked the way to communication with the Divine and thus the possible recognition of one's very own salvation.

The very foundation of Calvinist Puritan belief, as researched painstakingly three decades ago by Sacvan Bercovitch in his classic *Puritan Origins of the American Self* (1975), is the furious contrast between "personal responsibility and individualism." Though the typical Puritan was concerned with the "welfare of his own soul," he balked inwardly at the very mention of "own." Bercovitch writes that the way of the soul "starts with a 'holy despair in ourselves' and proceeds 'with a holy kind of violence' back to Christ; the advantage of self-knowledge [is] the terror it brings [to] exorcise our individuality."[22] This sense of alienation within the world was a shared characteristic at one stage of the Calvinist mind. The growth of this kind of religious introspection, so habituated in English Protestantism and German Pietism, is predicated upon the epistemological, inward emphasis seen in Western philosophy from Descartes to beyond Kant.[23]

Horror at one's subjectivity forces repentance. Further, it curiously instructs each believer to concentrate on oneself alone and to forget the lives of neighbors; it sets up the extreme dichotomy between the evil of self-concern and the good of concern for others. The self for the Puritan mind was "the great snare," the "false Christ," "a spider's webbe [spun out of] of our bowels," a "figure or type of hell."[24]

A sense of alienation within the world was a shared characteristic at one stage of the Calvinist mind.

In an attempt to purge the personal and therefore social body of this inherent tendency toward self-rumination, a variety of constant self-monitoring was enacted. This is the internal behavior of the Calvinist who is not assured of his salvation or state of grace, who attempts to root the "Devil's poison and venome or infection"[25] from his being by giving his interiority over to

Christ. This tendency and unceasing internal scanning and practice was developed in Jesuits and Puritans, and the latter did so to descry signs of grace, as well as to bring thoughts in line with a welcome to God, and, at the same time, to the community. Eventually, "The Protestant culture of introspection becomes secularized as a form of confessional autobiography."[26]

"Self" was to be overcome in favor of the godly "social." This was an identity that God desired the religious pilgrims to form. Thus to err was to do harm to the collective identity being created, one that undertook the transposition of secular into religious identity, as God inspired. The Puritans attempted to transform all that was secular into sacred identity. "Thus they personified the New World as America *microchrista*," Bercovitch writes; "they combined the genres of political and spiritual exhortation, and equated public with personal welfare."[27]

In this interpretation of the Puritan mind—admittedly, for the sake of this argument, loose and historically imprecise—one can interpose, as I will in a moment, the seeds of the current opposition between the earnestly engaged citizen and the ironist, who has been described as rejecting the implicit social contract—the covenant. By extension, to be saved, one must take the *errand* to heart, to have it be for someone else. But the reiterations of the errand only come when it has been trespassed. To be for oneself triggers the reminder (the jeremiad) that the errand is for others. To invest in the other becomes an indicator of salvation. This most recent outbreak of debate over civic trust and civic remove is thus a very old story and tactic in American life, however much it remains an immediate concern.

CHAPTER SEVEN

Inward, Christian Soldiers

Wee must entertaine each other in brotherly Affeccion,
wee must be willing to abridge our selves of our
superfluities, for the supply of others necessities, wee must
uphold a familiar Commerce together in all meekness, gen-
tlenes, patience and liberality, wee must delight in eache
other, make others Condicions our owne reioyce together,
mourne together, labour, and suffer together, allwayes
before our eyes our Commission and Community in the
worke, our Community as members of the same body, soe
shall wee keepe the unitie of the spirit in the bond of peace,
the Lord will be our God and delight to dwell among us
. . . we must Consider that wee shall be as a Citty upon a
Hill, the eies of all people are upon us.
    —John Winthrop, *A Modell of Christian Charity* (1630)

Each person, withdrawn into himself, behaves as though
he is a stranger to the destiny of all the others. His children and his good friends constitute for him the whole of
the human species. As for his transactions with his fellow
citizens, he may mix among them, but he sees them not; he
touches them, but he does not feel them. . . . There no
longer remains a sense of society. . . . Each man is forever
thrown back on himself alone, and there is danger that he
may be shut up in the solitude of his own heart.
    —Alexis de Tocqueville, *Democracy in America* (1835)

In perfect solitude, the American spirit leans against its
absolute isolation as a spark of God in a sea of space. . . .
the divine shall seek out each spirit only in total isolation.
—HAROLD BLOOM, *The American Religion* (1992)

In the ironic view, each individual is essentially alone.
—JEDEDIAH PURDY, *For Common Things* (1999)

I walk alone.
—GREEN DAY, "Boulevard of Broken Dreams" (2005)

Long before September 11, of course, the idea that American society
has been in decline because of a remove of citizens' private lives from
the public sphere, a lack of commitment to one's public duties and
responsibilities, has worried many interested in the health of the social
body. The threat of this remove has been a central narrative in the history of American social criticism. Such declinist literature, as it's
sometimes been called,* has its roots in the form of the religious jeremiad—America's first narrative genre—already present shortly after
the arrival of Puritans on New England shores.†

---

*Richard Posner, *Public Intellectuals: A Study of Decline* (Cambridge: Harvard
University Press, 2001), 281. The chapter on this subject is "The Jeremiah
School," which he wryly designates as "declinist literature," spelling out its
tradition and form. Charles Taylor has separated the camps of contemporary
cultural criticism into "boosters" and "knockers." The word *jeremiad* itself is
derived from the Old Testament prophet Jeremiah, someone who was often
depressed about the world. To his great sorrow and pain, Jeremiah believed
that the sins of the people and of all nations would bring about God's punishment. Oops! When he proclaimed this message and called for repentance, he
was arrested and then nearly lynched as a traitor. Lesson learned: Jeremiah's
prophecies soon became ones of comfort, restoration, and hope for a new
moral order. Just like the ones we have now.
†See Sacvan Bercovitch, *The American Jeremiad* (Madison: University of Wisconsin Press, 1978). Therein Bercovitch offers that "Miller rightly called the
New England jeremiad America's first distinctive literary genre; its distinc-

The early American jeremiads of Puritanism shared the dual threads of doom and optimism—indeed they saw themselves as inheriting Jeremiah's function—for a directedness toward the future of God's plan.* When the Pilgrims erred, divine punishments were seen as correctives, not a means to destroy the offenders. Calamity was a sign of God's will for redirection of individual souls toward the original errand; there was a larger universal project in which Americans played key role. All history, in John Winthrop's momentous words, was converging upon "the cosmic climax of Boston's founding." Cosmic climax!

Indeed, whether we like it or not, and however dangerously inconvenient and embarrassing the fanatical, loopy religious Right makes it,

---

tiveness, however, lies not in the vehemence of its complaint but in precisely the reverse. The essence of the sermon form that the first native-born American Puritans inherited from their fathers, and then 'developed, amplified, and standardized,' is its unshakable optimism. In explicit opposition to the traditional mode, it inverts the doctrine of vengeance into a promise of ultimate success, affirming the world, and despite the world, the inviolability of the colonial cause" (6–7). This is set in direct opposition to the European version of the jeremiad, which was "a lament over the ways of the world. It decried the sins of 'the people'—a community, a nation, a civilization, mankind in general—and warned of God's wrath to follow" (7). See also, in the modern European vein, *aber selbstverständlich*, Oswald Spengler, *The Decline of the West*, ed. Helmut Werner and Arthur Helps, trans. Charles Francis Atkinson (New York: Oxford University Press, 1991); John Lukacs, *The End of An Age* (New Haven: Yale University Press, 2002); Barzun, *From Dawn to Decadence*. For a historiographic study of how nineteenth-century writers of history utilized specific narrative structures and tropes to compose accounts of history, see Hayden White's *Metahistory: The Historical Imagination in Nineteenth-Century Europe* (Baltimore: Johns Hopkins University Press, 1973). Of American decline, many books recently.

*For the uninitiated: the Pilgrims believed in something we now call typology, which is the study of religious texts, specifically Old Testament texts in this case, for the purpose of identifying episodes in the present that appear to have been prophesied. This centuries-old form of thinking is still practiced among some religious fundamentalists in America.

the Christian tradition is the big inescapable fact of American intellectual history. Introduced by first arrivals to the new land, it was rein-
forced by generations as the dominant force in American life; it was
the chief unifier of early American society. As the Americanist Merle
Curti has written:

> No intellectual interest served so effectively as Christian thought
> to bring some degree of unity to the different classes, regions,
> and ethnic groups. Whatever differences in ways of life and what-
> ever conflicts of interest separated the country gentry and great
> merchants from the frontiersmen, poor farmers, artisans, and
> small shopkeepers, all nominally subscribed to Christian tenets
> and as least in theory accepted
> Christianity as their guide.[1]

*However dangerously inconve-
nient, the Christian tradition is
the big inescapable fact of American intellectual history.*

The combination of vast linguistic
and cultural groups throughout
the colonies of the eighteenth century—French Huguenots, Dutch
and German Calvinists, Swedish
and German Lutherans, Swiss
Baptists, English Calvinists, Presbyterians, Methodists, Quakers,
Mennonites, Anglicans, Baptists, and Catholics—made for a complex
organism. But as much as these groups differed in doctrine and worship, they all, with a few notable exceptions, shared an implied Judeo-
Christian conception of human nature, social relationships, and ideas
about knowledge and beauty.[2]

Much has changed since then, luckily for the sake of science, justice,
human knowledge, and decent television. But, importantly, seriously,
for this argument, Christians in the dissenting tradition shared the
fundamental agreement that there existed the possibility for an
inwardly "direct, subjective communication of every individual with
the Holy Spirit as the authentic way of arriving at the truth."[3] The idea
that the individual might determine and descry religious truth,

regardless of what it was called, without the aide of authority, was the outgrowth of these original yet long-tempered leanings. In Quakerism the deification of subjective feeling would find early and resolute expression. As the Quaker reformer John Woolman wrote, "The mind was moved by an inward principle to love God as an invisible, incomprehensible being, [and] by the same principle it was moved to love Him and all His manifestations in the visible world."[4] Slowly, this Protestant principle would continue to erode tradition and ecclesiastical authority in America. We are undoubtedly witnessing yet another revival to counter its staccatoed decay, however much of its religious phraseology now seems absurd.

To be sure, though, American spirituality would increasingly see the subjective detection of faith as the only indicator of a relationship with God; piety would become less convincing as individuals grew into self-possession. In the mid–eighteenth century this kind of subjectivity would find expression in a Great Awakening that would see Jonathan Edwards's sermons in New England, German Pietism's influence on the Lutheran and German Reformed churches of the middle colonies, the Presbyterian stress on emotional fervency in the middle and southern colonies, and the Methodist George Whitefield make his case for personal feeling in religion all over the eastern seaboard.* To lean inward for religious experience was to become the entire American way of life. Our own ethos is part and partial of this tradition, however devoid it now is of metaphysical, religious credibility.

This long excursus brings us finally to the mind-set of the earliest ideology to take root in the "American mind"—Protestant Christianity in its many emanations—and thus, circuitously, back to the contempo-

---

*In his passion to convert and spread the Word, George Whitefield made fifteen tours of Scotland, three tours of Ireland, and seven tours of the entire colonial territory, visiting each more than once, particularly his adopted home of Georgia. Even that wry skeptic Benjamin Franklin professed to be so moved by Whitefield when he visited Philadelphia that he "emptied his pockets into the collection plate." McDougall, *Freedom*, 132.

rary consideration of irony and civic trust in America.* The above quotations, indeed the above chapters, take two seemingly disparate mind-sets—Protestantism and the ironic worldview—and point them toward similar tendencies: consciousness directed toward inner life, a

---

*Two points of note on the clichéd myth of American foundings: Andrew Delbanco opens his book *The Real American Dream*—originally delivered as the William E. Massey Sr. Lectures in the History of American Civilization at Harvard University in 1998—with both poignant self-critique and subsequent overcoming: "Let me begin by proposing to do something that the historian Alan Taylor has recently described as 'quaint.' 'What could be more quaint,' he asks, 'than to seek [the roots of American identity] in colonial New England, the land of Puritans, Salem witches, the *Mayflower*, and Plymouth Rock?' Of course, he's right. Anyone who has been even half-awake in the last twenty years or so knows it is no longer safe to assume, as Tocqueville did, that there is 'not an opinion, not a custom, not a law' that the New England origin of American civilization does not explain. Nevertheless, that is where I shall look for some clues to understanding our culture as it was first established and as it has since evolved" (15). Additionally, the philosopher Jacob Needleman, anticipating the accusation of sentimentalism in his look to the Puritan heritage, remarks, "It is quite wrong to think of the origins of America only in economic or political terms without acknowledging the fundamental place of the inner search in the minds and hearts of the early colonists. It is true that over the years the religious motivation of the early colonists has been sentimentalized—to the point of absurdity and unreality. Scholarship and common sense have done much to correct this sentimentalized picture by pointing out the economic, political, and military factors involved in the movements of peoples from England and Europe to America and the westward expansion of the United States. But all this scholarship leads to an equally false and, in its way, equally absurd picture of the forces behind the origins of America when the power of authentic spiritual need and practice is not recognized. Among those who came first to the Northeast from England, Germany, and Holland were very many who brought with them plans for a life of interiority, even to the point of various forms of monastic communitarianism." *The American Soul: Rediscovering the Wisdom of the Founders* (New York: Tarcher/Putnam, 2002), 101. I take both Delbanco's and Needleman's points to heart, recognize the possible sentimentality involved, and have followed the same impulse as driving the motivation of this essay.

protection of this inwardness against exteriorities imagined as contaminants; a sense of absolute loneliness; the self—as the vessel of inwardness—imagined in a wild sea of social space.

This inward tendency—seen in Romantic irony and Protestantism—results in feelings both of inner liberation, experienced as freedom, and of an isolated and hermetic interior dwelling—experienced as a sense of aloneness or a sense of detachment. Importantly, this sort of inward turn in the narrative of the American identity—and thus the fundament of the American myth—is derived from the Protestant *location of freedom* in the individual inner self. It is a freedom with dual valence—religious and secular. And so there exists a tension between the outer component of freedom—that is, politics—and the inner location of personal freedom though joining with God, that is, its private religious tenor.

The January 20, 2005, presidential inaugural address by George W. Bush mentioned the word *freedom* twenty-seven times. His conception (or, at least his speechwriter's), repeated several times, is that "each individual has the seed of freedom planted within him by the Creator." Repetition, as Kierkegaard observed and as we are all aware, destroys meaning. Moreover, it emasculates once vivacious concepts. The mention of *freedom* now in political speech is met, if not with flag-waving applause, as either a placeholder synecdoche for "what America stands for," or as a hokey catch-

Spazzing-out President

phrase now entirely emptied. It's the equivalent of the rallying "U.S.A.!, U.S.A.!, U.S.A.!" Freedom, when used without regard for concretizing the *inward sense of what it feels like*, loses its meaning, the sense that it is alive, the sense that it has been a motivating force behind some of the most important political upheavals we've experienced as a country. "The deepest spiritual source of the early colonists' rejection of political and religious tyranny," writes the philosopher Jacob Needleman, "was that such tyranny prevented them from searching for *inner* freedom."[5]

> Harold Bloom asks: "How are we to understand, and judge, an American spirituality that, to be authentic, seems always fated to make the believer, ultimately, a worse citizen?"

There are, of course, slippery dangers of sentimentalism in looking to this spark of the original European emigration, of idealizing a past fraught with contradictions and mistakes, of glossing over hundreds of years of racial and gender injustice, indeed total, unyielding oppression. But the idea of freedom as a driving *inner narrative* in the American mind, nourished by religious and philosophical victuals, is unrepudiable. And so this friction between freedom's *inward* leaning and its subsequent *outward* requirements leads Harold Bloom to ask a question that has been the foremost concern of this entire essay: "How are we to understand, and judge, an American spirituality that, to be authentic, seems always fated to make the believer, ultimately, a worse citizen?"[6]

An American Religion

The idea that these inner longings have remained, that we retain the religiously serious intonations of civic trust, and that similarities in Americans' moral views have remained coherent despite dissimilar outward emanations, is something hard to believe; but, for the sociologist of American religion Alan Wolfe,

> When it comes to fundamental questions about human nature, the formation of character, qualities of good and evil, and the sources of moral authority . . . there is a common American moral philos-

ophy, and it is broad and inclusive enough to incorporate people whose views of the actual issues of the day are at loggerheads.[7]

This view is repeatedly expressed by other surveyors of the American religious and moral landscape. Harold Bloom writes in *The American Religion* (1992) that he finds stable characteristics in every authentic version of American religion, and that those characteristics have fundamentally to do with a person discovering God "in themselves," a lone interiority "finding God in total isolation," after "experiencing a total inward solitude." And, again: "In perfect solitude, the American spirit learns again its absolute isolation as a spark of God in a sea of space. . . . the divine shall seek out each spirit only in total isolation."[8]

Yes, ideas generated in past philosophy and religious precepts have made it into the present: "The deposited ideas of Christianity and civil religion are still the bedrock of our culture," writes Andrew Delbanco in *The Real American Dream* (1999), "whatever intellectuals may think of them. [The] history of ideas is usually [best] understood as a process of incorporation and transformation."[9] This Puritan idea of salvation conceived as a contradictory mechanism that happens through both the social union and a radically private impulsion is a "deeply paradoxical faith [that] is still alive in one form or another in America."[10] And, earlier, for Daniel Bell, in the *Cultural Contradictions of Capitalism* (1976), "The thought of Puritan theocracy is the great influential fact in the history of the American mind."*

---

*Daniel Bell, *The Cultural Contradictions of Capitalism* (New York: Basic Books, 1976), 56. Americanist Bettina Friedl crucially notes Bell's oversight in this instance: to claim that the influence of Puritan "theocracy" on successive thought is to confuse the influence of Puritan *thinkers* and the influence of social structure of political theocracy. The latter did not, in fact, and with intention, rule or overly influence Puritan New England. The exception, of course, was New Haven, which was run as a theocracy. All other colonies ran political structures with the explicit intent of keeping church and state separate entities. But the fear ran opposite of what it does today: that the state would influence the church.

The calling on these numerous quotations for support is simply to say that when we consider the current debate over irony and civic trust, these older notions play a crucial if less-than-immediately-detectable role in the assumptions about what it means to be a good citizen, about the seriousness of the social bond, and in the kinds of things we conceive of as corrosive to the coherence of the social body. We still live with these philosophical and religious ghosts and attempt to navigate the paths they travel.

There are, to be sure, *many* separate historical narratives that have helped foster the incredibly complicated American identity, that informed the American narrative, and those living within its sway, how to rely upon an "internal compass" and to shun that which does not point in the direction of that compass. The mythic American story—the abstracted narrative sewn from tales that resonate with recognition as somehow part of oneself—is filled with episodes of the individual's strong will, the location of certitude and ultimate truth inside the individual self's mysterious recesses.

From the Calvinist conviction of the battle between good and evil taking place in each person, presided over by the conscience, to the Quaker notion of Inner Light, and the secularized concept of "conscience as guide," Martin Luther King Jr.'s unrelenting moral force, or, even, "just do it," the American pantheon had long determined that moving forward is to be done so not out of strict adherence to external rules and regulations, but rather out of a sense of the *individual's inward conviction* of right.* This has yet another powerful propellant that ushers it further into the present: American romanticism.

---

*This is indeed the view that many European countries have of America and the way it behaves internationally. It is a point of pride not to "listen to polls," or "listen to much to what others think." Occasionally admirable, not always a good thing.

Emerson

At the same time the young Kierkegaard was finishing his thesis on irony, across the ocean a figure was feeling the effects of the same German Romanticism that Kierkegaard was struggling with. Ralph Waldo Emerson was constructing his own transcendence, rethinking the religious experience in America. Indeed, it is in Emerson, that fiery genius, wherein a Puritan, American urge toward collective salvation and the Romantic individual's antisocial needs are at once morally married and incongruous, such that the moral thought Emerson developed played on the same duality espoused by the Greeks, Augustine, and Luther, and later tinkered with by the Puritans and Quakers. There were two selves—inner and outer, spiritual and material; each played a part in the drama of human experience. The inner, for Emerson, was superior.

Emerson's American Romantic impulse toward transcendence and escape mingles with the conception of the inward self—and its snares—as the place of ultimate refuge so deliberated upon by the Calvinism of his forefathers. Even democracy has its roots, as he put it, "in the sacred truth that every man hath in him the divine Reason." In the sense that Emerson attempts to universalize the feeling for this bigger self, Transcendentalism represents the continuing democratization of religion begun by the Reformation. The glorification of the individual and the political sympathies (i.e., abolitionism) characteristic of many Transcendentalists corresponded to the democratic understanding that all men possess a sacred, irrevocable right to govern themselves. Every person was capable of making the internal "divine reason" their guide.[11]

In 1832, tired of the Unitarianism he was preaching—calling it "corpse-cold"—Emerson looked to the German idealism of Kant and others to escape the dominant Lockean view that *all* knowledge derives from the senses. The idealists provided for Emerson an extrication from the confines of sense perception, instead positing that the mind already knows things it did not glean from sensory input.[12] This view formed the basis of Emerson's conviction that there was an inward Over-Soul, something that, though not experienced, was individually sensed and unearthed through intuition. Such a perception could only be found in isolation, in Nature, leading Emerson into a life-long campaign for confident individualism, which comprises at least one element of American romanticism.*

In "Self-Reliance," published as part of his *Essays: First Series* in 1841 (the year Kierkegaard had published *The Concept of Irony*) Emerson extolled the virtues of this triumphant individualism, of the inward self's ability to be willingly nonconformist with regards to social rules and behaviors. As he famously penned,

> Whoso would be a man must be a nonconformist. He who would gather immortal palms must not be hindered in the name of goodness, but must explore if it be goodness. Nothing is at last sacred but the integrity of your own mind. Absolve you to yourself and you shall have the suffrage of the world. . . . What have I to do with the sacredness of traditions if I live wholly from within?[13]

This generalized resistance is so crucial to the soul's health—that is, by implication, every person's soul's health—and it depended on a willful antagonism between the world of one's peers and one's own perceived interiority, deemed the seat of virtuous action. Integrity of

---

*Indeed there were others. Some of that movement's most prominent literary figures—Emerson, Hawthorne, Melville, Poe, Thoreau, Whitman—appear to be more different than alike in their varied sentiments, views of humanity, use of literary forms, and pessimistic uncoverings. However, American romanticism was unified by a fascination with the recesses of the mind; even Romantic landscape painting often has more to do with its creators than with the physical world itself. Less interested in a sociological, objective, historical view, American romanticism as an ideology was obsessed with the mysteries, darknesses, and potentialities of the nationalized American individual and where that individual was going.

one's own mind, the self's relation to itself, was the supreme value. The end of this self-concentration for Emerson was a fusion with the Divine, an overcoming of small, egoistic concerns for self-presentation and social mores. The locus of authentic man is clear, for "everywhere society conspires against him."

This sentiment was something not wholly uninspired by the German romanticism that had occurred several decades prior. Beyond the idealism of Kant, Emerson borrowed as well from the inferno of German romanticism in Goethe and Schiller. Yet the influence of the Germans, he saw, was no longer limited to a geography. It was as widespread in the northeast United States as it was across the Black Forest:

> The Genius of the German nation, spreading from the poetic into the scientific, religious and philosophical domains, has made theirs now at last the paramount intellectual influence on the world, reacting with great energy on England and America.[14]

Emerson even proclaims that to look for the German "genius" in the wake of American romanticism in 1848, was to relocate it at home:

> How impossible to find Germany! Our young men went to the Rhine to find the genius which had charmed them, and it was not there. They hunted it in Heidelberg, in Göttingen, in Halle, in Berlin; no one knew where it was; from Vienna to the frontier, it was not found, and they very slowly and mournfully learned, that in the speaking it had escaped, and as it had charmed them in Boston, they must return to look for it there.[15]

What began in the lecture halls of Jena and Berlin had since spread throughout the world, arrived on the very shores of Massachusetts. The genius of the sensibility that so impressed Emerson had come home to roost. And it would stay.

Indeed the man with a fire in his mind in Concord was not alone in his admiration for things German; in a sense Emerson was absorbing the contemporary importation of German thought, predominantly that of idealism, romanticism, and their effects, that had been growing in the United States slowly for several decades, namely as part of increased trade relations with Hamburg and the Baltic ports.[16] In the years following the War of 1812, when interest in British culture not only declined but was looked upon scornfully, fascination with (and, importantly, translation of) German thinkers such as Fichte, Goethe, Schiller, Kant, Schelling, and Jacobi found a pleasant welcome in educated households and university settings.

In 1814 Madame de Staël's *De l'Allemagne* ("Germany"), for which Friedrich Schlegel was both inspiration and advisor, was full of enthusiastic praise for German originality in thought and culture and was published to great fanfare in New York City. Additionally, the first generation of young Americans began traveling abroad to study at German institutions; Edward Everett, George Ticknor, George Bancroft, and Joseph Cogswell all headed off to German universities, coming back full of enthusiasm for its scrupulous educational system and pulsating intellectual culture—some going so far as attempting to model schools after the German Gymnasium right in Emerson's neighborhood.*

Transcendentalism, as we know, was part of the larger Romantic movement that had swept western Europe up in its winds a few decades prior. And, indeed, in the 1830s and 1840s "Northern Germany played so important a role in American philosophy and education," writes the Americanist Merle Curti.[17] American periodicals had begun to find a place for German letters, philosophy, and scholarship in public life; translations abounded. Antecedent to this flowering,

---

*Ibid. See Curti, *The Growth of American Thought*, pp. 234–35. As for school structure in Emerson's neck of the woods, Edward Everett, after studying in Göttingen, tried to effect change in the Harvard curriculum to reflect a more German arrangement. He was unsuccessful. Not so with George Bancroft and Joseph Cogswell, however, who managed to revivify the famed Round Hill school in Northampton, Massachusetts, into something resembling the wide-reaching liberal education of a German Gymnasium.

Goethe had even handed over a full set of his works to Harvard University in 1819. Emerson was a sixteen-year-old junior.

The Wake of Romanticism

As mentioned at the outset of this long slog, both the Protestant mind and the Romantic ironist stress the need for consciousness to be focused on inner direction for the hope of salvation and in the belief in internal divinity. Predictably at this point, the Romantic worldview has its roots in the Reformation, or, as one authority blithely put it, "The link between Romantic and Puritan is obvious enough."[18] Okay.

Romanticism, then—in both its German and American appearances—runs a strain of the Reformation's aim to further remove all mediations (society, Church, politics, language) between the self and God, between man and Nature, between sacred interiority and the immediacy of experience. Relevantly, Pietism, the late seventeenth- and eighteenth-century movement within German Protestantism, aimed to replace the emphasis on institutions and dogmatic teaching in then-orthodox Protestant circles by concentrating on the everyday "practice of piety," which they held was ultimately rooted in inner experience, expressed in a life of religious commitment. This movement held great importance for German romanticism and the stress on inward experience. It forms an important bridge between romanticism in the United States and the push of Protestant directives toward inwardness as an escape. Historian Peter Heltzel contends:

A case could be made that with Pietism's "inward turn" much of modern American individualism was anticipated and mediated through Protestant thought. . . . The American expression of this Pietist theme (the heartfelt character of true religion) is Jonathan Edwards' concept of "religious affections." This "inward emphasis" of Protestant theology would have a big influence on mid-nineteenth century Transcendentalism (Emerson and Thoreau).

. . . One can argue that Protestant thought in America was an important tributary feeding the river of American Romanticism. Moreover, the inward turn of the subject was an essential move in the evolution of modern subjectivism.*

Heltzel connects Reformed Lutheran thought with the urge toward inwardness and feeling seen both in the Great Awakening and in American romanticism, and then in the modern deification of subjectivity, or "doing your own thing." The Reformers unleashed individuality, an inward possession of the self. The Romantics, running a similar track but allowing for even further freedom from history and society, freed the individual to invent even identity, and then to impose his own symbols upon experience, including upon history, nature, and God himself.[19]

This freely wandering, suspended, creative but estranged Romantic identity experienced a sense of profound isolation within the world and a terrifying alienation within society. These dual experiences, metaphysical isolation (incredulity toward big stories being told and believed about the nature of world and man) and social alienation (a consequence of the first experience), were the distinguishing signs of the Romantic mind.

Recall just briefly the quintessential (and now stereotyped, caricatured) image of the Romantic individual in Caspar David Friedrich's *The Wanderer Above the Mist* (1818), to put into visual terms the imaginative creation of individuality, the uncertainty of what exactly

---

*Peter Heltzel, "Philipp Jakob Spener and the Rise of Pietism in Germany," from the Boston Collaborative Encyclopedia of Modern Western Theology at http://people.bu.edu/wwildman/WeirdWildWeb/Wesley.html. Additionally, the little-remembered German literary historian Fritz Brüggemann has connected, in *Die Ironie als entwicklungsgeschichtliches Moment* (1909), as well, the ironic *Weltanschauung* to the Pietist revival in German romanticism. I found reference to this in Mueck's *Compass of Irony* but, unfortunately, could not locate Brüggemann's dissertation in German or English.

should be constructed.* It has become the caricatured (and poster-frenzied) illustration of the Romantic continuing the adventure into an unknown subjectivity.† The painting elaborates the late-eighteenth-century kinship between private feeling and nature, attempts to communicate the deep bond between the two. "Feeling can never be contrary to nature," Friedrich wrote; "it is always consistent with nature."[20]

In October 2006 at the Hamburg Kunstalle in Germany a massive and hyped exhibition was installed: "Casper David Friedrich, Inventing Romanticism." While art exhibitions are not necessarily the ultimate litmus test of the Zeitgeist, the fact that the exhibition was touted so loudly and entrance was nearly impossible without reservations is indicative of shared sentiments. The museum's site announced:

> Today everyone is again talking about Romanticism—in art and literature, in advertising and entertainment. This seems only logical as the increasing individualism and full aestheticisation of our world are both rooted in Romanticism. It is thus all the more important now to recall the origins of Romanticism and the initial ideas of the early Romantics. In a demystified reality, they clung to questions concerning unity, integrity and the meaning of life and created a world to counter the uniformity and normality of emerging middle-class life. Their contrasting world is just as attractive today.[21]

---

*This painting is located at the Hamburg Kunsthalle in Hamburg, Germany. It is irresistible to make a connection with a "gathering mist" comment D.C. Muecke made: "Getting to grips with irony seems to have something in common with gathering mist; there is plenty to take hold of if only one could. To attempt a taxonomy of a phenomenon so nebulous that it disappears as one approaches it is an even more desperate adventure" (*Compass of Irony*, 3). In both cases, something misty is going on.

†See the covers of, among many books dealing with the Romantic era, Erich Heller's *The Artist's Journey into the Interior* and Paul Johnson's influential *Birth of the Modern*.

And seemingly just as necessary to recall. As is now resoundingly clear, authenticity and integrity for Romantics circumvented the authority of society, and they believed in reconnecting to nature outside of it. Society was conceived of as confining, degrading, and limiting to a sense of true human fulfillment. Innocence and natural spontaneity become the opposite of the inauthenticity of society. This movement inward, this circumventing of normal social norms of expression, should simultaneously bring the individual into greater sincerity and authenticity of being through art, poetry, violence, sensuality, play, humor, mystery—things upsetting the normal patterns of modern life. It thus attempts to pierce the sheath of conventional morality, urging that the social world, ultimately, *negates* one's authenticity. Romanticism's origins—that is, Romantic irony's origins—lay in the Reformation's dislodgment of older values by a superlative one: sincerity.

And Now: The Debate Recast!

To return, yet again, to the present: The mounting concerns over civic engagement in the 1990s were the precursors to the outburst of anti-irony sentiment following 9/11. But the historical underpinnings of both of these positions, as I've tried to argue, are the Protestant notions of inner dependence, sacred interiority, "salvation" through faith alone, the implied duty of helping the social body to cohere, and interior protection from corrupting external influences. Again, Romantic irony is the secular continuation of the Protestant push toward the attainment of inner freedom.

Our differing opinions about public issues have less to do with those actual issues than with a fundamental split in the historical makeup of our moral traditions. On the one hand are the religious conservatives, who hold, too fundamentally, that moral behavior is "the commitment on the part of adherents to an external, definable, and transcendent authority," and, on the other, cultural progressives, who believe in "the tendency to re-symbolize historic faiths according to the prevailing assumptions of contemporary life."[22] These two basic differences in moral vision also characterize the differences in the debate about irony. For religious conservatives—literalists—irony represents a sort of moral relativism and hedonism that is corrosive to clear decision-making and ethical behavior. For secularists—interpreters—irony is often seen as an appropriate reaction to a postmodern world filled with contradictions, threats to integrity, rampant skepticism, and dubious political speech and behavior; irony is a method by which individuals retain and protect their authenticity.

Thus, in contrast to the "devout" vision of the world propagated by the social contract tradition, its religious tenor and seriousness, the ironic worldview stands, ostensibly, in direct opposition to this civic feeling in the American mind. It is because of this deep philosophical tension that the contemporary ironist receives such disdain. Where the ironic worldview recoils from collective understanding in favor of the "hidden truth of inwardness," the civic-minded subject is transparent to the others in his community. He speaks, like Aristotle's virtuous citizen, plainly; he does not boast or underestimate his capabilities. And "to speak plainly," writes Bercovitch of the Puritan emphasis on clarity of communication, of the perfect registration between avowal and meaning, "was not primarily to speak simply, and not at all to speak artlessly. It meant speaking the Word—making language itself, as self-expression . . . [conform] to scripture."[23] More than one-third of Americans believe that the Bible is the direct and exact word of God, not "just" a collection of parables or ethical instructions. Though this religious interpretation of speaking clearly is not explicit today, can we doubt that such an idea plays into our own interpretation of the *moral* value of speaking clearly?

We continue to live today with *both* the push of romanticism—witnessed in the production and consumption of ironic sentiment in popular culture, in the arts, in everyday communication and assumptions about politics, power, and motivation, and in skepticism toward power and self-proclaimed moral authority—*and* with the demands of the

Protestant-based social contract, which extended the individual's moral duty and salvation outwardly through society. What we are now calling ironic detachment could just as easily be called romanticism (as Kierkegaard maintained)—an inward leaning with Protestant beginnings, a tendency to protect the sacredness of the salvation of the individual self, a totalized worldview. Indeed, as the sociologist Harvie Ferguson has straightforwardly put it, "Selfhood . . . is simply religious reality within capitalist society."[24] It is the last remaining sanctity in a world divested of spiritual importance.* And what we are now calling civic trust can be seen as the extension of the demands and assumptions of the social contract that lie historically deep in our expectations of citizenship.

We continue to live with both the inward push of romanticism and the demands of the Protestant-based social contract.

Though each attitude shares the same foundation in the Protestant conception of the world and self, they appear in the contemporary debate as forceful opposites. On the conservative side, irony has often been cast as Hegel had cast it, as a sort of moral evil, as vanity, and as a radically self-absorbed subjectivity. On the communitarian side, disengaged ironists can be seen as persons who willingly shirk their civic

---

*For an update on this logical progression in the Germanic vein of the Romantic ideology, see Theodor W. Adorno's *Negative Dialectics*, trans. E. B. Ashton (New York: Routledge, 1973) and *Minima Moralia: Reflections from Damaged Life*, trans. E. F. N. Jephcott (London: Verso, 1984). In the latter, Adorno contends that "there is no way out of entanglement. The only responsible course is to deny oneself the ideological misuse of one's own existence, and for the rest to conduct oneself in private as modestly, unobtrusively and unpretentiously as required, no longer by good upbringing, but by the shame of still having air to breathe, in hell" (26). Commenting on this passage, Timothy Bewes notes that it seems to "reaffirm the position of the inner emigrant in the very process of disinterring it, and thereby lifts its inner emigration itself on to a new ironic plane of existential solitude" (*Cynicism and Postmodernity* [London: Verso, 1997], 173). Yikes.

responsibilities to the public of which they are a part, in favor of self-styling, close-knit circles, and narrow interests.

That is to say, the ironist seems to willfully choose individuality—chooses to focus on and construct personal identity—insists on his separateness from the whole, seems uncommitted to public betterment, and then condemns and judges the whole—conceived of in this case to represent the "mass" of middle-class American taste. By his choosing this individuality, he valuates the self and its unique composition, its style; he aestheticizes his life and language. He, for the later Kierkegaard and for Hegel, "moves away from the Absolute." To traditional religious moralists, this sort of position cuts off the ironist from any chance of personal salvation, for instead of ridding the self through absorption into the whole, into Christ (as they would conceive it), which would rid the ironist of his sense of alienation, the ironist denies the stories told by the traditional moralists—whether liberal communitarians or Born-Agains.

The social contract set the model for citizenship based on the Reformation's ideals of total commitment, willfulness, and Calvinistic notions of salvation through joining with others through the covenant. Romantic irony, while leaning on the inwardness of Protestantism and the removal of intermediaries between man and God/nature, rejects the social contract because the Romantic cannot see his spiritual course being run within society—something he now conceives, since the "fall of public man," as filled with "mere" roles, not with the authenticity of personality, and certainly not as he sees society being run by others with power. This distinction is continued in the debates insofar as the Romantic ironist believes that he needs to achieve salvation alone and connect with something outside of what he perceives as a deadening and vicious social world, while the more "serious" pundits and intellectuals believe that the social contract provides not only the model of good citizenship, but also the means of salvation through collective agreement and social "coherence."

The crucial difference between these two strands of modern thought, and why they are and have been at loggerheads in America for several decades, is this: where the social contract tradition demands that salvation can come only *through one's relations with others,* Romantics are convinced, as Rousseau was, that we *must circumvent society altogether* in order to be authentic, sincere, and true to ourselves. In the first instance, society becomes a key to salvation, but in the Romantic vein, its absolute hindrance.

Today, the entire contemporary culture—as one invested in the triumphant individualism of our Protestant-Romantic heritage—is built upon individual customization. The supernarrative of Self has surpassed prior guiding narratives of God and Nation.[25] In an intellectual and literary culture with waning credible belief in Christian metaphysics, the culture that today holds sway over much of Europe and influential sectors of the American population, existential longings result in changes in terminology, in redescription. Philosophy, like everything, fits itself to the contemporary environment or risks annihilation. Thoughtful people foster new phrases that become believable once the old is no longer credible. As political philosopher Charles W. Anderson aptly confides,

> I have no idea what some people mean by a "personal savior," nor do I know what Quakers mean by the "inner light" or how they know when they are in its presence. Our experiences, and our interpretations of the human spirit, are radically different; often they are mutually incomprehensible. Are we then talking about different aspects or expressions of the same phenomenon? Or are we perhaps talking about entirely different things? . . . We really do need to say *something* collectively, publicly, about this vision of human nature that, as a core value in our liberal political philosophy, may be our strongest common bond.[26]

Regardless of outward description, as this passage attests, our historical yearnings remain. Given the (albeit shrinking) percentage of Americans who today claim Protestantism as their religious affiliation (currently accounting for 52 percent of the population) one can safely assume the influence that these deeply held notions of social duty, of "brotherly affections," have had on the construction of individual personality and, by extension, shared ideas and sentiments that have become institutionalized, legalized, and reified.*

---

*According to a 2004 survey by the National Opinion Research Center at the University of Chicago, between 1993 and 2002 the percentage of Americans who claimed they were Protestant dropped from 63 percent to 52 percent, after years of generally sustained levels. According to Rachel Zoll of the Associated Press, "Respondents were defined as Protestant if they said they were members of a Protestant denomination, such as Episcopal Church or Southern Baptist Convention. The category included members of the Church of Jesus Christ of Latter-day Saints and members of independent Protestant churches. . . . The study was based on three decades of religious identification questions in the General Social Survey, which the opinion center conducts to measure public trends." Catholics numbered 25 percent of the population; Jewish, 2 percent; and other faiths, such as Islam, Orthodox Christianity, or Eastern religions, increased from 3 percent to 7 percent. The study also controversially concludes that in the coming years the United States will no longer be a predominantly Protestant nation.

This has some pundits and scholars up in arms. A debate about the fundamentally Protestant character of the United States flared up again with the publication of Samuel Huntington's *Who Are We? The Challenges to America's National Identity* (New York: Simon and Schuster, 2004). Huntington claims that America remains a resolutely Protestant nation by virtue of the fact that the structures set up by the British colonialists are the ones that guided the country into existence. Among those defining traits are "the English language, Christianity, religious commitment, English concepts of the rule of law, the rights of individuals, Protestant values of individualism, work, and the belief that individuals have a shared duty to create a heaven on earth, a 'city upon a hill'" (quoted in *Foreign Affairs*, September–October 2004, 156). Among the challenges Huntington perceives is (primarily Catholic) immigration from Mexico, with which Alan Wolfe, in his criticism of Huntington, takes issue in *Foreign Affairs*, July–August 2004. Perturbed, Huntington responded to Wolfe in the September–October issue, which also printed a reply from Wolfe and another response from Huntington. This sort of back-and-forth is unorthodox for a national publication; it speaks to the troubled situation of national identity and its crucial intertwining with personal identity—and why it is thus guarded with teeth bared.

Indeed, in the contemporary American climate, such religiously informed notions of the person's ethical relationship to the community must have residual sway and influence: 94 percent of Americans believe in God; nearly half of Americans believe that their country has special protection from him; 68 percent believe in a literal Devil (even among those with college and postgraduate degrees: 68 percent and 55 percent, respectively); 40 percent that the earth will end in Armageddon and a battle between Jesus and the Antichrist; 45 percent believe that Jesus will return to Earth in their lifetime; and 82 percent of Americans believe in a literal Heaven, to which 63 percent believe they're headed. Only 1 percent believe they're going to Hell.

To be sure, Americans are the most religious people in the advanced industrial world, or, at least they publicly identify themselves in polls as believing, going to church, following the Word, and so forth.[27] Yet, for the scientifically, agnostically, or secularly inclined, it is an unsettling reality that Americans' religious beliefs most accurately compare not to those of European and other advanced industrialized nations, but to those of developing countries.* This is strange, indeed frightening.

This statistical backdrop of powerful religiosity in America, when joined with discussions of social decline, is what fuels the forever-renewable notion that the American populace is erring, is somehow slipping from its original moorings—those built by the Puritans, the Founders, Native Americans, Nature, God's Laws, the British gentry, aliens implanted in the Earth, what have you. Unlike the pulpit correctives of old, however, social science and punditry now supply the

---

*Rifkin., 21. Compared with Europe: while six of ten Americans say that religion is very important in their daily lives, it is barely so in most European nations, even in Catholic Italy and Poland. In Germany "only 21% say that religion is very important to them, while the percentage in Great Britain drops to 16% and in France to 14%, and in the Czech Republic, 11%. In Sweden, the numbers are even lower, 10 %, and in Denmark, 9%. In Korea, only 25% of the population considers religion to be very important in their lives, and in Japan only 12% consider themselves to be very religious" (20–21).

necessary fodder for today's jeremiads, which are still delivered from, of course, upon high. The ebbing of civic spirit and the growth of cancerous civic malaise, of disengagement and of anomie, has been a central anxiety (and family of metaphors) among many critics alarmed at the state of American society over the past three decades, and not without statistical warrant.

"Between waves of patriotism and troughs of skepticism about government," William Chaloupka observes, "civic belief somehow vanished as an overarching way of life. It ceased to be the only practical master strategy for life in democratic society."[28] The causes intimated for this loss vary wildly, but the results always bear the same descriptions: decline, cynicism, cultural twilight.* Correctives are needed. People held accountable. Decisions made. Blame distributed. Statements of what exactly these correctives are, what these modern-day jeremiads suggest we do, though ultimately political, frequently surface in cultural debate over social and moral issues.

Thus the heated disagreements over irony come down not to uses of "whatever," or a like or dislike of *Seinfeld*, but over a second-level disagreement about how man achieves salvation. Calls for civic renewal are essentially saying the Romantic ironist has it wrong: man needs to achieve salvation through others, through subsuming his will to the common good, not by or for himself. The first-level agreement, however, is that in order to do so, one must value the sacredness of the inward self, that the individual conscience is the seat of all that is valuable.

Resolve

This contest of worldviews looks less philosophically abrasive if we accept that Protestantism's insistence on the turn inward *results in* dis-

---

*Quite literally. See Morris Berman's uplifting *Twilight of American Culture* (New York: W. W. Norton, 2000) and *Dark Ages America: The Final Phase of Empire* (New York: W. W. Norton, 2006).

220 CHIC IRONIC BITTERNESS

tancing and ironic detachment rather than causes it. The introspection originating in the religious precepts of Reformed Christianity brings in tow what can now be seen to form the basis of ironic posturing in the American mind—a position that is simultaneously destructive of civic trust and preserving of the Christian inwardness that allows civic trust to flourish. The ironist mind-set, seen in this tradition, can be described as encouraged by the American Puritan introspective sensibility, by the Protestant encouragement of the "inner man," but—through modernity and metaphysical skepticism born of the postmodern destruction of metanarratives (more simply: big stories becoming unbelievable)—one that does not discover God while turned inward; that is to say, one that does not find a credible narrative with which the ironist can contextualize the experience of selfhood.

As Charles Anderson notes above, so many of us don't even know what something like "personal savior" or "salvation" even *means*. Seriously! These words just don't make sense. They are empty. Yet in the face of secular and technological change, in the postmodern "condition," the religious sense—a sense of authentic being in the world, the search for a sense of connection, of Emersonian self-identity through resistance, of ineffability, of purpose larger than self—remains present and acted upon even as it escapes inwardly and battens down the hatches against the winds of perceived inauthenticity, corruption, and moral vacuity in the society in which it finds itself. It attempts to "survive" the current environment. It protects itself. It dwells internally until true outwardness can flourish. It arms itself with ironic detachment.

Devoid of an outwardly credulous religious belief in a God that unifies all beings—Kant's transcendental subjectivity and the aim of much modern philosophy generally, up to Habermas's yearning for philosophy to "hang things together"—the contemporary ironist is conceived of as not contributing to society, of being uncommitted because of his refusal to join with the now-metaphorical social contract, of having no faith because he has no trust; he cannot phrase his inwardness in outward religious terms, because they are no longer credible; they seem like stories for those too unimaginative or fearful to create their own. The ironist is thus left with himself alone, which only reaffirms his separation, which again leads to detachment (the existentialist stance). Humor that is bleak is funny because it seems the most real. What the American self has found, in both religious and nonreligious arenas, since about 1800, Harold Bloom writes, "is its own freedom—from the world, from time, from other selves. But this freedom is a very expensive torso, because of what it is obliged to leave out: society, temporality, the other. What remains, for it, is solitude and the abyss."[29]

The cyclical nature of this inward turn and outward confirmation of belief leads to a further battening down of subjectivity within itself. Unable to sense the connectedness with others, namely resolutely Red states, through a shared metaphysical story or feeling of social alliance, the contemporary Romantic attempts then to connect with others through, on one hand, outward associations—and television stations—or, more solidly, through irony itself, which, without doubt, serves to protect and defend. This is how the Romantic of today navigates a way through the world.

Yet while this modernized consciousness, the Romantic mind bereft, would like to come to a different conclusion, he must admit that in order to be *sincere and authentic*—in order to openly say, "This is my predicament," to maintain the Protestant values that he cannot shed and did not choose—is to enact *private* melancholy through public irony as the only sincere, authentic, moral, and intelligent way to be in the world. "Naïve idealism," Toby Young of the *Modern Review* wrote, was the only other option, and "for the intellectually honest [this] is not an option."

For the ironist, then, the only way to maintain integrity of private personality, to be honest about the world and self, to live up to the Protestant-Romantic demand of authenticity, is to live within the ironic worldview because it guards, ultimately, against spiritual and social pain. And part of that pain in modernism and romanticism is the weighty lumbering of self-awareness, of others' awareness of us that so many have described: "I know what I am doing now," Dave Eggers writes on throwing his mother's ashes into Lake Michigan, "that I am doing something both beautiful but gruesome because I am destroying its beauty by knowing that it might be beautiful, that it's no longer beautiful. . . . I am a monster. . . . She would do this without the thinking, without the thinking about the thinking."[30] Melancholy and irony form the twin poles of the contemporary mood: the "depth of modern life" and the "romance of distance."[31] The latter is an attempt to cure the former.

If nothing else, and for all the complaints about it as a social corrosive, then, ironic activity among those who "get it" urges a connection to others by alternative means, by showing what is true and real by avoiding the display of it through the confines of corrupted literalist representation, through dominant social constructions and forms given. Irony is the way to navigate attempts at some degree of existential peace, of the recognition of like sensibilities, the confirmation of not being alone in one's sensibility within the grand, grand world.

The current complaints about irony as a worldview reflect a position that has limited the understanding of irony to its surface—to its literal emanation historically understood as dishonesty.

The current complaints about irony as a worldview reflect a position that has limited the understanding of irony to its surface—to its literal emanation historically understood as dishonesty, as the misregistration between avowal and meaning—the opposite of sincerity. Detractors have failed to see the deeper commitment and trust that irony entails by its sacrificing of its own overtness, its social role, its *name,* in order to foster a more complex and nuanced understanding of the modern predicament, a silent understanding that says more by implication than by words alone.

In religiously oriented parts of American society, where the values of literalness and overtness hold sway, ironic understanding is interpreted as elitist, selective, dodgy, uncommitted. But these kinds of critics of contemporary irony have failed to see that irony ultimately *values* moral commitment and consistency, at times more profoundly and religiously than anyone else. Distracted by its methodology of dissembling exteriorities and undercutting (exposing) dominant forms of representation that deaden the mind to all good and worthy things, irony's detractors "fail miserably" to see the impetus behind its use. They fail to see behind the mask, the *use* of exteriority as a means. "The ironist is ironical not because he does not care," the writer Randolph Bourne whispered in 1913, "but because he cares too much."

Elected Official, Heal Thyself

An increase in devious or deceptive actions by political figures—entrusted by the public to take care of the common good—leads to the electing public's withholding its trust; the second Trilateral Commission on Democracy's work uncovered such a now widely known fact. When corporations, representatives, and institutions act deceptively, lie, and mislead, the breakdown of trust spreads from skepticism toward authority (already handicapped in the American mind) to a general social skepticism toward trust in those one does not know—strangers, or the public itself. Institutions or authority figures within a democracy that allow, propagate, or fail to detect lies, that are unable to enforce contracts and honor promises, that allow unfair advantage, and, especially, that fail to iron out social inequalities, appear to be, as extensive research has shown, "the only legitimate reasons for 'systematic' distrust and eventually cynicism."[32]

In this sense, ironic detachment from public life—conceived of as the subject viewing himself as separate from a more broadly shared experience—can be seen as a consequence, not a cause, of the current state of affairs. "Citizens are becoming more cynical," remarks political scientist Mark Warren, "because their expectations have increased without a corresponding increase in the trustworthiness of officials."[33] Not that we need a political scientist for corroboration, for "everybody knows" the disjunction between citizens' expectations and officials' actual behavior results in psychological disengagement, in "whatever." But the complaint that irony or cynicism, rather than the behavior of officials, *is the poison* comprises a frequent refrain among some of the self-appointed moral authorities. Taking good aim, writer Benjamin DeMott fired this back:

> While the citizen disengagement from public life that civility pro-moters term "mysterious" is clearly a complex phenomenon, some influences on it aren't arcane. Rude, abusive speech and action reflects, in one of its dimensions, belief in the need for an atti-tude—*some kind of protection against sly, sincerity-marketing politicos and boss-class crooks.* "Uncivil" refusal by ordinary citizens to labor unpaid in the cause of points-of-light good works reflects, in one of its dimensions, the daily exposure of ordinary citizens to pow-erful anti-mutuality instruction from above—oblique but persua-sive lessons on how to pull your oar ceaselessly for the benefit of Number One; how not to fret about hungry children in the street; how to feel good when, in the age of homelessness, a corporate bright boy spends $45 million on his own one-family dwelling; how to avoid being suckered into caringness. The "new incivility" needs to be recognized, in short, for what it is: a flat-out, *justified rejection* of leader-class claims to respect, a demand that leader-class types start looking hard at themselves.*

---

*Benjamin DeMott, "Seduced by Civility: Political Manners and the Crisis of Democracy," *The Nation*, December 9, 1996, 11; emphasis mine. "Sincerity marketing" is a fantastic phrase that everyone knows is true, which irony helps to counter: at my father's local bar there are two regular gentlemen. One is not fond of the other one because he is a crook. One day the crook gen-tleman asked the former why he was always so nice to him, nicer to him than any others. "Because I don't like you." Being overtly and constantly nice, as so many of us know, is now grounds for suspicion.

Physician, heal thyself. And Alan Wolfe, in a similar mood of frustration, writes,

> Moral authority is too important to people who have experienced moral freedom to be accepted just because those who would exercise moral authority claim that they have a monopoly over it. Moral authority must be earned before it can be exercised. As they look out on the world around them, not all Americans are convinced that their institutions—as well as their practices and their leaders—have done enough to earn it, which is why they reserve some of it for themselves.[34]

Three's a charm: political scientist William Chaloupka offers a succinct claim:

> The cynicism so easily diagnosed in political talk resists spectacles, sermons, and editorials. Its resilience raises an interesting possibility: . . . We are a cynical society [because] we have good reason.[35]

It's tough medicine, but the bond of social trust is fragile; it is the sole glue between a shared public life and individuals' private concerns and moral commitments. When that bond is broken or in doubt, detachment and skepticism result. And it's directed not only toward the institutions and officials whose offenses against public trust are touted loudly by a media ready to pounce (an entirely other litany of problems), but as well against the strangers that those institutional relations were supposed to support. It is a question of the maintenance of legitimacy and credibility. The more a society seems to be without viable responses to its current problems, the more it will allow itself to be cynical toward the things it used to hold dear. This is evidenced in a society and its culture becoming ironical about the legitimacy of its own political statements and representations.[36]

"I make the decisions. I'm the decider."

"He's *'The Decider!'*"

"The Great Decider." (This one from, five years on, Graydon Carter, *Vanity Fair*, October 2006—the one where we get to *finally* get to meet Suri Cruise!)

CHAPTER EIGHT

Conclusion (i.e. Everything
Summed Up Nicely)

I did not have sex with that woman.
—PRESIDENT BILL CLINTON, 1998

I did not have sex with that woman . . . I wanted to . . .
—ROBIN WILLIAMS, *Man of the Year* (2006)

If I criticize somebody it's because I have higher hopes for
the world, something good to replace the bad.
—MORT SAHL

The ironic life is a life keenly alert, keenly sensitive, reacting promptly with feelings of liking or dislike to each bit
of experience, letting none of it pass without interpretation and assimilation, a life full and satisfying—indeed a
rival of the religious life. . . . The ironist is ironical not
because he does not care, but because he cares too much.
—RANDOLPH BOURNE, 1913

Attempts to pull irony and some contrary element apart, to *oppose*
"irony" and "earnestness," "sincerity," or "moral values"—as the
debate over the "end of irony" attempts to do—will never work. Not
only have political figures and leaders of business and public life been
repeatedly shown to be corrupt and hypocritical (even "been repeat-

edly shown to" sounds naïve, our cynicism so confirmed it's hardly worthy of the term *cynicism*, but rather, more simply, "observation"), but also both ironists and "serious" pundits know the value of critique, however much bluster to the contrary. We are now set up internally to deflect any calls to believe. The alternative is political and moral blindness.

Yet, importantly, the ironically disengaged person still longs for the connection, commitment, and belonging to a *better* civic body and culture that social belief brings. He unwittingly calls on some of the deepest American historical means for inward freedom—particularly against public figures who blather on about morality while committing crimes and misdemeanors. The ironist more than the figure of uprightness thus holds "a conviction so deep . . . an emotion so strong, as to be able to command itself, and to suppress its natural tone, in order to vent itself with greater force."[1] See again, Colbert's White House Correspondents' Association Dinner speech.

Max Horkheimer as Bat

Thus the contemporary Romantic personality—the ironically detached modern psyche—wears a mask of social adeptness or coy absorption when it must, and looks on from a position of detachment. Yet this worldview does not completely float and adapt to everything internally. Rather this perspective, though both fascinated and disgusted with its general social context (it must always believe that it is marginal, no matter if it is not), retains solidity because it leans inward; it believes itself to be self-possessed, autonomous, even if slightly melancholic. It does not morph into what it observes. Oppositely, it resists the forms and demands of any given culture where it finds itself.

Analysts supreme of modernity, Theodor Adorno and Max Horkheimer, had this internal resistance in mind in the *Dialectic of Enlightenment* (1944) when they maintained that the "culture industry" forces a violent incursion into the subject, who was then forced to keep a foothold on his own integrity through a deep recursion into subjective space, to a resolute commitment to one's own experiences and thoughts.* This inward commitment was set against the advocates of total communicability, namely, the invisibility that Fascism and Communism demanded of its subjects. This inward flight toward a staunch integrity was something that could sustain resistance, something that could escape the ever-more depressing march of commodification and kitsch.

Importantly, the Romantic of today finds a real connection, a sense of groundedness, with others *through* irony, with those who under-

---

*Max Horkheimer and Theodor W. Adorno, *The Dialectic of Enlightenment* (New York: Continuum, 1944), chap. 2: "The Culture Industry: Enlightenment as Mass Deception," 120. Though hyperbolically victimized, overly suspicious, and impossibly bleak, as much by Adorno and Horkheimer seems to be, this passage from the same chapter is particularly depressing because it rings so true: "Not only are the hit songs, stars, and soap operas cyclically recurrent and rigidly invariable types, but the specific content of entertainment itself is derived from them and only appears to change. The details are interchangeable . . . ready-made clichés to be slotted in anywhere; they never do anything more than fulfill the purpose allotted them in the overall plan. . . . [T]he man with leisure has to accept what the culture manufacturers offer him" (124–25). Grim. But even more grim, perhaps, is that the film, record, and television companies actually call themselves industries. We have to think about that a moment. See the episodes of *The Simpsons* and *South Park* that skewer technologically enhanced boy bands for a much clearer explanation than I could ever give.

stand what is meant without having to say it, with those who also
question the saccharine quality of contemporary commercial culture,
who are certain that all diatribes of
virtue-lament will turn out to have
been made by some gambling,
lying, hypocritical talk-show host/
senator overly fond of interns/
pages. This they see as doing an
injustice to the depth of human
possibility and the complexity and
goodness of human feeling, to the
power of the imagination over all
forms of potential constraint, to a
basic ethics that they themselves
are proud to uphold. But ironists,
above all else, are certain that we
must live in this world as best as
we can, "whether or not it suits our
own moral outlook," writes
Charles Taylor. "The only alternative seems to be a kind of inner
exile."[2] Ironic detachment is
exactly this sort of inner exile—an

Theodor Adorno with Paxil®

inner emigration—maintained with humor, chic bitterness, and a sometimes embarrassing but abidingly persistent hope.*

Both the contemporary ironist and the critics who lambaste the
stance, then, aim to achieve the same end: an honest society and commitment to the common good, a better America, one that will not

---

*The term *innere Emigration* was first used by the German-Jewish philosopher Hannah Arendt in her famous description of Adolf Eichmann and other
Nazis who "frequently had held positions, even high ones, in the Third Reich
and who, after the end of the war, told themselves and the world at large that
they had always been 'inwardly opposed' to the regime." *Eichmann in
Jerusalem: A Report on the Banality of Evil* (Harmondsworth: Penguin, 1977),

humiliate them, one for which they won't have to make excuses: "Oh, *that* proposed law/cultural nightmare/Hollywood schlock film/hollow rhetoric/protracted war? Yeah, funny thing about that . . ." Those lamenting the dissolution of civic trust due to cynicism or irony hold the same valuation of inwardness that cynicism and irony help ultimately to *protect*, particularly in a culture widely perceived to be dense with superficiality, mindless consumerism, incivility, and ubiquitous political spin. Moreover, it protects—good Lord it protects—against the fanaticism of belief that seems to be ever more polarized between Allah believers and God believers. I mean, *Sharia law? Jesus*

We have come into a cultural situation where jokes seem to make themselves.

camp?! Jesus! (unfortunately so, so far from camp). Robertson and Dobson are still thinking with a mind of the middle ages.

Luckily, ironists' jobs are now much easier than they have been. We have come into a cultural situation where jokes seem to make themselves. The vice president blasted a man in the face with a shotgun while hunting quail. News anchors stand in hurricanes for hours to tell

---

126–27. *Innere Emigration* was originally used by the German expressionist writer Frank Theiss to refer to writers who had stayed in Germany after 1933 but who detached themselves emotionally and psychologically from the political realities (and thus reality generally) of the Nazi regime. The term had come to signify a movement into the inner recesses of the soul as caused by the unbearable circumstances surrounding the agents in question. It had also come to signify a tradition: that of a mythologized European Christian inwardness over pragmatic utilitarianism. This is precisely the view of Dostoyevsky's *Underground Man*, the motivation behind Adorno's "negative dialectics," as well as those of the British magazine *The Idler*, and perhaps even, for us Yanks, *Beavis & Butthead* and *The Big Lebowski*, all of which, to varying degrees of intellectual acrobatics, were basic humanistic justifications for, or investigations of, *inaction* in defense of personal integrity and nonutilitarianism. Appropriately, the subtitle to *America: The Book* by Stewart, Karlin, Javerbaum & Co., is *A Citizen's Guide to Inaction*.

us it is windy in hurricanes. Timid intellectuals write books about manliness. A full media week dedicated to Britney Spears's shaven head. A piece of the earth's crust is "missing." Political authorities hit-on their underlings via gay chat-rooms. Entire countries riot because of caricature. "There will be no cartoon today," wrote the political cartoonist Doug Marlette following the violent outbreaks, "because the world, in fact, has become a cartoon." Each day brings new and more absurd news, threats, and *so-fucking-bleak-that-you-can-only-laugh-in-order-not-to-self-combust-in-panic* information than the day before. In June 2006 Stephen Hawking told a conference in Hong Kong, "It is important for the human race to *spread out into space* for the survival of the species. Life on Earth is at the ever-increasing risk of being wiped out by a disaster, such as sudden global warming, nuclear war, a genetically engineered virus or other dangers we have not yet thought of."[3] Hey, Stephen, not a problem. How's next week for you? Say, Thursday? Thursday for me *WORKS GREAT* for an intergalactic jaunt. I'll bring the Tang! And the revolver.

But, then again, maybe Larry Flynt is right (yes, Homer makes it to the end). Suggestions for and complaints about American culture, society, and the world situation will always take variegated forms—even flying into space to escape a collapsing Earth—as they always have. Still, betterment remains the motive. But, now, somehow eerily and more so gallows-humorously, our own deaths remain a *not-entirely-awful* final release from the world that will be. "What do I care? I'll be dead by then! Ha-ha!" Yeah. Ha-ha. Hi. Larious.

Playing on humorous dread, addressing dark realities otherwise panned, the contemporary ironist figures—from Sacha Baron Cohen, *South Park*, Sarah Silverman, David Rees, David Foster Wallace, Todd Phillips, Matt Groening, John Waters, *Wundershowzen*, Conan O'Brien, Amy and David Sedaris, George Saunders, Aaron Sorkin, John Stewart, Samantha Bee, Ben Karlin, David Javerbaum, Stephen Colbert, Steve Carrell, Will Farrell, Rob Corddry, Ed Helms, Mo Rocca, *The Believer, The Onion*, and scores and scores and scores of others I am too tired to include because I'm wrapping up now—all somewhere within are harboring an idea of an intellectually challenging public life, a culture of un-self-conscious honesty and good deeds, one that is simultaneously smart and consistent, one less threatening than our current predicament, and one not hindered by the passivity, existential worry, spin, and dishonesty that now preclude it. They are not attempting to wreck the social fabric (they'd be out of jobs), but rather to prod it into a vision of what counts as the good society. And because this is true, they'll never speak it.

Whereas the ironists see the present age as something not measuring up to their ideas of what social life and culture could be—that is, they are most often progressives—the critics of irony sees it as *the cause of* the uneasiness in social life—that is, they are most often conservative insofar as they want to retain the models and forms of citizenship of the past.* The latter believe that without the ironist character, we would "no longer fail to take things seriously." But for the ironists who are, yes, committed to social and political change through the long tradition of satire and critique, taking things *seriously* in a culture widely perceived to be ignoring environmental catastrophe, driving Hummers, misusing power, spinning politics and media, Wal-Marting, corporate branding—swaddled in insincerity, egoism, and crappy taste—can only be done (as Oscar Wilde and H. L. Mencken, so sorely missed, believed) through irony and artifice—the last of the Romantic weapons in their arsenal.

This is the irrevocable device they retain to avoid sacrificing the integrity of individual judgment and reduction of their inner measures for culture and humanity. It gives them some degree of power and autonomy, some modicum of resistance, some remembrance of why this is all worth it, some ability to define their culture, nation, and identity. It will help them avoid, as Adorno asserted, "the misuse of

---

*There is, to be sure, conservative irony, mostly on websites for invigorated young Republicans or in quips by Ann Coulter, but it always seems gratuitous and awkwardly gloating, as conservatives now run, until 2008 at least, the executive roost.

one's own existence" by a social world that seems ever ready to espouse a logic of brute utilitarianism, the market, and the apotheosis of survivalism at all costs—even at the expense of one's own integrity, the most valuable of all things.

The ironists of frequent lament, then, far from being the evidentiary beings that willfully corrode society, in fact withhold their trust from a politics and culture undeserving of it. In doing so they hold dearly and implicitly the ultimately Protestant values of sincerity and authenticity that civic trust needs but has forgotten. In a world that seems to value the opposite, they must express these values ironically. Through this move they take temporary inward recourse, leaving the world to realize just how upside down it has become. And as they lean inward, they take their trust with them.

Or, like, whatever. ; -)

Notes

INTRODUCTION

1. Portions of these examples excerpted from "Silva Rhetoricae," compiled by Gideon O. Burton at humanities.byu.edu/rhetoric/Figures/I/irony.html.

2. Stephen Colbert on *Fresh Air with Terry Gross*, National Public Radio, January 24, 2005.

3. Søren Kierkegaard, *The Concept of Irony with Constant Reference to Socrates*, trans. Lee M. Capel (London: Collins, 1966), 265.

4. Elise Harris, "Infinite Jest," *The Nation*, week of March 2, 2000.

5. Benjamin Anastas, "Irony Scare: How Did A Literary Device Become A Public Enemy?" *The New Republic Online*, May 18, 1999, www.tnr.com/online/anastas051801.html.

6. Anastas, "Irony Scare."

7. Rodger D. Hodge, "Thus Spoke Jedediah," *Harper's*, September 1999, 84.

8. When looking for the tradition of witty satirists in America, start here (alphabetically, not chronologically): William Austin (1778–1841); George W. Bagby (1828–83); Joseph Glover Baldwin (1815–64); Lewis Gaylord Clark (1810–73); Willis Gaylord Clark (1810–41); William Cox (?–1851); Frederick Swartout Cozzens (1818–69); David Crockett (1786–1836); Charles Augustus Davis (1795–1867); George Horatio Derby (1823–61); Samuel Griswold Goodrick (1793–1860); Joseph Green (1706–80); Asa Greene (1788–1837); Charles Graham Halpine (1829–68); Samuel A. Hammett (1816–65); George Washington Harris (1814–69); Johnson Jones Hooper (1815–62); John Pendelton Kennedy (1795–1870); David Ross Locke (1833–88); Augustus Baldwin Longstreet (1790–1870); John Ludlum McConnel (1826–62); Cornelius Matthews (1817–89); George Pope Morris (1802–64); Robert Henry Newell (1836–1901); Henry Junius Nott (1797–1837); George Denison Prentice (1802–70); John Sanderson (1783–1844); John Godfrey Saxe (1816–87); Henry Wheeler Shaw (1818–85); Seba Smith (1792–1868); William Tappan Thompson (1812–82); John Trumbull (1750–1831); Nathaniel Ward [1578(?)–1652]; Mrs. Frances Miriam Berry Whitcher (1811–52); Henry Augustus Wise (1819–69). The above collated from *The Cambridge History of English and American Literature*, 18 vols. (Cambridge: Cambridge University Press, 1907–21).

9. Marc and Marque-Luisa Miringoff, *The Social Health of the Nation: How America is Really Doing* (New York: Oxford University Press, 1999).

CHAPTER 1

1. Roger Rosenblatt, "The Age of Irony Comes to An End: No Longer Will We Fail To Take Things Seriously," *Time*, September 20, 2001.

2. Rosenblatt, "Age of Irony."

3. Blurb from *The Onion's* book *Dispatches From the Tenth Circle* (New York: Three Rivers Press, 2001).

4. Bill Carter, "CNN Will Cancel Crossfire and Cut Ties to Commentator," *New York Times*, January 6, 2005.

5. John Colapinto, "The Most Trusted Name In News," *Rolling Stone*, October 28, 2004.

6. William Chaloupka, *Everybody Knows: Cynicism in America* (Minneapolis: University of Minnesota Press, 1999), 45.

7. Andrew Delbanco, *The Death of Satan: How Americans Lost Their Sense of Evil* (New York: Farrar, Straus and Giroux, 1995), 208.

8. See Richard Sennett's *The Fall of Public Man* (New York: Knopf, 1992) for a sociologically powerful overview of how and why this happened in the twentieth century.

9. David M. Halbfinger, "ABC Tells Robin Williams: Drop Comic Song from Oscars," *The New York Times* News Service, *Philadelphia Inquirer*, February 27, 2005, A12.

10. Stanley Cohen and Laurie Taylor, *Escape Attempts: The Theory and Practice of Resistance to Everyday Life* (London: Routledge, 1992), 47–48.

11. Dave Eggers, *A Heartbreaking Work of Staggering Genius* (New York: Vintage, 2000), in the unnumbered "Acknowledgments" section.

12. David Foster Wallace from the *Review of Contemporary Fiction* quoted in Robert Fulford's "Column About Irony" in the Canadian *Globe and Mail*, September 18, 1999.

13. Wyatt Mason, "My Satirical Self," *New York Times Magazine*, August 17, 2006.

14. Robert Storr, "The Rules of the Game," in *Alex Katz: American Landscape* (Baden-Baden: Staatliche Kunsthalle Verlag, 1995), 27.

15. Peter N. Stearns. *American Cool: Constructing a Twentieth-Century Emotional Style* (New York: New York University Press, 1994), 300.

16. Richard Majors and Janet Mancini Billson, *Cool Pose: The Dilemmas of Black Manhood in America* (New York: Lexington, 1992), 8.

17. Ernst Behler, *Irony and the Discourse of Modernity* (Seattle: University of Washington Press, 1990), 112.

18. Christopher Lasch, *The Miminal Self: Psychic Survival in Troubled Times* (New York: W. W. Norton, 1984), 96.

19. Alan Wilde, *Horizons of Assent: Modernism, Postmodernism, and the Ironic Imagination* (Philadelphia: University of Pennsylvania Press, 1987), 16.

20. David Worcester, *The Art of Satire* (New York: W. W. Norton, 1969), 75.

21. See "The Metropolis and Mental Life," trans. Edward A. Shils in *On Individuality and Social Forms*, ed. David Levine (Chicago: University of Chicago Press, 1971).

22. Behler, *Irony*, 4–5.

23. John Evan Seery, *Political Returns: Irony and Politics in Theory from Plato to the Antinuclear Movement* (Boulder, Colo.: Westview Press, 1990), 169.

24. Linda Hutcheon, *Irony's Edge: The Theory and Politics of Irony* (London: Routledge, 1995), 3.

25. Samuel Hynes, *The Pattern of Hardy's Poetry* (Chapel Hill: University of North Carolina Press, 1961), 41–42, quoted in D. C. Muecke, *Irony and the Ironic* (London: Methuen, 1969), 31. Reference from Seery, *Political Returns*, 206 n. 21.

26. "A Quiet Joke at Your Expense," *The Economist*, December 16, 1999.

27. Chaloupka, *Everybody Knows*, xiv.

28. Søren Kierkegaard, *The Journals of Kierkegaard*, trans. A. Dru (London: Collins, 1958), 50—51.

29. This idea about dignity as the last bourgeois concept is Theodor W. Adorno's.

30. Peter Sloterdijk, *The Critique of Cynical Reason* (Minneapolis: University of Minnesota Press, 1987), 5.

31. C. Thirwall, "On the Irony of Sophocles," *The Philological Museum 1832–3*, ed. Christopher Stray (London: Thoemmes Press, 2005), 434.

32. Delbanco, *The Death of Satan*, 217. Delbanco is here referring to the ironist specifically through the model of Humphrey Bogart's public persona.

33. Sloterdijk, *Critique of Cynical Reason*, 143.

CHAPTER 2

1. For these twin poles of nostalgia and irony, see Linda Hutcheon, "Irony, Nostalgia, and the Postmodern," http://www.library.utoronto.ca/utel/criticism/hutchinp.html; Fredric Jameson, "Nostalgia for the Present," *South Atlantic Quarterly* 88.2 (1989); and, naturally, *Postmodernism, or the Cultural Logic of Late Capitalism* (Durham, N.C.: Duke University Press, 1991); Svetlana Boym, "From the Russian Soul to Post-Communist Nostalgia," *Representations* 49 (Winter 1995) and her *Future of Nostalgia* (New York: Basic Books, 2001); Andreas Huyssen's *Twilight Memories: Marking Time in a Culture of Amnesia* (New York: Routledge, 1995); Allison Graham, "History, Nostalgia, and the Criminality of Popular Cul-

ture," *Georgia Review* 38.2 (1984); Elizabeth Wilson, *Adorned in Dreams: Fashion and Modernity* (London: Virago, 1985), where she says that nostalgia in fashion is a "strangely *unmotived* appropriation of the past" (172). Whaaa?

2. Contrariwise, in a rare exception to the rule, literary historian D. C. Muecke writes that G. G. Sedgewick's research found that "'*Eironeia*, as the Periclean Greeks conceived it, was not so much a mode of speech as a *general mode of behaviour*,' and the word, down to Aristotle, was a term of abuse connoting 'slyfoxery' with 'a tinge of 'low-bred.'" *The Compass of Irony* (London: Methuen, 1969), 47. The consensus I have found throughout the literature on the genesis on the term, specifically in Knox (note below), is that this conception was not a significant enough departure to warrant adjustments to the idea of irony in classical Greece as primarily a rhetorical device.

3. Norman Knox, *The Word Irony and Its Contexts, 1500–1755* (Durham, N.C.: Duke University Press, 1961), 4.

4. Knox, *The Word Irony*, 4.

5. Aristotle, *Nicomachean Ethics*, 105–6.

6. Knox, *The Word Irony*, 4.

7. Quintilian, *Institutio Oratorica*, 9.22.44 ("contrarium ei quod dicitur intelligendum est").

8. Knox, *The Word Irony*, 8. The English classical period, taken generally to range from 1500–1660, a.k.a the English Renaissance, refers to the influence of classical tragedies and comedies on authors of the time, or to the lasting quality of the literature into the present day. For more on the qualifications of such a distinction, see C. Hugh Holman, *A Handbook to Literature*, 4th ed. (Indianapolis: Bobbs-Merrill Educational Publishing, 1980), 82–84, 156–59.

9. Earl of Shaftesbury, *Characteristics of Men, Manners, Opinions, Times* (New York: Cambridge University Press, 2000), 194–95.

10. Ibid. Capitalization of nouns for that old Englishy effect. Did you believe it?

11. For an informed discussion of the importation of literary culture from London to the colonies and the effects it had on the self-defined sophistication of eighteenth-century cosmopolitans in America, see Ned C. Landsman, *From Colonial to Provincials: American Thought and Culture, 1680–1760* (Ithaca: Cornell University Press, 2000), specifically chapter 2, "Transatlantic Republic of Letters," 31–56.

12. Jonathan Swift, "A Modest Proposal," *The Norton Anthology of English Literature* (New York: W. W. Norton, 1979), 2146.

13. Swift in Muecke, *The Compass of Irony*, 65.

14. Jacob Axelrad, *Philip Freneau: Champion of Democracy* (Austin: University of Texas Press, 1967), 60.

15. Axelrad, *Philip Freneau*, 51.

16. Axelrad, *Philip Freneau*, 190; originally from *The Daily Advertiser*, New York City, February 5, 1791.

17. Philip Freneau, *Letters on Various and Important Subjects* (Del Mar, N.Y.: Scholars' Facsimiles and Reprints, 1976), iii.

18. Axelrad, *Philip Freneau*, 226.

19. Hugh Henry Brackenridge from preface of 1792 edition of *Modern Chivalry*, quoted in Claude Milton Newlin, *The Life and Writings of Hugh Henry Brackenridge* (Mamoroneck, N.Y.: Paul P. Appel, 1971), 114–15.

20. Brackenridge, *Modern Chivalry* ,79–81, in Newlin, *Life and Writings*, 120.

21. Brackenridge, *Modern Chivalry* ,51–52; in Newlin, *Life and Writings*, 121.

22. Walter A. McDougall, *Freedom Just Around the Corner: A New American History, 1585–1828* (New York: HarperCollins, 2004), 379. Of note: "Artemus Ward" is a character created by Charles Farrar Brown (1834–67); Artemus Ward, the actual person, was a commander in Massachusetts during the Revolutionary War. Works by Augustus Baldwin Longstreet include *Patriotic Effusions*, by "Bob Short" (1819) (Attributed to Longstreet); *Georgia Scenes, Characters, Incidents, etc., in the first Half Century of the Republic. By a Native Georgian* (1835); *Know Nothingism Unveiled* (1855); *Master William Mitten* (1864, 1889); *Stories with a Moral, Humorous and Descriptive of Southern Life a Century Ago* (1902).

CHAPTER 3

1. Jacques Barzun, *Romanticism and the Modern Ego* (Boston: Little, Brown, 1943), 137.

2. For an account of how this major narrative—the psychologistic account of the mind being a reflection of nature—plays out in the history of modern philosophy, see the groundbreaking volume by Richard Rorty, *Philosophy and the Mirror of Nature* (Princeton: Princeton University Press, 1979).

3. Michael J. Hoffman, *The Subversive Vision: American Romanticism in Literature* (Port Washington, N.Y.: Kennikat, 1972), 46; emphasis added.

4. See Raymond Immerwahr, "The Subjectivity or Objectivity of Friedrich Schlegel's Poetic Irony," *Germanic Review* 26 (October 1951): 190; and Alfred E. Lussky, "Friedrich Schlegel's Theory of Romantic Irony," *Tieck's Romantic Irony* (Chapel Hill: University of North Carolina Press, 1932), 2–4. Muecke contends that Schlegel used the term *romantische Ironie* only in the *Notebooks;* see *The Compass of Irony*, 182.

5. Harvie Ferguson, *Melancholy and the Critique of Modernity: Søren Kierkegaard's Religious Psychology* (London: Routledge, 1995), 38.

6. Earl Wasserman, *The Subtler Language* (Baltimore: Johns Hopkins University Press, 1968), 10–11.

7. Seery, *Political Returns*, 233.

8. Muecke, *Irony and the Ironic*, 22–23.

9. Steven E. Alford, *Irony and the Logic of the Romantic Imagination* (New York: Peter Lang, 1984), 5.

10. Hayden White, *Metahistory: The Historical Imagination in Nineteenth-Century Europe* (Baltimore: Johns Hopkins University Press, 1973), 37.

11. Muecke, *The Compass of Irony*, 9.

12. Norman D Knox, "Irony," *Dictionary of the History of Ideas: Studies of Selected Pivotal Ideas*, ed. Philip P. Wiener (New York: Charles Scribner's Sons, 1973), 2:626–34.

13. Quoted in Clair Colebrook, "Romantic Irony," http://www.englit.ad.ac.uk. See also Colebrook's *Irony in the Work of Philosophy* (Lincoln: University of Nebraska Press, 2002).

14. Ferguson, *Melancholy*, 48.

15. Fredrick C. Beiser, *Enlightenment, Revolution, and Romanticism: The Genesis of Modern German Political Thought, 1790–1800* (Cambridge: Harvard University Press, 1992), 223.

16. Frederick Neuhauser, *Fichte's Theory of Subjectivity* (Cambridge: Cambridge University Press, 1990), 43.

17. Hans Eichner, *Friedrich Schlegel* (New York: Twayne, 1970), 76.

18. Friedrich Schlegel, *Lucinde and the Fragments*, trans. Peter Firchnow (Minneapolis: University of Minnesota Press, 1971), fragment 42, p. 148.

19. Schlegel, *Lucinde and the Fragments*, 148.

20. Friedrich Schlegel, *Literary Notebooks, 1797–1801*, ed. Hans Eichner (Toronto: University of Toronto Press, 1957), 114, 62, quoted in Muecke, *The Compass of Irony*, 183.

21. Alford, *Irony*, 10.

22. Muecke, *The Compass of Irony*, 182.

23. Quoted in J. Bronowski and Bruce Mazlish, *The Western Intellectual Tradition* (New York: Harper Torchbooks, 1960), 480–81.

24. Georg Wilhelm Friedrich Hegel, *The Philosophy of Law*, quoted in Behler, *Irony*, 88.

25. Capel in Kierkegaard, *Journals*, 35.

26. Hegel in Kierkegaard, *Concept of Irony*, 507.

27. Kierkegaard quoted in Alistaire Hannay, *Kierkegaard: A Biography* (New York: Cambridge University Press, 2001), 139.

28. Hannay, *Kierkegaard*, 140.

29. Kierkegaard, *Concept of Irony*, 292.

30. Kierkegaard, *Concept of Irony*, 274.

31. Kierkegaard, *Concept of Irony*, 242.

32. Kierkegaard, *Concept of Irony*, 261.

33. Gary J. Handwerk, *Irony and Ethics in Narrative* (New Haven: Yale University Press, 1985), 8.

34. Schlegel, *Lucinde and the Fragments*, 155.

35. Harvie Ferguson, *Religious Transformation in Western Society: The End of Happiness* (London: Routledge, 1992), 133.

CHAPTER 4

1. Thomas Carlyle, *Sartor Resartus: The Life and Opinions of Herr Teufelsdröckh, in Three Books* (New York: AMS Library, 1969), 104–5.
2. See Mark E. Warren, ed., *Democracy and Trust* (New York: Cambridge University Press, 1999).
3. Christopher Lasch, *The Culture of Narcissism: American Life in An Age of Diminishing Expectations* (New York: W. W. Norton, 1979), 96.
4. Robert Putnam and Susan J. Pharr, eds., *Disaffected Democracies: What's Troubling the Trilateral Countries?* (Princeton: Princeton University Press, 2000), xv.
5. Putnam and Pharr, *Disaffected Democracies*, 9.
6. Jeffrey C. Goldfarb, *The Cynical Society: The Culture of Politics and the Politics of Culture in American Life* (Chicago: University of Chicago Press, 1991), 1.
7. Michael Lerner, *The Politics of Meaning: Restoring Hope and Possibility in an Age of Cynicism* (Reading, Mass.: Addison-Wesley, 1996), 3, 9.
8. Delbanco, *The Death of Satan*, 210.
9. Michael Portillo, "Poison of a New British Disease," *Independent on Sunday*, January 16, 1994, quoted in Timothy Bewes, *Cynicism and Postmodernity* (London: Verso, 1997), 15.
10. Toby Young and Tom Vanderbilt, "The End of Irony," *Modern Review* 1.14 (1994).
11. Anastas, "Irony Scare."
12. Quoted in William J. Bennett, *The Death of Outrage* (New York: Free Press, 1998), 35.
13. Putnam and Pharr, *Disaffected Democracies*, 8.
14. Bill Bradley, "Civil Society and the Rebirth of Our National Community," *Responsive Community* 5, no. 29 (1995): 5.
15. Robert Putnam, "Bowling Alone, Revisited," *Responsive Community* 5, no. 2 (1995): 28.
16. John Marks, "The American Uncivil Wars," *U.S. News and World Report*, April 22, 1996, 68. The above three statistics quoted in Christopher Beem, *The Necessity of Politics* (Chicago: University of Chicago Press, 1999), 1.
17. Quoted in Lewis Lapham, "Tentacles of Rage: The Republican Propaganda Mill, a Brief History," *Harper's*, September 2004, 41.
18. Gail Appleson, "Poll Shows U.S. Trust of Politicians 'Epidemic,'" Reuters, September 28, 2004.
19. This term makes reference to Christopher Lasch's book of the same title,

Haven in A Heartless World: The Family Besieged (New York: W. W. Norton, 1977).

20. Friedrich Hayek, quoted in Robert H. Bork, *Slouching Towards Gomorrah* (New York: HarperCollins, 1996), 83.

21. Bork, *Slouching Towards Gomorrah*, 53.

22. Goldfarb, *The Cynical Society*, 12–13.

23. www.tikkun.com.

24. www.washingtonpost.com/wp-srv/style/longterm/books/chap1/politics.htm.

25. Chaloupka, *Everybody Knows*, 5.

26. Jedediah Purdy, *For Common Things: Irony, Trust, and Commitment in America Today* (New York: Knopf, 1999), 10.

27. Purdy, *For Common Things*, 11.

28. Gregory Wolfe, "Editorial Statement: In Defense of Irony," *Image: A Journal of the Arts and Religion* 25 (Winter 1999–2000).

29. "Controversial Event in American Letters," quoted from Kevin Mattson, "Irony's Irony: Jedediah Purdy and the Plight of the Young Writer," *Social Policy*, Spring 2001.

30. Benjamin DeMott, "The West Virginian," *New York Review of Books*, March 9, 1999, 17.

31. Rodger D. Hodge, "Thus Spoke Jedediah," 84.

32. Caleb Crain, from Salon.com, September 7, 1999, www.salon.com/books/review/1999/09/07/Purdy/.

33. Adam Begley, "Against Irony, Really (Truly): Spongy Screed Wrings False," *New York Observer*, August 23, 1999.

34. Christopher Lehmann-Haupt, "Why Seinfeld (Irony Incarnate) Is So Menacing," *New York Times*, September 9, 1999.

35. Jesse Walker, "Jedediah the Ironist." *Reason Online*, January 2000, www.reason.com/0001/bk. jw.jedediah.shtml.

36. Quoted in Delbanco, *The Death of Satan*, 193.

37. Chaloupka, *Everybody Knows*, 15.

38. Charles Taylor, *The Ethics of Authenticity* (Cambridge: Harvard University Press, 1991), 90.

CHAPTER 5

1. Adam Seligman, "Trust, Confidence, and the Problem of Civility," in *Civility*, ed. Leroy S. Rouner (Notre Dame: University of Notre Dame Press, 2000), 68.

2. Friedrich Nietzsche, *Human, All Too Human*, trans. Marion Faber and Stephen Lehmann (Lincoln: University of Nebraska Press, 1984), aphorism 304.

3. Christopher Beem, *The Necessity of Politics: Reclaiming American Public Life* (Chicago: University of Chicago Press, 1999), 45.

4. Beem, *The Necessity of Politics*, 11.

5. Stephen Carter, *Civility* (New York: Basic Books, 1998), 15.

6. Carter, *Civility*, 67.

7. Robert B. Pippin, "The Ethical Status of Civility," in Rouner, *Civility*, 110.

8. Stanley Kurtz, "Freedom and Slavery: Our Moral Predicament and Bill Bennett's," *National Review Online*, May 13, 2003.

9. Charles Taylor, *Sources of the Self: The Making of Modern Identity* (Cambridge: Harvard University Press, 1989), 193.

10. John Demos, *A Little Commonwealth: Family Life in Plymouth Colony* (New York: Oxford University Press, 2000), 5–6.

11. Sacvan Bercovitch, *Puritan Origins of the American Self* (New Haven: Yale University Press, 1975), 18.

12. Taylor, *Sources*, 194.

13. Delbanco, *Real American Dream: A Meditation on Hope* (Cambridge: Harvard University Press, 1999), 43.

14. Robert A. Ferguson, *The American Enlightenment, 1750–1820* (Cambridge: Harvard University Press, 1997), 51; emphasis added.

15. Ferguson, *The American Enlightenment*, 53–62.

16. Ferguson, *The American Enlightenment*, 53.

17. Ferguson, *The American Enlightenment*, 62.

18. Ferguson, *The American Enlightenment*, 55.

19. Ferguson, *The American Enlightenment*, 60.

20. Adam B. Seligman, *The Problem of Trust* (Princeton: Princeton University Press, 1997), 49. Aside from the Latin phraseology, italics mine.

21. Michael Walzer, *The Revolution of the Saints* (Cambridge: Harvard University Press, 1965), 213.

22. Taylor, *Sources*, 229.

23. Lionel Trilling, *Sincerity and Authenticity* (London: Oxford University Press, 1974), 10, 6.

24. For a unique examination of what Luther may have meant by "meaning it," see Erik Erikson's enduring study *Young Man Luther* (New York: W. W. Norton, 1958), specifically chapter 6, "The Meaning of 'Meaning It.'"

25. Trilling, *Sincerity and Authenticity*, 31.

26. J. M. Roberts, *History of the World* (New York: Oxford University Press, 1992), 553.

27. Taylor, *Ethics*, 90.

28. Thomas Frank, *What's the Matter with Kansas?* (New York: Metropolitan Books, 2004).

29. Rosenblatt, "Age of Irony."

30. Friedrich Nietzsche, *On the Genealogy of Morals and Ecce Homo*, ed. Walter Kaufmann (New York: Vintage, 1969), 61.

CHAPTER 6

1. Charles W. Anderson, *A Deeper Freedom: Liberal Democracy as an Everyday Morality* (Madison: University of Wisconsin Press, 2002), 54.

2. For accessible readings on the history of Stoic spiritual practice and its intertwining with Western philosophy, see works by the French historian of ancient philosophy Pierre Hadot, *What Is Ancient Philosophy?* trans. Michael Chase (Cambridge: Harvard University Press, 2002) and *The Inner Citadel: The Meditations of Marcus Aurelius*, trans. Michael Chase (Cambridge: Harvard University Press, 1998). See also Marcus Aurelius's *Meditations*, Epictetus, Seneca, Cicero, etc.

3. Taylor, *Sources*, 131.

4. For a detailed account of this autobiographical shift in writing and visual representation, see the thoroughgoing *History of Private Life: Revelations of the Medieval World*, ed. Georges Duby, trans. Arthur Goldhammer (Cambridge: Belknap Press of Harvard University Press, 1988), specifically chapter 5, "The Emergence of the Individual," by Georges Duby and Philippe Braunstein, 507–630.

5. Duby and Braunstein, "Emergence of the Individual," 513.

6. Taylor, *Sources*, 215.

7. Taylor, *Sources*, 185. Additionally, for Augustine on total commitment, see *Confessions*, book 8, section 9.

8. See Lewis W. Spitz, *The Protestant Reformation, 1517–1559* (New York: Harper and Row, 1985); and Alister McGrath, *The Intellectual Origins of the Protestant Reformation* (Oxford: Basil Blackwell, 1987).

9. Marcell Mauss, "A Category of the Human Mind: The Notion of the Person, the Notion of the Self," in *The Category of the Person*, ed. Michael Carrithers, Steven Collins, and Steven Lukes (Cambridge: Cambridge University Press, 1985), 19, 21–22.

10. Martin Luther quoted in Ralph Barton Perry, *Puritanism and Democracy* (New York: Vanguard Press, 1944), 89.

11. Ferguson, *Religious Transformation*, 120.

12. Ferguson, *Religious Transformation*, 120.

13. Thomas H. Greer, *A Brief History of Western Man* (New York: Harcourt, Brace, and World, 1968), 314.

14. Ferguson, *Religious Transformation*, 124.

15. Thomas Adams quoted in Max Weber, *The Protestant Ethic and the Spirit of Capitalism*, trans. Stephen Kalberg (New York: Routledge, 2001), 179.

16. Miller, *The New England Mind*, 67.

17. Miller, *The New England Mind*, 67.

18. McDougall, *Freedom*, 56.

19. McDougall, *Freedom*, 59.

20. Perry, *Puritanism and Democracy*, 192.

21. Quoted in Weber, *Protestant Ethic*, 58.

22. Bercovitch, *Puritan Origins*, 17–18.

23. Muecke, *The Compass of Irony*, 189.

24. Bercovitch, *Puritan Origins*, 18.

25. Bercovitch, *Puritan Origins*, 18.

26. Taylor, *Sources*, 184.

27. Bercovitch, *Puritan Origins*, 114.

CHAPTER 7

1. Merle Curti, *The Growth of American Thought* (New Brunswick, N.J.: Transaction, 1995), 3.

2. Curti, *The Growth of American Thought*, 4.

3. Curti, *Growth of American Thought*, 8.

4. John Woolman. *The Journal and Essays of John Woolman*, ed. Amelia M. Gummere (New York: Macmillan, 1922), 156.

5. Jacob Needleman, *The American Soul: Rediscovering the Wisdom of the Founders* (New York: Tarcher/Putnam, 2002), 101.

6. Harold Bloom, *The American Religion* (New York: Simon and Schuster, 1992), 32.

7. Alan Wolfe, *Moral Freedom: The Impossible Idea That Defines the Way We Live Now* (New York: W. W. Norton, 2001), 168.

8. Bloom, *American Religion*, 32.

9. Delbanco, *Real American Dream*, 112.

10. Delbanco, *Real American Dream*, 43.

11. Curti, *Growth of American Thought*, 297.

12. For a careful discussion of Emerson's oversimplification of Kantian philosophy and its hoary details, see Lawrence Buell, *Emerson* (Cambridge: Belknap Press of Harvard University Press, 2003), 199–206.

13. Ralph Waldo Emerson, "Self-Reliance," in *Essays and Lectures* (New York: Library of America, 1983), 261.

14. Ralph Waldo Emerson, quoted in Perry Miller, *Nature's Nation* (Cambridge: Belknap Press of Harvard University Press, 1967), 191.

15. Miller, *Nature's Nation*, 191.

16. Curti, *Growth of American Thought*, 234.

17. Curti, *Growth of American Thought*, 296, 235.

18. Bercovitch, *Puritan Origins*, 164.

19. For more on how Reformers and Romantics differ on the construction of identity, see Bercovitch, *Puritan Origins*, 164.

20. Caspar David Friedrich, quoted in Taylor, *Ethics of Authenticity*, 86.

21. www.hamburger-kunsthalle.de (accessed October 15, 2006).

22. James Davidson Hunter, *Culture Wars: The Struggle to Define America* (New York: Basic Books, 1991), 44–45.

23. Bercovitch, *Puritan Origins*, 29.

24. Ferguson, *Religious Transformation*, 138.

25. See Delbanco, *Real American Dream*, for how and when each of these narratives replaced the last.

26. Anderson, *Deeper Freedom*, 56–57.

27. Statistical information culled from Jeremy Rifkin, *The European Dream: How Europe's Vision of the Future is Quietly Eclipsing the American Dream* (New York: Tarcher/Penguin, 2004), 19; Rifkin's sources include the Gallup Organization (www.gallup.org), the Pew Research Center for People and the Press (www.people-press.org) and *The Washington Post*/Kaiser/Harvard Survey Project (www.kff.org).

28. Chaloupka, *Everybody Knows*, 16.

29. Bloom, *American Religion*, 37.

30. Eggers, *Heartbreaking Work*, 399–400.

31. See these chapters in Ferguson, *Melancholy*.

32. Claus Offe, "How Can We Trust Our Fellow Citizens?" in Warren, *Democracy and Trust*, 75.

33. Warren, conclusion to *Democracy and Trust*, 350.

34. Alan Wolfe, "Are We Losing Our Virtue?" in Rouner, *Civility*, 139.

35. Chaloupka, *Everybody Knows*, 9, 28.

36. The founding address for the discussion of the legitimacy of authority in modernity is Jürgen Habermas, *Legitimation Crisis*, trans. Thomas McCarthy (Boston: Beacon Press, 1975).

CHAPTER 8

1. Thirwall, "Irony of Sophocles," 434.

2. Taylor, *Ethics of Authenticity*, 97.

3. http://www.marsnews.com/newswire/humans_to_mars/.

Bibliography

Adorno, Theodor Wiesengrund. *The Jargon of Authenticity*. Trans. Knut Tarnowski and Frederic Will. London: Routledge and Kegan Paul, 1973.

Adorno, Theodor Wiesengrund. *Minima Moralia*. Trans. E. F. Jephcott. London: Verso, 1984.

Adorno, Theodor Wiesengrund. *Negative Dialectics*. Trans. E. B. Ashton. New York: Routledge, 1973.

Alford, Steven E. *Irony and the Logic of the Romantic Imagination*. New York: Peter Lang, 1984.

Anderson, Amanda. *Powers of Distance*. Princeton: Princeton University Press, 2001.

Anderson, Charles W. *A Deeper Freedom: Liberal Democracy as an Everyday Morality*. Madison: University of Wisconsin Press, 2002.

Anderson, Walter Truett, ed. *The Truth About The Truth*. New York: Tarcher/Putnam, 1995.

Arendt, Hannah. *Eichmann in Jerusalem: A Report on the Banality of Evil*. Harmondsworth: Penguin, 1977.

Aristotle. *Nicomachean Ethics*. Trans. Martin Ostwald. New York: Macmillan/ Library of Liberal Arts, 1962.

Aurelius, Marcus. *Meditations*. Trans. Maxwell Staniforth. London: Penguin, 1964.

Baker, Keith Michael, and Peter Hanns Reill. *What's Left of Enlightenment: A Postmodern Question*. Stanford: Stanford University Press, 2001.

Baritz, Loren. *Sources of the American Mind: A Collection of Documents and Texts In American Intellectual History*. New York: John Wiley and Sons, 1966.

Barzun, Jacques. *From Dawn to Decadence: 500 Years of Western Cultural Life: 1500 to the Present*. New York: HarperCollins, 2000.

Barzun, Jacques. *Romanticism and the Modern Ego*. Boston: Little, Brown, 1943.

Baudrillard, Jean. *America*. Trans. Chris Turner. London: Verso, 1989.

Baym, Nina, et al., eds. *The Norton Anthology of American Literature*. Shorter 5th ed. New York: W. W. Norton, 1999.

Beem, Christopher. *The Necessity of Politics: Reclaiming American Public Life*. Chicago: University of Chicago Press, 1999.

Behler, Ernst. *Irony and the Discourse of Modernity.* Seattle: University of Washington Press, 1990.

Beiser, Fredrick C. *Enlightenment, Revolution, and Romanticism: The Genesis of Modern German Political Thought, 1790–1800.* Cambridge: Harvard University Press, 1992.

Bell, Daniel. *The Cultural Contradictions of Capitalism.* New York: Basic Books, 1976.

Bell, Daniel. *The End of Ideology: The Exhaustion of Political Ideas in the Fifties.* New York: Free Press, 1960.

Bellah, Robert. *The Good Society.* New York: Vintage, 1992.

Bellah, Robert. *Habits of the Heart: Individualism and Commitment in American Life.* Berkeley and Los Angeles: University of California Press, 1996.

Benjamin, Walter. *Illuminations: Essays and Reflections.* Ed. Hannah Arendt. Trans. Harry Zohn. New York: Schocken, 1968.

Bennett, Jane. *The Enchantment of Modern Life: Attachments, Crossings, and Ethics.* Princeton: Princeton University Press, 2001.

Bennett, William. *The Death of Outrage.* New York: Free Press, 1998.

Bennett, William. *The De-Valuing of America: The Fight for Our Culture and Our Children.* New York: Simon and Schuster, 1992.

Bercovitch, Sacvan. *The Puritan Origins of the American Self.* New Haven: Yale University Press, 1975.

Bercovitch, Sacvan. *American Jeremiad.* Madison: University of Wisconsin Press, 1978.

Bewes, Timothy. *Cynicism and Postmodernity.* London: Verso, 1997.

Bloom, Allan. *The Closing of the American Mind.* New York: Simon and Schuster, 1987.

Bloom, Harold. *The American Religion.* New York: Simon and Schuster, 1992.

Bloom, Harold. *The Anxiety of Influence.* New York: Oxford University Press, 1973.

Bloom, Harold, ed. *Romanticism and Consciousness.* New York: W. W. Norton, 1970.

Booth, Wayne C. *A Rhetoric of Irony.* Chicago: University of Chicago Press, 1974.

Bork, Robert H. *Slouching towards Gomorrah.* New York: HarperCollins, 1996.

Bottomore, T. B. *Social Criticism in North America.* Vancouver: Canadian Broadcasting Corporation, 1966.

Boym, Svetlana. *The Future of Nostalgia.* New York: Basic Books, 2001.

Branham, R. Bracht, and Marie-Odile Goulet-Cazé. *The Cynics: The Cynic Movement in Antiquity and Its Legacy.* Partial translation by Michael Chase. Berkeley and Los Angeles: University of California Press, 1996.

Bremer, Francis J. *The Puritan Experiment: New England Society from Bradford to Edwards.* Rev. ed. Hanover, N.H.: University Press of New England, 1995.

Brinkley, Alan. *The Unfinished Nation.* 4th ed. Boston: McGraw-Hill, 2004.

Brogan, Hugh. *The Penguin History of the USA.* London: Penguin, 1999.

Burke, Kenneth. *The Philosophy of Literary Form: Studies in Symbolic Action.* New York: Vintage, 1957.

Bronowski, J., and Bruce Mazlish. *The Western Intellectual Tradition: From Leonardo to Hegel.* New York: Harper and Row, 1960.

Capper, Charles, and David A. Hollinger, eds. *The American Intellectual Tradition.* 4th ed. 2 vols. New York: Oxford University Press, 2001.

Carlyle, Thomas. *Sartor Resartus: The Life and Times of Herr Teufelsdröckh, in Three Books.* New York, AMS Press, 1969.

Carter, Steven L. *Civility: Manners, Morals, and the Etiquette of Democracy.* New York: Basic Books, 1998.

Ceasar, James W. *Reconstructing America: The Symbol of America in Modern Thought.* New Haven: Yale University Press, 2000.

Chaloupka, William. *Everybody Knows: Cynicism in America.* Minneapolis: University of Minnesota Press, 1999.

Cohen, Stanley, and Laurie Taylor. *Escape Attempts: The Theory and Practice of Resistance to Everyday Life.* London: Routledge, 1992.

Colebridge, Clair. *Irony in the Work of Philosophy.* Lincoln: University of Nebraska Press, 2002.

Coles, Robert. *Irony in the Mind's Life.* Charlottesville: University Press of Virginia, 1974.

Commager, Henry Steele. *The American Mind: An Interpretation of American Thought and Character since the 1880s.* New Haven: Yale University Press, 1950.

Dane, Joseph. *The Critical Mythology of Irony.* Athens: University of Georgia Press, 1991.

Dasilva, Fabio, et al. *Politics at the End of History.* New York: Peter Lang, 1993.

Delbanco, Andrew. *The Death of Satan: How Americans Lost the Sense of Evil.* New York: Farrar, Straus and Giroux, 1995.

Delbanco, Andrew. *The Real American Dream: A Meditation on Hope.* Cambridge: Harvard University Press, 1999.

Demos, John. *A Little Commonwealth: Family Life in Plymouth Colony.* New York: Oxford University Press, 2000.

Dionne, E. J. *Community Works: The Revival of Civil Society in America.* Washington, D.C.: Brookings Institution Press, 1998.

Du Bruyne, Edgar. *The Esthetics of the Middle Ages.* Trans. Eileen B. Hennessy. New York: Frederic Ungar, 1969.

Duby, Georges, ed. *A History of Private Life: Revelations of the Medieval World.* Trans. Arthur Goldhammer. Cambridge: Belknap Press of Harvard University Press, 1988.

Dyson, A. E. *The Crazy Fabric: Essays in Irony.* New York: St. Martin's Press, 1966.

Eagleton, Terry. *Ideology: An Introduction.* London: Verso, 1991.

Eco, Umberto. *Art and Beauty in the Middle Ages.* Trans. Hugh Bredin. New Haven: Yale University Press, 1986.

Eggers, Dave. *A Heartbreaking Work of Staggering Genius.* New York: Vintage, 2000.

Eichner, Hans. *Friedrich Schlegel.* New York: Twayne, 1970.

Eitner, Lorenz. *Neoclassicism and Romanticism, 1750–1850: Sources and Documents.* Vol. 2. Englewood Cliffs, N.J.: Prentice-Hall, 1970.

Elias, Norbert. *The Civilizing Process: The History of Manners and State Formation and Civilization.* Trans. Edmund Jephcott. Oxford: Blackwell, 1994.

Emerson, Ralph Waldo. *Essays and Lectures.* Ed. Joel Porte. New York: Viking Press, 1983.

Enright, D. J. *The Alluring Problem: An Essay on Irony.* New York: Oxford University Press, 1986.

Erikson, Erik. *Young Man Luther: A Study in Psychoanalysis and History.* New York: W. W. Norton, 1962.

Ferguson, Harvie. *Melancholy and the Critique of Modernity: Søren Kierkegaard's Religious Psychology.* London: Routledge, 1995.

Ferguson, Harvie. *Religious Transformation in Western Society: The End of Happiness.* London: Routledge, 1992.

Fernandez, James W., and Mary Taylor Huber, eds. *Irony in Action: Anthropology, Practice, and the Moral Imagination.* Chicago: University of Chicago Press, 2001.

Frank, Thomas. *What's the Matter with Kansas?* New York: Metropolitan, 2004.

Friedman, Lawrence. *The Horizontal Society.* New Haven: Yale University Press, 1999.

Fukuyama, Francis. *Trust: The Social Virtues and the Creation of Prosperity.* New York: Free Press, 1995.

Gilmore, Jonathan. *The Life of a Style: Beginnings and Endings in the Narrative History of Art.* Ithaca: Cornell University Press, 2000.

Girgus, Sam, ed. *The American Self.* Albuquerque: University of New Mexico Press, 1981.

Goffman, Erving. *The Presentation of the Self in Everyday Life.* New York: Anchor Books, 1959.

Goldfarb, Jeffrey C. *The Cynical Society: The Culture of Politics and the Politics of Culture in American Life.* Chicago: University of Chicago Press, 1991.

Greenberg, Clement. *Art and Culture.* Boston: Beacon Press, 1961.

Greven, Philip J., Jr. *The Protestant Temperament: Patterns of Child-Rearing, Religious Experience, and the Self in Early America.* New York: Knopf, 1977.

Gurko, Leo. *Crisis of the American Mind.* London: Rider, 1956.

Habermas, Jürgen. *Legitimation Crisis.* Trans. Thomas McCarthy. Boston: Beacon Press, 1975.

Habermas, Jürgen. *The Philosophical Discourse of Modernity: Twelve Lectures.* Cambridge: MIT Press, 1987.

Habermas, Jürgen. *The Theory of Communicative Action.* Trans. Thomas McCarthy. 2 vols. Boston: Beacon Press, 1981.

Hadot, Pierre. *The Inner Citadel: The Meditations of Marcus Aurelius.* Trans. Michael Chase. Cambridge: Harvard University Press, 1998.

Hadot, Pierre. *What Is Ancient Philosophy?* Trans. Michael Chase. Cambridge: Harvard University Press, 2002.

Hammond, Jeffrey. *The American Puritan Elegy.* New York: Cambridge University Press, 2000.

Handwerk, Gary J. *Irony and Ethics in Narrative from Schlegel to Lacan.* New Haven: Yale University Press,1985.

Hannay, Alistaire. *Kierkegaard: A Biography.* New York: Cambridge University Press, 2001.

Harris, Daniel. *Cute, Quaint, Hungry, and Romantic: The Aesthetics of Consumerism.* New York: Basic Books, 2000.

Hegel, Georg Friedrich Wilhelm. *The Phenomenology of Spirit.* Trans. A. V. Miller. Oxford: Oxford University Press, 1977.

Heidegger, Martin. *Basic Writings.* Ed. David Farrell Krell. New York: Harper and Row Publishers, 1977.

Heidegger, Martin. *Being and Time.* Trans. John Macquarrie and Edward Robinson. New York: Harper and Row, 1962.

Held, David. *Introduction to Critical Theory.* Berkeley and Los Angeles: University of California Press, 1980.

Heller, Erich. *The Ironic German: A Study of Thomas Mann.* Boston: Little, Brown, 1958.

Himmelfarb, Gertrude. *One Nation, Two Cultures.* New York: Alfred A. Knopf, 1999.

Hoffman, Michael J. *The Subversive Vision: American Romanticism in Literature.* Port Washington, N.Y.: Kennikat, 1972.

Holman, C. Hugh. *A Handbook of Literature.* 4th ed. Indianapolis: Bobbs-Merrill Educational Publishing, 1980.

Honderich, Ted, ed. *The Oxford Companion to Philosophy.* New York: Oxford University Press, 1995.

Horkheimer, Max. *Eclipse of Reason.* New York: Seabury Press, 1974.

Horkheimer, Max, and Theodor W. Adorno. *The Dialectic of Enlightenment.* New York: Continuum, 1944.

Howe, Daniel Walker. *Making the American Self.* Cambridge: Harvard University Press, 1997.

Hunter, James Davidson. *Culture Wars: The Struggle to Define America.* New York: Basic Books, 1991.

Hutcheon, Linda. *Irony's Edge: The Theory and Politics of Irony.* London: Routledge, 1995.

Huzinga, Johannes. *The Waning of the Middle Ages.* Trans. F. Hopman. London: Harmondsworth, 1965.

Hynes, Samuel. *The Pattern of Hardy's Poetry.* Chapel Hill: University of North Carolina Press, 1961.

Jameson, Frederic. *Postmodernism or, the Cultural Logic of Late Capitalism*. Durham, N.C.: Duke University Press, 1991.

Johnson, Paul. *The Birth of the Modern: World Society, 1815–1830*. New York: HarperCollins, 1991.

Kaplan, Robert D. *The Coming Anarchy*. New York: Random House, 2000.

Kierkegaard, Søren. *The Concept of Irony: With Constant Reference to Socrates*. Trans. Lee Capel. Bloomington: Indiana University Press, 1965.

Kierkegaard, Søren. *Either/Or*. Trans. David F. Swenson and Lillian Marvin Swensom. 2 vols. Princeton: Princeton University Press, 1959.

Kierkegaard, Søren. *Journals*. Trans. A. Dru. New York: Oxford University Press, 1938.

King, Andrew, ed. *Postmodern Political Communication*. Westport, Conn.: Praeger, 1993.

Knox, Norman. *The Word Irony and Its Contexts, 1500–1755*. Durham, N.C.: Duke University Press, 1961.

Kuklick, Bruce. *A History of Philosophy in America, 1720–2000*. New York: Oxford University Press, 2001.

Kuspit, Donald. *Psycho-Strategies of Avant-Garde Art*. New York: Cambridge University Press, 2000.

Kuspit, Donald. *Signs of the Psyche in Modern and Post-modern Art*. New York: Cambridge University Press, 1993.

Landsman, Ned C. *From Colonials to Provincials: American Thought and Culture, 1680–1760*. Ithaca, N.Y.: Cornell University Press, 1997.

Lane, Robert E. *The Loss of Happiness in Market Democracies*. New Haven: Yale University Press, 2000.

Lasch, Christopher. *The Culture of Narcissism: American Life in An Age of Diminishing Expectations*. New York: W. W. Norton, 1979.

Lasch, Christopher. *The Minimal Self: Psychic Survival in Troubled Times*. New York: W. W. Norton, 1984.

Lasch, Christopher. *The True and Only Heaven: Progress and Its Critics*. New York: W. W. Norton, 1991.

Leach, William. *Country of Exiles: The Destruction of Place in American Life*. New York: Pantheon, 1999.

Lerner, Michael. *The Politics of Meaning: Restoring Hope and Possibility in an Age of Cynicism*. Reading, Mass.: Addison-Wesley, 1996.

Lessnoff, Michael. *Social Contract*. London: Macmillan, 1986.

Levine, David, ed. *On Individuality and Social Forms*. Chicago: University of Chicago Press, 1971.

Lowrie, Ernest Benson. *The Shape of the Puritan Mind: The Thought of Samuel Willard*. New Haven: Yale University Press, 1974.

Lukacs, John. *The End of An Age*. New Haven: Yale University Press, 2002.

Luther, Martin. *Selected Political Writings*. Ed. J. M. Porter. Philadelphia: Fortress Press, 1974.

MacIntyre, Alasdair. *After Virtue.* Notre Dame: University of Notre Dame Press, 1984.

MacKenzie, G. Calvin. *The Irony of Reform: Roots of American Political Disenchantment.* Boulder, Colo.: Westview Press, 1996.

Mailer, Norman. *Advertisements for Myself.* Cambridge: Harvard University Press, 1992.

Majors, Richard, and Janet Mancini Billson. *Cool Pose: The Dilemmas of Black Manhood in America.* New York: Lexington, 1992.

Martinez, Roy. *Kierkegaard and the Art of Irony.* Amherst, N.Y.: Humanity Books, 2001.

McDougall, Walter A. *Freedom Just Around the Corner: A New American History, 1585–1828.* New York: HarperCollins, 2004.

McGrath, Alister E. *The Intellectual Origins of the European Reformation.* London: Blackwell, 1987.

Mellor, Anne K. *English Romantic Irony.* Cambridge: Harvard University Press, 1980.

Miller, Perry. *Errand into the Wilderness.* Cambridge: Harvard University Press, 1975.

Miller, Perry. *The New England Mind: The Seventeenth Century.* Cambridge: Harvard University Press, 1939.

Miller, Perry. *Nature's Nation.* Cambridge: Harvard University Press, 1967.

Mills, C. Wright. *White Collar: The American Middle Classes.* New York: Oxford University Press, 1951.

Miringoff, Marc, and Marque-Luisa. *The Social Health of the Nation: How America Is Really Doing.* New York: Oxford University Press, 1999.

Mosier, Richard. *The American Temper: Patterns of Our Intellectual Heritage.* Berkeley and Los Angeles: University of California Press, 1952.

Muecke, D. C. *The Compass of Irony.* London: Methuen, 1969.

Muecke, D. C. *Irony and the Ironic.* London: Methuen, 1982.

Mullett, Michael A. *Martin Luther.* London: Routledge, 2004.

Murphy, Paul V. *The Rebuke of History: The Southern Agrarians and American Conservative Thought.* Chapel Hill: University of North Carolina Press, 2001.

Myers, David G. *The American Paradox: Spiritual Hunger in An Age of Plenty.* New Haven: Yale University Press, 2000.

Needleman, Jacob. *The American Soul: Rediscovering the Wisdom of the Founders.* New York: Tarcher/Putnam, 2002.

Neuhauser, Frederick. *Fichte's Theory of Subjectivity.* Cambridge: Cambridge University Press, 1990.

Newman, C. *The Post-Modern Aura.* Evanston, Ill.: Northwestern University Press, 1985.

Nietzsche, Friedrich. *Human, All Too Human.* Trans. Marion Faber and Stephen Lehmann. Lincoln: University of Nebraska Press, 1984.

Nietzsche, Friedrich. *The Joyful Wisdom.* Trans. Thomas Common. New York: Frederic Ungar, 1960.

Nietzsche, Friedrich. *On the Genealogy of Morals and Ecce Homo.* Trans. Walter Kaufmann. New York: Random House, 1967.

Pappano, Laura. *The Connection Gap: Why Americans Feel So Alone.* New Brunswick, N.J.: Rutgers University Press, 2001.

Parrish, Tim. *Walking Blues: Making Americans from Emerson to Elvis.* Amherst: University of Massachusetts Press, 2001.

Pascal, Blaise. *Pensées.* Trans. John Warrington. London: J. M. Dent and Sons, 1960

Peckham, Morse. *Romanticism: The Culture of the Nineteenth Century.* New York: George Braziller, 1965.

Perry, Bliss. *The American Mind.* Boston: Houghton Mifflin, 1912.

Perry, Ralph Barton. *Puritanism and Democracy.* New York: Vanguard, 1944.

Pharr, Susan, and Robert D. Putnam, eds. *Disaffected Democracies: What's Troubling the Trilateral Countries?* Princeton: Princeton University Press, 2000.

Phillips, Adam. *On Kissing, Tickling, and Being Bored.* Cambridge: Harvard University Press, 1993.

Posner, Richard. *Public Intellectuals: A Study of Decline.* Cambridge: Harvard University Press, 2001.

Pountain, Dick, and David Robbins. *Cool Rules: Anatomy of an Attitude.* London: Reaktion Books, 2000.

Purdy, Jedediah. *For Common Things: Irony, Trust, and Commitment in America Today.* New York: Knopf, 1999.

Putnam, Robert. *Bowling Alone: The Collapse and Revival of American Community.* New York: Simon and Schuster, 2000

Riesman, David, with Nathan Glazer and Reuel Denney. *The Lonely Crowd.* New Haven: Yale University Press, 1961.

Rifkin, Jeremy. *The European Dream: How Europe's Vision of the Future is Quietly Eclipsing the American Dream.* New York: Tarcher/Putnam, 2004.

Riley, Denise. *The Words of Selves: Identification, Solidarity, Irony.* Stanford: Stanford University Press, 2000.

Roberts, J. M. *History of the World.* New York: Oxford University Press, 1992.

Rojek, Chris. *Celebrity.* London: Reaktion Books, 2001.

Rorty, Richard. *Achieving Our Country.* Cambridge: Harvard University Press, 1998.

Rorty, Richard. *Contingency, Irony, and Solidarity.* New York: Cambridge University Press, 1989.

Rorty, Richard. *Philosophy and Social Hope.* New York: Penguin, 1999.

Rorty, Richard. *Philosophy and the Mirror of Nature.* Princeton: Princeton University Press, 1979.

Rosenau, Pauline Marie. *Post-Modernism and the Social Sciences: Insights, Inroads, and Intrusions.* Princeton: Princeton University Press, 1992.

Rosenblum, Nancy L., ed. *The Obligations of Citizenship and the Demands of Faith.* Princeton: Princeton University Press, 2000.

Rossiter, Clinton, and James Lare, eds. *The Essential Lippman: A Political Philosophy for Liberal Democracy.* New York: Vintage, 1963.

Rouner, Leroy S. *Civility.* Notre Dame: University of Notre Dame Press, 2000.

Scheibe, Karl E. *The Drama of Everyday Life.* Cambridge: Harvard University Press, 2000.

Schlegel, Friedrich. *Literary Notebooks, 1797–1801.* Trans. Hans Eichner. Toronto: University of Toronto Press, 1957.

Schlegel, Friedrich. *Lucinde and the Fragments.* Trans. Peter Firchnow. Minneapolis: University of Minnesota Press, 1971.

Serry, John, and Daniel W. Conway. *Political Returns: Irony in Politics and Theory from Plato to the Antinuclear Movement.* Boulder, Colo.: Westview Press, 1990.

Serry, John, and Daniel W. Conway. *The Politics of Irony: Essays in Self-Betrayal.* New York: St. Martin's/Macmillan, 1992.

Seligman, Adam B. *The Problem of Trust.* Princeton: Princeton University Press, 1997.

Seligman, Martin. *Learned Optimism.* New York: Pocket Books, 1990.

Sennett, Richard. *The Corrosion of Character: The Personal Consequences of Work in the New Capitalism.* New York: W. W. Norton, 1998.

Sennett, Richard. *The Fall of Public Man.* New York: Knopf, 1992.

Shaftesbury, Anthony Ashley Cooper, Earl of. *Characteristics of Men, Manners, Opinions, Times.* New York: Cambridge University Press, 2000.

Shi, David E. *The Simple Life: Plain Living and High Thinking in American Culture.* Athens: University of Georgia Press, 1985.

Shields, John C. *The American Aeneas: Classical Origins of the American Self.* Knoxville: University of Tennessee Press, 2001.

Shinn, Roger L. *The Search for Identity: Essays on the American Character.* New York: Institute for Religious and Social Studies, 1964.

Shklar, Judith. *After Utopia: The Decline of Political Faith.* Princeton: Princeton University Press, 1957.

Shusterman, Richard. *Performing Live: Aesthetic Alternatives for the Ends of Art.* Ithaca, N.Y.: Cornell University Press, 2000.

Sirianni, Carmen, and Lewis Friedland. *Civic Innovation in America.* Berkeley and Los Angeles: University of California Press, 2001.

Sloterdijk, Peter. *The Critique of Cynical Reason.* Minneapolis: University of Minnesota Press, 1983.

Spengler, Oswald. *The Decline of the West.* Ed. Helmut Werner and Arthur Helps. Trans. Charles Francis Atkinson. New York: Oxford University Press, 1991.

Spitz, Lewis W. *The Protestant Reformation, 1517–1559.* New York: Harper and Row, 1985.

Sontag, Susan. *Against Interpretation.* New York: Anchor Books, 1966.

Stearns, Peter. *American Cool: Constructing a Twentieth Century Emotional Style.* New York: New York University Press, 1994.

Steinberg, Ted. *Down to Earth: Nature's Role in American History.* New York: Oxford University Press, 2002.

Stivers, Richard. *The Culture of Cynicism: American Morality in Decline.* Cambridge: Blackwell, 1994.

Storr, Robert. "The Rules of the Game." *Alex Katz: American Landscape.* Baden-Baden: Staatliche Kunsthalle, Baden-Baden, 1995.

Stringfellow, Jr., Frank. *The Meaning of Irony: A Psychoanalytic Investigation.* Albany: State University of New York Press, 1994.

Susman, Warren J. *Culture as History.* New York: Pantheon, 1985.

Swanson, Matthew. *The Social Contract Question and the Question of Political Legitimacy.* Lewiston, N.Y.: Edwin Mellen Press, 2001.

Swift, Jonathan. "A Modest Proposal." *The Norton Anthology of English Literature.* Ed. M. H. Abrams et al. New York: W. W. Norton, 1979.

Tartarkiewicz, Wladyslaw. *History of Aesthetics.* Trans. C. Barrett. 3 vols. The Hague: Mouton, 1970–74.

Taylor, Charles. *The Ethics of Authenticity.* Cambridge: Harvard University Press, 1991.

Taylor, Charles. *Sources of the Self: The Making of Modern Identity.* Cambridge: Harvard University Press, 1989.

Taylor, Mark C. *Journeys To Selfhood: Hegel and Kierkegaard.* Berkeley and Los Angeles: University of California Press, 1980.

Tocqueville, Alexis de. *Democracy in America.* 2. vols. New York: Vintage, 1990.

Trilling, Lionel. *Sincerity and Authenticity.* London: Oxford University Press, 1974.

Warren, Mark E., ed. *Democracy and Trust.* New York: Cambridge University Press, 1999.

Weber, Max. *The Protestant Ethic and the Spirit of Capitalism.* Trans. Stephen Kalberg. New York: Routledge, 2001.

White, Hayden. *Metahistory: The Historical Imagination in Nineteenth-Century Europe.* Baltimore: Johns Hopkins University Press, 1973.

Wiener, Philip P., ed. *Dictionary of the History of Ideas: Studies of Selected Pivotal Ideas.* New York: Charles Scribner's Sons, 1973.

Wilde, Alan. *Horizons of Assent: Modernism, Postmodernism, and the Ironic Imagination.* Philadelphia: University of Pennsylvania Press, 1987.

Wolfe, Alan. *Moral Freedom: The Impossible Idea That Defines the Way We Live Now.* New York: W. W. Norton, 2001.

Wolfe, Alan. *Whose Keeper? Social Science and the Moral Imagination.* Berkeley and Los Angeles: University of California Press, 1989.

Wuthnow, Robert. *Christianity and Civil Society: The Contemporary Debate.* Valley Forge, Pa.: Trinity Press International, 1996.

Worcester, David. *The Art of Satire.* New York: W. W. Norton, 1969.

Žižek, Slavoj. *The Sublime Object of Ideology.* London: Verso, 1998.

Index

Harris, Sam, 3n–4
Harris Poll, 122–23
Hawking, Stephen, 232
von Hayek, Friedrich, 133
Heartbreaking Work of Staggering Genius, A (Eggers), 6, 7n, 36, 124–25
Hegel, G. W. F., 4, 56, 60n*, 87, 102–4; ironists' individualism and, 214, 215; Kierkegaard and, 104, 105; morality and, 110; negativity and, 107
Heine, Heinrich, 99n
Heller, Erich, 211n†
Heltzel, Peter, 209–10
Hermenaut (magazine), 140
Hersh, Seymour, 61
Hesiod, 72
Hesychasm, 178n
High Fidelity (film), 47
high school, 43–44
Himmelfarb, Gertrude, 136–37
History of Cynicism from Diogenes to the Sixth Century A. D. (Dudley), 114n
History of the Decline and Fall of the Roman Empire (Gibbon), 48n*
Hodge, Rodger, 8, 142
Holocaust, 11n†
Holy Spirit, 198–99
Homer, 72
honesty, 7n, 20, 61, 75; ironist and, 38, 66, 233
hope, 66
Horace (Quintus Horatius Flaccus), 77
Horizons of Assent (Wilde), 73
Horkheimer, Max, 42n, 167n, 228, 229
Howard, Gerry, 16
"How Did A Literary Device Become A Public Enemy?" (Anastas), 8
Huber, Mary Taylor, 46n
Human, All Too Human (Nietzsche), 1, 87–88

human nature, 41, 216; relationships and, 186–87, 193–94
humor, 96, 169–70; advertising and, 120n; bleak, 221; British, 79
Huntington, Samuel P., 116, 217n
Hutcheon, Linda, 57
Hynes, Samuel, 57
hypocrisy, 66, 81, 227–28

idealism, 124, 138, 221
identity, 54, 193; national, 10–11, 34, 122–23, 160, 217n
"I Did It My Way" (song), 166n
Image: A Journal of Arts and Religion, 140
imagination, 94
immediacy, 29
inconsistency, 21
Independence Day (film), 17, 31n
individualism, 39, 71, 79, 135–37, 144, 216; Calvinism and, 184; civic trust and, 155; divine communication and, 198–99; Emerson and, 206; French Revolution and, 91n; German romantic irony and, 97–98; ironist and, 214, 215; Kurtz on, 154–55; personal responsibility and, 192; Puritanism and, 157; trust and, 162
inner Emigration, 230n–31
inner self, 230; Christianity and, 102–3; divinity of, 93–94; Emerson and, 205–9; as escape, 209; freedom of, 49, 51, 182, 201–2, 212; Heltzel on, 209–10; of ironist, 44, 52; Kurtz and, 154; nature and, 92–93; protection of, 89, 114, 231; Protestantism and, 54n, 200–201, 209; subjectivity and, 98. *See also* inwardness
insiderness, 3, 5, 25, 29
Institute for Civil Society, 134
Institutio Oratorica (Quintilian), 77
integrity, 12, 229

interiority, 95, 165, 200n; exteriority, 201, 223
Internet, 20, 27, 141
interpretation, 29, 37
intimacy, 149
intuition, 206
inwardness, 174–94, 230; Augustine and, 175–78; Calvinism and, 183–94; civic responsibility and, 180; Reformation and, 178–83. *See also* Calvinism; inner self
iPod, 73
Iran, 61
"Ironic" (song), 168n
ironie, 99
Ironie als entwicklungsgeschichtliches Moment, Die (Brüggemann), 210n
ironist, the, 5, 29–44, 74, 144, 220; civic responsibility of, 114; culture industry and, 31–34; *vs.* cynic, 61; enthusiasm and, 39–40; European romanticism and, 88, 89; faith and, 155; "getting it" of, 29–31; honesty and, 38, 66, 233; individualism of, 214, 215; inner self of, 44, 52; Kierkegaard on, 106–7; nostalgia and, 65–66; *vs.* pundit, 147; Purdy on, 140; as romanticist, 105; Seinfeld as quintessential, 43; self-consciousness and, 35–37; social contract and, 194; social roles and, 35–36, 37–38; television and, 41–43
irony. *See* attitude of irony; German romantic irony; ironist, the; literary device of irony; romantic irony; Socratic irony; worldview of irony
Irony and the Discourse of Modernity (Behler), 53
Irony in Action: Anthropology, Practice, and the Moral Imagination (Fernandez and Huber), 46n
Irony's Edge: The Theory and Politics of Irony (Hutcheon), 57

isolation, 92, 210
I Want A Famous Face (TV program), 54n

Jacobs, Jane, 128n
Jacobs, Marc, 70n
Jamestown colony, 188n
Jefferson, Thomas, 82, 83
Jennings, Peter, 20n
Jeopardy! (tv program), 29
Jephcott, Edmund, 152n
jeremiads, 130–45, 151, 161, 196n*–97, 219; conservative think tanks and, 132, 134; criticism of Left by, 132–34; cynicism and, 138–39; liberty and equality and, 135–37; pop culture and, 130–32; Purdy and, 139–43
Jeremiah, book of, 186
Jeremiah (prophet), 196n*
Jerry Maguire (film), 31n
Jesus Christ, 179, 188
Jewish population, 217n
John F. Kennedy School of Government, 127
Johnson, Paul, 211n†
Johnson, Samuel, 81, 163
judgment, 190
Juvenal (Decimus Junius Juvenalis), 76–77

Kant, Immanuel, 53n, 90, 98n, 205, 207
Kaplan, Robert, 137
Karlin, Ben, 28
Katz, Alex, 46
Kennedy, John F., 118
Kennedy, Robert, 118
Kierkegaard, Søren, 5, 13, 46n, 56, 110; Absolutes and, 215; *Concept of Irony*, 15, 52n†, 73, 87, 103, 104; *Either/Or*, 106; Emerson and, 205; Hegel and, 104, 105; on ironist,

200–201, 209; Reformation of, 78, 161, 164, 178–83; seriousness and, 167–71; sincerity and, 92, 162–67, 181

Pruzan, Todd, 142

Public Intellectuals: A Study of Decline (Posner), 196n*

Pullman, Bill, 31n

pundits, 5, 147, 149

Purdy, Jedediah, 8, 35, 139–43, 196

Puritanism, 157–58, 191, 193–94, 203, 213; jeremiads and, 196n*–97

Puritan Origins of the American Self (Bercovitch), 192

Purpose Driven Life, The (Warren), 3n

Putnam, Robert, 10, 126

Quakerism, 199, 204, 216

Quayle, Dan, 131–32, 144

Quintilian (Marcus Fabius Quintilianus), 77, 81

race, 49–50, 60n†

racism, 50

Rameau's Neighbor (Diderot), 163–64

Rather, Dan, 20n, 24

Real American Dream, The (Delbanco), 200n, 203

reality, 61, 90, 95, 176

reality shows, 30, 41–42, 55n, 167

reason, 155

Reason (magazine), 132n, 142

Reebok, 69

Rees, David, 40n†

Reformation, Protestant, 78, 161, 164, 178–84

relationships, 153–54; to God, 178–79, 180; human nature and, 186–87, 193–94

relativism, 101, 103

religion, 13, 98n, 110, 193, 201; American, 202–4; civic trust and, 155, 202, 204; politics and, 155, 158, 180;

prayer and, 178n, 185–86; secularization of, 158–59; self-possessed, 198–200; social contract and, 157–60. *See also* faith(s); spirituality

religious Right, 124

repetition, 201

Republican National Convention, 132n

Reuters/DecisionQuest poll, 129

revenge, 44n

revivalism, 158–60

Revolutionary War, 81–86, 159–60

rhetoric. *See* literary device of irony

Rhetoric (Aristotle), 75

ridicule, 77

Roberts, J. M., 164

Roberts, Julia, 31n

Rocca, Mo, 168n

Rock, the, 44n

Roman (novel), 93

romantic irony, 96, 105–8, 109, 201, 212, 215. *See also* German romantic irony

romanticism, 87, 89–96; authenticity and, 92–94, 97, 165–67, 212, 221; detachment as, 214; influence of, 91n; Kierkegaard and, 87, 104–8; mind and, 89–91; modernism and, 108–10; nature and, 90–93; nostalgia and, 91n, 92; objectivity and, 94–95; Schlegel and, 98–102; self and, 174; sincerity and, 92, 212, 221. *See also* American romanticism; German romantic irony

Rorty, Richard, 38

Rosenblatt, Roger, 15–16, 143, 167–68, 170

Rousseau, Jean-Jacques, 92–93, 99n, 216

routine, 120n–21

Saguaro Report, 127–28

Sahl, Mort, 227

saints, 190

salvation, 179–80, 183, 220; American
Revolution and, 159–60; Augustine
and, 184; Calvinism and, 186–89,
191–94; ego and, 103; Emerson and,
205; inwardness and, 176; of ironist,
215; reconstruction of, 160–61; sincerity and, 164–65; social contract
and, 156, 214; through relations *vs.*
through self, 215–16, 219; trust
and, 158

sarcasm, 8, 74, 87, 112, 114, 153; in
Simpsons, 1–2, 3, 43

Sartor Resartus (Carlyle), 112

Sartre, Jean-Paul, 166

satire, 9, 100, 233, 235n8; of American
Revolution, 82–86; *vs.* cool, 45–46;
English renaissance and, 78–81;
fake news and, 22; of Juvenal,
76–77; as modern, 108; Purdy and,
142; romantic irony and, 96; seriousness and, 169–70

Saturday Night Live (tv program), 18,
27

schema, 77

Schiller, Friedrich, 207

von Schlegel, Friedrich, 18n–19, 87,
93–94, 96–97, 108, 208; morality
and, 110; romanticism and, 98–102

*Schluss mit lustig: Das Ende der Spassge-
sellschaft* (Hahne), 101

Schneider, William, 128

Schroeder, Gerhard, 166n

Schroeder, Pat, 134

scientific reasoning, 91, 99

secularism, 130, 158–59, 161–62, 204;
Puritans and, 193–94

Sedaris, Amy, 34

Sedgewick, D. D., 238n2

Seery, John, 57

Seinfeld, Jerry, 43

Seinfeld (TV program), 43n, 149, 154

self, the, 155–56, 174, 216

self-awareness, 43, 98, 140, 183,
221–22

self-consciousness, 53, 96, 102, 121,
179; of inwardness, 182; ironist and,
35–37; Kierkegaard and, 104

self-depreciation, 75n*

"Self-Reliance" (Emerson), 206

Seligman, Adam, 161

selling out, 165

Seneca, 176

September 11, 2001: civic engagement
after, 212; end of irony and, 15–19;
national identity and, 10–11; Rosenblatt and, 167

seriousness, 29, 167–71, 233; about
civic responsibility, 149; civic trust
and, 147; post 9/11, 15–19; romantic irony and, 105, 108; Schlegel
and, 100; social critique and, 27–29;
survivalism and, 41–42

Servetus, Michael, 190n

Shaftesbury, Earl of (Anthony Ashley
Cooper), 78–79

Shakespeare, William, 163

Sha-Na-Na (tv program), 68

*Shapes of Things to Come: Prophecy and
the American Voice* (Marcus), 100n

Shyalamalan, M. Night, 136n

Silverman, Sarah, 34

Simmel, Georg, 56

simplification, 52n*

Simpson, Homer, 1–2

Simpsons, The, 1–2, 3, 5, 20, 43

sin, 180, 184, 185, 196n*

Sinatra, Frank, 166n

sincerity, 169, 222; authenticity and,
162, 165; Christianity and, 103,
167n; civic trust and, 147; *vs.* cool,
45; insincerity and, 167n; of ironist,
38; marketing of, 224n–25; modernism and, 109; moral values and,
163–67; Protestantism and, 92,
162–67, 181; Purdy and, 142;